REA

E X P L O R I N G

PRAGUE

FODOR'S TRAVEL PUBLICATIONS, INC.

NEW YORK • TORONTO • LONDON • SYDNEY • AUCKLAND

While every care has been taken to ensure the accuracy of the information in this guide, time brings change, and consequently the publisher cannot accept responsibility for errors that may occur. Prudent travelers will therefore want to call ahead to verify prices and other "perishable" information.

Published in the United States by Fodor's Travel - Publications, Inc.
Published in the United Kingdom by AA Publishing.

Fodor's and Fodor's Exploring Guides are registered trademarks of Fodor's Travel Publications, Inc.

ISBN 0–679–02822–6
First Edition

Fodor's Exploring Prague

Author: **Michael Ivory**
Series Adviser and Copy Editor: **Christopher Catling**
Joint Series Editor: **Susi Bailey**
Cartography: **The Automobile Association**
Cover Design: **Louise Fili, Fabrizio LaRocca**
Front Cover Silhouette: **BKA/Network Aspen**

Special Sales
Fodor's Travel Publications are available at special discounts for bulk purchases (100 copies or more) for sales promotions or premiums. Special editions, including personalized covers, excerpts of existing guides, and corporate imprints, can be created in large quantities for special needs, For more information, contact your local bookseller or write to Special Markets, Fodor's Travel Publications, 201 East 50th Street, New York, NY 10022.

MANUFACTURED IN ITALY
10 9 8 7 6 5 4 3 2 1

After studying modern languages at the University of Oxford, **Michael Ivory** qualified as a landscape architect and town planner, and now works as a freelance lecturer and travel writer. His books include *Essential Hungary, Essential Czech Republic,* and Fodor's *Exploring Australia*, and he also contributed to *Exploring Germany* and *Exploring France*.

View from Dětský ostrov (Children's Island) across the Vltava river

How to use this book

This book is divided into five main sections:

❏ ### Section 1: *Prague Is*
Discusses aspects of life and living today, from people to pollution problems

❏ ### Section 2: *Prague Was*
Places the country in its historical context and explores those past events whose influences are felt to this day

❏ ### Section 3: *A to Z Section*
Breaks down into regional chapters, and covers places to visit, including walks and drives. Within this section fall the Focus-on articles, which consider a variety of subjects in greater detail

❏ ### Section 4: *Travel Facts*
Contains the strictly practical information that is vital for a successful trip

❏ ### Section 5: *Hotels and Restaurants*
Lists recommended establishments throughout Prague, giving a brief summary of what they offer

How to use the star rating
Most of the places described in this book have been given a separate rating:

▶▶▶ **Do not miss**

▶▶ **Highly recommended**

▶ **Worth seeing**

Not essential viewing

Map references
To make the location of a particular place easier to find, every main entry in this book is given a map reference, such as176B3. The first number (176) indicates the page on which the map can be found, the letter (B) and the second number (3) pinpoint the square in which the main entry is located. The maps on the inside front cover and inside back cover are referred to as IFC and IBC respectively.

Contents

Top: view over the rooftops and cupolas of Malá Strana from the summit of Petřín hill
Below: ornate house number and lamp shadow near Karlova in Staré Město

Quick reference

This quick-reference guide high-lights the features of the book you will use most often: the maps; the introductory features; the Focus-on articles; the walks and the drives.

7

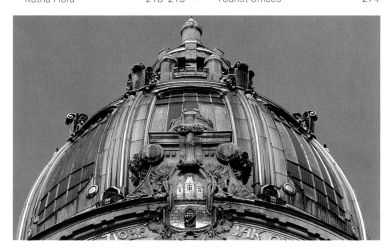

MY PRAGUE

Eva Jiřična
Eva Jiřična left her native Czechoslovakia in 1968 and, unable to return due to that summer's dramatic events, remained in London to pursue a career in architecture. In 1992 Eva Jiřična Architects became a limited company, based in Central London, and the following year Eva was invited to become a member of the Prague Presidential committee by President Havel. In 1994 Eva Jiřična was made a CBE for her services to interior design.

Alan Levy
Alan Levy became Editor-in-Chief of the *Prague Post*, an English-language weekly newspaper, when it was founded in 1991. He is the author of *Rowboat to Prague* (published in the UK as *So Many Heroes*), considered the definitive eyewitness account of the 1968 invasion, as well as the more recent *The Wiesenthal File*.

My Prague
by Eva Jiřična

During the Prague Spring of 1968 I managed to get to London just before the Russian invasion, and was then unable to return home for 22 years until after the Velvet Revolution of November 1989. The return was initially disappointing: on my journey from the airport, itself in the same poor state as when I had left, I passed terrible complexes of high-rise concrete apartment houses and empty stores, badly neglected roads and streets, and the infamous building where political prisoners were interned for investigation and punishment.

I was beginning to regret having come back at all when the car reached the top of the hill just by the castle, and the famous panorama over the city unfolded before me. In the morning sunshine of that early spring day I saw what I had looked at so often in my youth but had never really appreciated: a view of the most incredibly varied red-tiled roofs, spires and towers, hills and valleys, and palaces and gardens tumbling around the sparkling ribbon of the river with its picturesque bridges—an image as close to that of a fairytale as is possible.

I walked and walked, all the old memories and new discoveries overwhelming me. The combination of styles, details and materials, the clamor of different architectural and artistic statements, and the simple human touches all required special attention. All kinds of builders, architects, artists and experts have passed through Prague, each in some way leaving his or her signature and influence, this then being absorbed, reinterpreted and reinvented by the Czechs. Go and see for yourself, I promise you will not be disappointed.

My Prague
by Alan Levy

My visitors to Prague come off the plane bewildered and sometimes even a little belligerent: "What am I doing," they ask or wonder, "in the capital of an abbreviated land when there are so many challenges to be met and creature comforts to be enjoyed back home?" I say nothing, but, as soon as darkness falls, I take them walking on the Charles Bridge, a symphony in stone and statuary that is the song and soul of my city. Well before the end of the evening, they have stopped wondering why they are here and have started scheming and dreaming of coming back for a longer stay.

Above us, from the sgraffitoed (sculpted plaster of) Schwarzenberg Palace to the White Tower at the foot of Golden Lane, the quarter-mile of floodlit grandeur that is Prague Castle glows like a mirage, no longer the baleful and sinister citadel of Stalinist power. A generation after my family and I were expelled for my sins of truth-telling, Prague has proved to be "Second Chance City" for me, as well as for so many Czechs—one of whom holds office in that brooding castle: Václav Havel, the jailed playwright who, in one eventful year, 1989, went from prisoner of conscience to president of the republic.

PRAGUE IS

■ **Restored to the heart of Europe by the Velvet Revolution of 1989, the capital of the Czech Republic more than lives up to its reputation as the most beautiful city north of the Alps. The city's incomparable architectural heritage spans a thousand years of history, while its political, economic and cultural life is being rejuvenated by the release of the energies pent up by the long decades of Communism....■**

Magical beauty

Prague is a true metropolis—large (population 1,250,000) but not so large that it cannot be grasped as a whole. The focus of national life since the early Slav princes built their stronghold on the Hradčany heights, the city has no rival for significance or size in the Czech Republic. The four historic quarters of Hradčany, Malá Strana, Staré Město (Old Town) and Nové Město (New Town) contain buildings of every era in neighborly proximity to one another. The elegance of the Baroque age may seem to predominate, but there are monuments from every phase of the city's history, spared from war and redevelopment to form one of the most harmonious townscapes in Europe.

Nature fills out the picture; the classic view of Pražský hrad (Prague Castle) from the medieval Karlův most (Charles Bridge) takes in not only the broad sweep of the Vltava river but also waterside trees, terraced gardens and, in the background, the wooded heights of Petřín Hill.

Nowhere else in Europe is it possible to experience such a perfect vision of the pre-industrial city, an experience made all the more enjoyable by the sensitive planning which has removed traffic from much of the historic center.

But Prague is not just a spectacle: its stones are suffused with mystery. It was here that the alchemists and astrologers assembled by Emperor Rudolf II plied their strange trades, and that the Frankenstein figure of the Golem stalked the streets and alleyways of the Jewish ghetto. Prague was surreal before the term surrealism was dreamed up.

Modern capital If Prague is old, it is also very modern and, paradoxically, has been so for some time. After centuries of suppression, the Czech nation came alive again in the 19th century, in time to make its distinctive contribution to the modern world. At the turn of the century, even before the creation of Czechoslovakia, Prague was one of the focuses of European Art

City lights—a traditional lamp-standard in Hradčany

Nouveau, then of the Modernist style-in art and design, which included a unique architectural movement inspired by Cubism.

Communism brought an end to the free experimentation enjoyed in the liberal days of the interwar Republic, and severed the links which had bound Prague so closely to the other cities of Central and Western Europe. In the days of the Cold War it was easy to forget that Prague lay well to the west of Vienna.

Into the future Since the breathless days of late 1989, Prague has had a rollercoaster ride, leaving many inhabitants dizzy. First it seemed that the time of magic had returned: the Communist bogeymen vanished without protest in a puff of smoke, and a dissident playwright was suddenly transformed into a president. Thousands flocked from abroad to see these miraculous changes at first hand, soon followed by an army of tourists whose presence threatened at times to turn the city into a theme park. Unaccustomed advertisements replaced the worn-out slogans of the old regime on the façades of buildings which received their first coat of paint for 50 years.

The streets filled with peddlers and performers of all kinds. Foreign businesspeople arrived, pushing the prices of apartments and office space into the stratosphere. Czechs returned who had been exiled in 1968, 1948 and even 1938. The country split suddenly and painlessly into separate Czech and Slovak Republics. The changes continue, adding a layer of unprecedented excitement to the experience of this unique city as it continues its magical mystery tour into the future.

The busy boulevard of Václavské náměstí (Wenceslas Square)

■ The extraordinary events of 1989 freed Czechoslovakia from Communism, but delivered it up to the harsh realities the old regime had simply suppressed. The economy was crumbling, the environment was devastated and the people were unused to making decisions. The specter of nationalism appeared at freedom's feast, and by 1993 Czechoslovakia had ceased to exist, replaced by an independent Slovakia and by the Czech Republic....■

Western orientation The euphoria of the Velvet Revolution has long since evaporated and Václav Havel has overcome his trauma at Czechoslovakia's disintegration, returning as president of a truncated country comprising only the "historic provinces" of Bohemia and Moravia. A government consisting mostly of former dissidents, which had wanted to employ Frank Zappa as cultural ambassador, gave way to an altogether harder-nosed regime led by the committed free-marketeer, Václav Klaus.

The instincts of this regime were to look for a "market" rather than a "social" solution to problems of all kinds, and to integrate the country as quickly as possible into the economic and security structures of the western world. Restitution and privatization were two of its bywords; businesses and properties were returned to their pre-1948 owners, and the public was

Václav Havel—the country's dissident author turned president

encouraged to invest in privatized state enterprises by means of a voucher system.

One result of these changes has been an influx of western capital and the creation of many joint ventures, but state subsidies have been slashed, leaving many cultural institutions gasping for life. Uncoupling the economy from the former Soviet

The Czech tricolor flutters proudly atop many buildings, including the republic's Foreign Office headquarters at the Černín Palace

12

bloc—on which it was dependent for raw materials such as gas and oil—has not been easy.

Freedom and licence The hope that the country would catch up with western standards within a couple of years or so has been replaced by more realistic expectations. The inequalities opening up are resented: a surgeon can more than double his or her salary by working as an office cleaner for a foreign firm. Even so, unemployment has so far been kept within reasonable bounds, particularly in Prague, where there is a shortage of skilled labor.

The problem of the Communist past has not yet been overcome; the process of "lustration," or screening, was begun in order to illuminate the degree to which people had been contaminated by contact with the secret police. But in a state where virtually everyone's activities were subject to scrutiny, there are few who are not on the state security's files, not least one Havel, V.

Not everyone has interpreted freedom in a responsible way: crime has soared to levels which cause deep despondency among locals but which most Westerners would accept with equanimity. The rebuilding of a social and political order cannot be completed overnight and gaps remain in the law through which villains and opportunists can slip. Communism chose to ignore certain prejudices, sweeping those views about which it was ambivalent under the carpet; some unpleasant creatures have since emerged in the

shape of racists and extreme nationalists, venting their personal paranoias on victimized minorities, such as gypsies. The law, so long the servant of a discredited regime, has yet to regain its full authority.

As a result of all this, ordinary Czechs are confused; even so, they remain cautiously hopeful about taking their place in a Europe from which they have been forcibly excluded for more than 40 years.

Blue-uniformed guard at Prague Castle's gate

■ No city in Europe can match Prague's bristling skyline. Capital of a coastless country, the city seems to be reaching for the heavens, its towers and steeples the equivalent of the piers and jetties of sea-girt nations. To describe Prague as hundred-towered is no exaggeration, but that figure would be a gross underestimate if it included all the city's spires, spikes, and turrets, domes and cupolas, pinnacles and belfries, countless numbers of them rising over an undulating terrain of red roofs, themselves pierced by upward-sweeping dormer windows and graced with pointing weathervanes....■

14

Well-grounded city As well as straining for the sky, Prague is firmly anchored to the ground. The city is considered by many to be the supreme example of architecture working with Nature to enhance the appeal of a site. The early Bohemian princes may not have settled here because of the beauty of the location—who knows?—but the combination of a broad and curving river, the gentle undulations, the swelling hills and rocky bluffs, must have had a more than straightforward military appeal. Subsequent generations have built on this natural heritage, crowning the heights with a proud castle and a tall cathedral, giving form to the steep slopes with terraced gardens, precipitous streets and flights of steps, beautifying the river with bridges, and laying out an endlessly fascinating pattern of streets, squares and buildings.

Time has given Prague deep roots. The very beginnings of the city can

❑ Historic Prague—Hradčany, Staré Město and Nové Město (the Old and New Towns), Malá Strana and Vyšehrad—covers a total of nearly 23 sq m. In 1971 the Czechoslovak government declared the whole of this area to be a conservation zone, protected by law, while its global importance was recognized in 1992 by its inclusion on UNESCO'S World Heritage List.

still be traced in the foundations of 10th-century churches and in the Romanesque cellars of many a town house. Every age has left its mark: a Baroque façade of the 17th or 18th century may well be supported by deep-set Gothic arcades, while behind may lie the rooms lived in by a medieval family hundreds of years

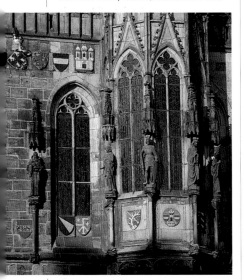

Detail of the Old Town Hall

previously. The 19th century left many new landmarks, such as the Národní divadlo (National Theater) and the Národní muzeum (National Museum), while the architects of the early 20th century managed to insert their array of radically modern buildings into the historic fabric of the city with consummate tact. Most miraculous of all, this accumulated treasure of townscape was left largely untouched, not only by war but, thanks to Communism, by the cruder forms of modern commercial development.

Labyrinthine Prague Prague is one of the most coquettish of cities, revealing and concealing itself at one and the same time. Few places offer themselves so completely to the eye (see page 64), but few are so

intriguing to explore in detail or so easy to get lost in. The maze of medieval streets is still intact—there are few straight lines or vistas here. Doorways and entries invite you into courtyards, passageways and arcades; some claim that it is possible to scurry all over the city "like a mouse behind the wainscoting" (Michael Frayn) without ever having to venture out on to a single street.

Nové Město has many decorative Secession buildings; this one is on Masarykovo nábřeží

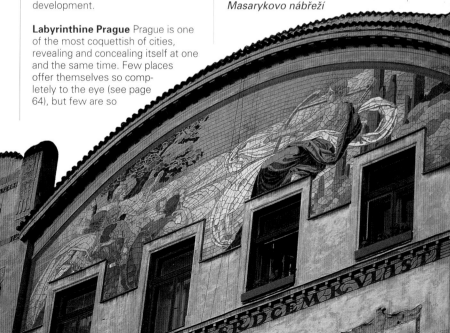

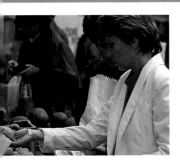

■ **The vast majority of Prague's million and a quarter inhabitants are native Czechs, the westernmost of all the Slav peoples. It still hurts some of them to be described as Eastern Europeans; if you do so you are likely to be reminded that Prague lies a long way west of Vienna, and that for most of its history the country has been firmly tied to a Western world which it is now, not without pain, doing its best to re-enter....■**

Central Europeans As you observe Praguers going about their business, you are likely to notice all kinds of contrasting characteristics. There are traces of Habsburg formality in the use of "Doctor this" and "Professor that," though you won't see much kissing of hands. If you understand the language you will notice that people use "Sir" and "Madam" instead of the once-pervasive "Comrade," and no one, not even in the head office of the reformed Communist Party, uses the greeting "Honor to Work!" any more.

Manners and ways of doing things generally are Central European and different from, say, American or French, though many Czechs pride themselves, especially since 1989, on their informality. Communism has left an overlay of apparent rudeness and indifference which is not characteristically Czech, but which persists among some waiters and shop assistants, the kind whose day is made when they tell the customer that something is unobtainable.

Private lives It would be a mistake to think of Czechs as fiery Slavs. Their history has taught them to keep their heads down, and to make an ironic comment or quiet joke rather than declaim a passionate speech. Subverting the system rather than confronting it head-on seemed a sensible approach when rulers held all the cards that counted. After 1968, most people concentrated on their private lives, making sure there was enough money to pay for the car, the cottage in the country and the occasional foreign vacation, leaving protest to a handful of diehard dissidents. Most women worked and they somehow managed to run a home as well, without overmuch help from a usually unreconstructed male partner.

Difficult days Confusion reigns in the post-1989 world. Life wasn't easy under Communism, but at least it was predictable. A few people

Elderly accordionist and friend in Václavské náměstí

Taking time out to enjoy some excellent local beer

Crime pays Communism suppressed crime and the reporting of it. When newly elected President Havel declared an amnesty for most of the prison population, the freed offenders went on an orgy of theft and vandalism, and criminals of all kinds have had something of a field day ever since. Crime rates rose by something like 300 per cent after 1989, not least because the police, faithful servants of the previous regime, suffered a serious crisis of morale. Even more serious, their Lada cars were incapable of catching the better class of criminal driving a BMW. Praguers enjoy recounting horror stories to their visitors, but you will eventually realize that the crime situation in Prague is roughly the same as it is at home.

Young Praguers face an exciting but uncertain future

have taken to the new order with alacrity; notably the sort of people who make life miserable in expensive restaurants through overuse of their mobile phones. Most people find they have to struggle harder than ever to make ends meet, and have little energy left over for the civic responsibilities so neglected under Communism. After 40 years of being made to mouth meaningless slogans, few people have confidence in politicians or in their own ability to influence the future. Political correctness is unheard of, and there's a feeling that anything suppressed by the previous regime must have a good side—so don't be surprised to hear old prejudices resurface that you thought had been buried way back in the 1940s.

■ **The Czech Republic has some of the most severe environmental problems in Europe. Power stations and heating plants fueled on soft brown coal pour out sulfurous smoke, while forests wither and die, and unpalatable water flows from the taps. Prague suffers particularly badly from environmental ills, sited as it is in a basin where polluted air can be trapped for weeks on end by temperature inversions, sometimes creating conditions so severe that motor vehicles have to be turned back at a cordon surrounding the city....■**

18

National disgrace Many buildings have all too obviously been affected by acid rain and atmospheric dirt. But Prague's biggest conservation problems have been caused not by pollution but by neglect and misuse. Communist Czechoslovakia was a country in which practically nothing escaped nationalization; not only did buildings pass into state ownership, but so did the responsibility for maintaining and restoring them. The state might find the wherewithal to conserve or rebuild some of the buildings in its charge, but neither its resources nor its inclination was enough to care for the whole of the capital's architectural heritage.

Sagging city The uses to which some structures were put, after their original owners had been dispossessed, were not always compatible with their character. Palaces were crudely subdivided and turned into tiny apartments; churches were used as warehouses, convents as libraries. Maintenance was carried out according to a plan, not according to need. Plaster ornaments fell off façades, window frames rotted, roofs fell in and birch trees grew in clogged

Above: Malá Strana statues undergoing restoration
Left: trees damaged by acid rain

gutters. Walls might eventually be shored up with the timber scaffolding that has become such a prominent—and permanent-seeming—feature in the townscape. The legacy is a sagging city, 90 per cent of which is urgently in need of repair.

But... The 40 years of Communism had an up as well as a down side. Money *was* made available for certain projects, and support was given to bodies like SURPMO, the Building Conservation Institute. The SURPMO team of surveyors, architects and craftsmen built up a formidable range

of expertise in the restoration of individual buildings and even of whole towns. Historic structures such as Anežský klášter (St. Agnes's Convent), were rescued from centuries of neglect (and, in this case, turned into an exemplary home for part of the National Gallery).

All along the "Royal Way"—the route from Staré Město (the Old Town) to Pražský hrad (the Castle) once followed by the monarch's coronation procession—house fronts were renovated with exquisite taste and care, though the buildings behind the façades might continue to crumble away. The House at the Stone Bell (Dům U kamenného zvonu) in Staroměstské náměstí (Old Town Square), which everyone had assumed was a Baroque palace, was found, after careful investigation, to be a much altered Gothic house, now lovingly restored to its original state.

Perhaps even more important than these positive achievements, the city was cocooned in time, sealed off from all those destructive forces of commercialism which have ruined the character of many a Western city by insensitive redevelopment, intrusive advertising and the replacement of houses by shops and offices.

Tall story It remains to be seen whether exposure to the pressures of contemporary finance and enterprise will favor the conservation of Prague's heritage any more than the discredited priorities of Communism, which at least handed the city down complete, if not wholly intact. A city council whose basic priority is to expand its tax base may find it difficult to turn down such preposterous (but very real) proposals as the one to build a 900-ft.-high office tower just behind the castle, ruining the integrity of the city's romantic skyline once and for all.

Škodas clog the urban highway

PRAGUE IS *Cultured*

■ **The creative spirit of the Czechs has expressed itself vigorously but unevenly throughout the 20th century, in the visual arts, in music of all kinds and in literature. In retrospect, the interwar republic seems to have been a cultural Golden Age, and when Communism faltered artists again seized the opportunity of voicing the nation's deeper thoughts and wishes....■**

Culture in the springtime The Prague Spring of 1968 was preceded by an outburst of cultural activity, particularly in film and theater. Plays by previously banned Western dramatists were performed, and new theatrical ensembles—such as the Theater on the Balustrade—put on shows whose subversive subtext fooled the censors but not the audience. The cinemas were crammed with audiences enjoying the thinly disguised satirical content of films such as Jiří Menzel's *Closely Observed Trains* (1966) and Miloš Forman's *Loves of a Blonde* (1965), both of which also won international acclaim for their wry observation of human failings.

Exodus and underground After the invasion of 1968, cultural life was put on hold. The country lost many of its cultural leaders, some of whom made new careers abroad, including Forman, who brought his particular touch to Hollywood productions such

Multi-media exuberance at the famous Laterna Magika

as *One Flew over the Cuckoo's Nest*, and the novelists Milan Kundera (*The Unbearable Lightness of Being*) and Josef Škvorecký (*The Engineer of Human Souls*). Škvorecký continued to write while running an adventurous publishing house (68 Publishers) from his base in Toronto. Some of those who stayed at home, such as Bohumil Hrabal, managed to write to their satisfaction (*I Served the King of England*) in spite of censorship; others, including Václav Havel (plays, essays and letters) and Ivan Klíma (novels and short stories), were published in *samizdat* (underground) editions for their friends, for posterity and for an audience abroad. These authors were sometimes able to earn respectable sums in foreign royalties, but were unable to speak to their fellow-countrymen, the public that really mattered.

Money counts The triumphs of 1989 removed the cultural straitjacket of party control and censorship on the country's cultural life, but exposed it immediately to equally formidable financial disciplines. The withdrawal

for a Czech would be the equivalent of a week's wages just to hear a performance of, say, a Mozart opera.

Pop people The subversiveness of rock music never went down well with the Communists, who promoted the blander offerings of brass bands and balladeers. This attitude increased the allure of "underground" music by persecuted performers, such as The Plastic People of the Universe, prolonging 1960s style into the 1990s. All kinds of pop are now performed in Prague (get to see the rock band Laura and her Tigers if you can), some of it retaining an edge of real protest that has disappeared elsewhere, and the John Lennon Wall (see page 114) remains a much-revered icon.

Left: the National Theater
Below: promotional material from the Laterna Magika theater

of subsidies left many theaters in a vulnerable position, and the wonderfully equipped Barrandov film studios are now engaged in providing top-quality technical backup for foreign producers rather than turning out another "Czech New Wave."

All the previously banned authors' books are now in the shops, but the public seems more interested in reading science fiction and romantic fantasy, or manuals on management and accountancy, than in catching up on the thinking that was forbidden under Communism. The most successful theaters are those that appeal to the visitors from abroad, visitors who can afford to pay what

■ "Enchanting," "magical" and "spellbinding" are some of the epithets commonly applied to the "Golden City." Like all clichés they are true, and not least because the truth they contain has more than one side to it. Scratch the entrancing surface of this city and you soon reveal layers of mystery, eccentricity and even horror....■

Eccentric emperors Emperor Charles IV had a mania for collecting odd bits and pieces of the bodies of holy men and women and putting them on display; this may only have been a slight exaggeration of typical medieval behavior, though it contrasts oddly with the rational grandeur of his replanning of Prague.

22

Two centuries later Emperor Rudolf II created a courtly environment in which the rationality of the Renaissance was melded into a strange amalgam with the still-strong

Above: Emperor Rudolf II
Left: astronomer Johannes Kepler

superstitions of the waning Middle Ages. Alchemists, such as the earless Edward Kelley, struggled in smoky laboratories to transmute mercury into gold, while astronomers, such as the noseless Tycho Brahe and the more-or-less intact Johannes Kepler, investigated the mysteries of the heavens (the latter taking time off to defend his mother against a charge of witchcraft).

The Emperor Rudolf himself toiled to understand an increasingly complicated world, driven in part by intellectual curiosity, in part by his own unusual desires—the latter hinted at in the erotic overtones

of some of the works of art which his network of agents brought here for his delectation from all over Europe.

The Golem On one occasion Rudolf sought advice from the famous Rabbi Loew, though the content of their conversation remains a secret. The learned Rabbi would have had a lot to tell his curious ruler; it was he, according to legend, who fashioned a man of mud from the alluvium of the Vltava, then brought it to life as the Golem. Accounts of the Golem's exploits vary; in some he is the guardian of the ghetto against its Christian persecutors, while in others he is a kind of clumsy sorcerer's apprentice. In all accounts he runs amok, like any satisfactory man-made monster, and has to be destroyed by his maker. Both the Golem and the magical Prague in which he lived are brilliantly evoked in Paul Wegener's classic Expressionist film of the early 1920s.

Modern monsters The countless windows of Prague's castle often seem to have a sinister glint to them. For centuries their blank stare pro-claimed the remoteness of Habsburg rule. In 1939, Hitler's head popped cuckoo-like from one of them, though his cruel-faced henchman, "Hangman" Heydrich, exercised his cat-and-mouse rule over the Czechs from Černínský palác (Černín Palace), a building equally suited to be a sym-bol of implacable power. With the advent of Communist rule, Klement Gottwald, First Working Class President and alcoholic, moved back into the castle, but the Reds' real shrine was the Národní památník (National Memorial) on Na Vrchu

Žižkově (Žižkov hill). Here the fore-most of their number became pharaohs of the Proletariat, embalmed in bizarre imitation of their Soviet gods, Lenin and Stalin. Previously pickled in *slivovice*, Klement's corpse responded poorly to preservation, putrefying slowly from the feet up. Seemingly in robust good health, his jowly features peered out from the lurid green 100-crown bill that was issued, with a sublime sense of timing, only weeks before the Velvet Revolution, then rapidly withdrawn to become an instant collector's item.

Source of power—the fountain in the castle's Second Courtyard

■ **Under Communism, Prague sometimes seemed more gray than golden, its drabness relieved on occasion by a rash of red banners proclaiming "Towards a Happy Future with the Soviet Union" or "Work, Learn and Live for the Progress of our Socialist Republic." Since 1989, however, the street scene has become a kaleidoscope of color promoting the products of an international economy long craved for by the Czechs....■**

Consumer city Among the items the Communist order failed to deliver in sufficient quantity and variety was paint. Showpiece buildings might have received their quota of retouching, but most façades remained a slowly darkening shade of elephant gray. What color there was really stood out, like the red and yellow of the city trams, or the variegated parkas and satchels of a line of schoolchildren.

Press here for information

The public transportation department has now transformed some of its vehicles into mobile billboards for cigarettes and computers. New owners have given their old buildings their first coat of paint for 50 years, and the Communist slogans, which no one read anyway, have given way to infinitely more persuasive promises of happiness, courtesy of Coca-Cola, Benetton, McDonald's, Marlboro, Bitburger...

Bazaars and bars The townscape has been further enlivened by the opening of countless bars, boutiques, bureaux de change, shops, cafés and restaurants, each with their own advertisements, displays or inventive menu cards. In front of the new shops, much to the annoyance of the owners, stand hopeful street traders offering everything from T-shirts to smuggled cigarettes (although their numbers have been greatly reduced in recent years). Conceived originally as a way of crossing the river, Karlův most (Charles Bridge) has now become a bazaar where crowds of tourists are offered souvenirs, entertained by street performers or relieved of the contents of their wallets and purses by pickpockets.

Cops and robbers Surveying the changing scene—and not always sure of how to deal with it—are the police, plus an array of auxiliaries: the dark-uniformed guards hired out by a surprising total of 600 or so security firms. The Prague police were once modeled on the British bobby, with a blue uniform and a helmet that looks impractical. After 1968 they were put into intimidating khaki. Their new uniforms, like their changed name ("Police" rather than "Public Security"), are intended to reassure, just like the natty outfits tailored for the castle guard. The role of intimidation seems to have been taken on by the private security men, whose

credentials are sometimes less than confidence-inspiring; in one case a guard attacked the soccer crowd he was supposed to be protecting, then turned on the police who were called to restrain him.

Press released The return of press freedom has made life easier for the visitor from abroad, as well as packing the news kiosks with any number of new titles. No longer does the tourist have to make do with the turgid texts of such party-approved papers as London's *Morning Star* or East Berlin's *Neues Deutschland*; newspapers are now available from all over the world. Local publications cater for all tastes, though the appetite for crude home-grown porn, printed on what looks like blotting-paper, seems to be waning.

The ubiquitous McDonald's

25

■ Draped over hills and riverbanks, Prague has always known how to exercise its allure on foreigners, beckoning to them from behind the veils of forested mountains that seem to form such a formidable barrier on the Bohemian borders, but which are no obstacle to the determined. Ever since the Arab merchant Ibrahim ibn Jakub described Prague in the 10th century as "the richest of all cities," traders from abroad have displayed their wares in its streets and markets....■

Immigrants and tourists Germans came to Prague from the earliest times, both as monks and priests to strengthen Christianity, and as mercenaries and opportunists to grab what they could from a country often plagued by turmoil. Italians brought their skills as designers and craftsmen to help restyle the townscape in the frenzy of rebuilding that took place in Baroque times, settling in the part of town still named after them: Vlašská (Italian Street).

The first true tourists were those early 19th-century Germans imbued with a Romantic sensibility who sailed up the Elbe from Saxony, marveling at the drama of its gorge and the horror of the great rock at Schreckenstein, before settling down to sample the picturesque pleasures of the capital.

After World War I, the new state of Czechoslovakia tried to seduce

Below: a 1920s Čedok charabanc pauses in the Old Town Square

Above: a 1930s ad for the Czech Tatra tourer

tourists by promoting both Golden Prague and the landscapes and folk-lore of the country as a whole. Even when Czechoslovakia was absorbed into the Third Reich in 1939, strenuous but short-lived efforts were made to promote the "Protectorate of Bohemia and Moravia" as an ideal holiday destination for the people of the Master Race.

Traditional tourism died with the coming of Communism. For decades, virtually the only foreigners to cross the frontier were those from other Soviet bloc countries, or else subsidized trade unionists visiting from the West on tours of nurseries, blast furnaces and other "Socialist achievements." After 1989, the expected happened; thousands upon thousands of visitors flocked to Prague to participate in the euphoria following the collapse of Communism and to see for themselves whether the city really was as beautiful as it was reputed to be. Along with the casual tourists came many businesspeople, media folk and students, some here for the short term, but many to stay, committing themselves to a city whose outward charm helps soothe the many frustrations of everyday life.

***Rive gauche* revived** Prague casts the same kind of spell on some Americans as Paris did in the 1920s. Estimates of the number of U.S. citizens living here vary from

the thousand or two who have official work permits to tens of thousands of semi-permanent "tourists." The proudest boast is to have been a pioneer, to have arrived when Prague was still a "one Mac city" (McDonald's has opened several restaurants since its first outlet began operating in 1991).

The *Prague Post* The presence of a substantial American community has encouraged the development of a network of institutions and support services to aid survival in what can be a difficult or confusing environment. Books in English and Brooklyn-style bagels are now available, but the key institution is the English-language weekly newspaper, the *Prague Post*, launched in October 1990. Its editor-in-chief is the old Prague hand Alan Levy, thrown out of the country by the Communists in 1971 and given a 5,615-year jail sentence in absentia. Bought by Czechs as well as visitors, it is essential reading, filled with a highly stimulating mixture of news, editorials, and cultural goings-on.

English-language newspapers keep Prague's expatriate population posted

■ Ever since Parisians identified a group of itinerant gypsies as "Bohemians" the word has been used as a tag for those who lead an unconventional life. Communism kept its subjects firmly clamped inside a limited number of categories, but its demise has allowed all kinds of individuals to crawl out of the woodwork and behave in ways that would have been unthinkable a few years ago....■

Bohemian sleaze For Cecil Parrott, former British Ambassador, the original "Bad Bohemian" was the author of *The Good Soldier Švejk*, Jaroslav Hašek (1883–1923). Hašek's life was led on society's margin before alcoholism sent him to an early grave. Bigamist and brawler, boozer and

Individual style: a hat-seller on the Charles Bridge

Above: exotic characters crowd the front of the Martinic Palace

prankster, founder of the pub-based "Party of Moderate Progress within the Bounds of the Law," Hašek's anarchic exploits often ended with his arrest or with his carriage home as a "beer corpse" aboard that peculiar Prague institution, a wickerwork trolley in which the casualties of the night were delivered to their doorsteps. The trolley has long since disappeared, and the army of determined drinkers who daily fill Prague's bars now seem more or less able to make their own way home.

Bohemian tease As far back as the 15th century, rumor credited Hussite splinter groups with nudism, free love, and indulgence in orgies. Prague's atmosphere has always carried a high erotic charge. Young women here are as pretty as anywhere; under Communism, some were tempted to become "Tuzex Girls," exchanging their favors for hard currency to be spent in the special shops of that name. The dullness of life at that time led many people into sexual adventuring as a substitute for other frustrated ambitions, a phenomenon explored in the writings of Milan Kundera.

"Tuzex Girls" were closely controlled by the police, but since 1989 there has been an explosion of free enterprise in this field. Its exponents can be seen in Václavské náměstí (Wenceslas Square), or waiting hopefully by roads in country districts close to border crossings.

PRAGUE WAS

PRAGUE WAS *A legend*

■ **Centuries of glory began for the Czechs when soothsaying Princess Libuše stood on a high cliff above the Vltava and revealed a vision of a city "whose splendor shall reach unto the stars." Persuaded by her followers to ally masculine muscle power to feminine intuition, the noble lady married a plowman prince, one Přemysl, and together they founded Prague at a place where the stone sill (*prah* in Czech) of a house was being constructed....■**

Myth and reality Princess and plowman are, of course, myths, but ones based on some sort of historical reality; the dynasty which ruled the Czech Lands for hundreds of years between the 9th and the 14th centuries were known as the Přemys-

30

lids. Libuše's prototype may have reigned in the 6th century, the time when Slav tribes moved into Bohemia from the northeast, replacing the Germanic clans who had lived here beforehand.

Royal rocks In its early years, Pražský hrad (Prague Castle) was just one stronghold among many. The original ruler's seat was at Levý hradec (Left Castle), a clifftop site so named because it stood above the left bank of the Vltava. The high bluff at Vyšehrad where Libuše had celebrated her marriage to Přemysl was the preferred royal residence in the 11th and 12th centuries. In the end, though, the overwhelming advantages of the castle site prevailed, and over the years Hradčany developed as the "Bohemian Acropolis," a fortified complex comprising cathedral, royal palace, convents and chapels, residences, stables, and workshops.

❑ Prehistoric people left many traces of their presence in and around present-day Prague, and it was the Celts who gave the country its name. The Celtic tribe known as the Boii to the Romans lived in Bojohemum (Bohemia) before being pushed out by the Germanic Marcomans in the 1st century BC. ❑

Top: Prague's founding figure, the proud Princess Libuše
Left: legends and leisure-seekers in Vyšehrad Park

■ **The rule of the Czech kings once extended far beyond the natural boundaries of Bohemia. The Great Moravian Empire of the 9th century was smashed by the onrush of the heathen Hungarians, severing the Czechs from their Slovak cousins for a thousand years, but in the 13th century the realm of ambitious Otakar II reached as far as the Adriatic, briefly bestowing on Bohemia that seacoast referred to so puzzlingly by Shakespeare in *The Winter's Tale*....■**

Urban nuclei At the foot of the castle and on the far bank of the Vltava, trading townships grew up from the 10th century onwards. The Jews arrived in Malá Strana at this time, and in the 13th century they were given the ghetto district (today called Josefov) in Staré Město (the Old Town). Otakar II walled in Malá Strana and encouraged industrious German immigrants to settle not just here and in the Old Town, but also in newly founded royal towns all over the country.

The Old Town, too, had a semicircle of walls 36 ft. high, punctuated at intervals by 13 towers up to 90 ft. tall, and further protected by a deep moat. The moat is recalled by today's Na příkopě ("On the Moat") and by the arches of one of the bridges that used to cross it, now exposed in Můstek metro station. Within the walls, fine stone houses were built along the winding streets. The streets themselves followed the alignment of ancient trackways straggling over the fields towards the fords across the Vltava; in the 10th century the fords were replaced

The country's patron saint

King Wenceslas IV (1361–1419)

first by a wooden bridge, and then, in 1170, by the first stone structure, the Judith Bridge (itself now defunct).

The Good King The Wenceslas who rides his sprightly steed in front of the Národní muzeum (National Museum) is "Our Prince" to the Czechs, not a king as in the Christmas carol. He is also the country's foremost patron saint, having died a martyr's death in AD 929 at the hands of his brother, Boleslav. Wenceslas is supposed to slumber with his knights deep beneath a cliff, ready to rescue the nation on the day that real disaster strikes.

■ **Emperor Charles IV (1316–78) continues to inspire awe and affection among the Czechs. Brought up in France, Charles chose Prague as his residence and set about transforming what was already a substantial city into an imperial metropolis. By the end of his reign, Prague was Europe's third-largest city....**■

King-Emperor Charles Charles ascended the throne of Bohemia in 1346 and became head of the Holy Roman Empire in 1355; by the time of his death in 1378 he had thrown a great Gothic-arched bridge across the Vltava, begun to build St. Vitus's Cathedral, established the first university in Central Europe, founded the spa-town of Carlsbad, and erected the fortress-shrine of Karlštejn on the banks of the Berounka. His most ambitious project was the construction of Prague's Nové Město (New Town), whose streets and squares remain in use today, though the site of its walls is now occupied by the Magistral motorway.

architect of the age, Petr Parléř of Cologne. The arts flourished under Charles's rule, and artists were given enviable official commissions, including Master Theodorik, entrusted with the decoration of the Kaple svatého Kříže (Chapel of the Holy Cross) at Karlštejn, with its 100-plus panel paintings. Charles is also remembered for a great gift to the Czech Lands, that of viticulture, importing vines from Burgundy to be planted at Mělník, still the wine center of Bohemia.

Relaxed ruler Charles IV ruled his kingdom with wisdom and restraint, perhaps mindful of the horrors of war. He had been wounded as a young man at the battle of Crécy, where many a flower of Bohemian chivalry had perished. While dealing firmly with treachery (he once put the noose round a rebel's neck with his own hands), he tolerated growing radicalism among the clergy, even forgiving a denunciation of himself as the Antichrist by one intemperate priest!

Karlštejn Castle in its glorious setting of crag and forest

Charles was a cosmopolitan who felt at home in Bohemia and was happiest when speaking Czech, a language he insisted be mastered by all his officials. Under his rule the cathedral was begun by Matthew of Arras and continued by the greatest

Charles IV greets visitors to his bridge

■ A century before Luther and the Reformation, Czech clerics defied the Church authorities. Protesting against corruption and worldliness, they insisted on their right to preach in Czech, the language of the common people. Foremost among these was Master Jan Hus (John Huss in English), a man of humble origin....■

A turbulent priest Hus taught at the university founded by Charles IV, and in 1409 his promotion of Czech interests upset his German colleagues and students so much that they quit Prague and founded their own university in Leipzig. More upsetting to his superiors was his insistence on the supremacy of the Bible as the source of divine wisdom, rather than the Church itself. This was heady stuff to the city crowd, who filled the Betlémské kaple (Bethlehem Chapel) in Staré Město (the Old Town) to hear God's word preached in language they could understand.

Eventually Hus was run out of town, though he continued to write and to preach to congregations in the countryside. Summoned to Konstanz in 1414 to give an account of himself, Hus faced his interrogators proudly, refused to recant and went to the stake without a qualm in 1415.

Jan Hus surveys Old Town Square

The Hussite heritage Hus is still a hero to many Czechs today. Following his execution, his followers founded the holy city of Tábor, in South Bohemia, and wars were fought in his name. Erected in the 1920s, the Národní památník (National Memorial) stands on the hill to the east of the city center where the Hussite army, led by one-eyed Jan Žižka, trounced the Crusaders sent against them in 1420. In 1457 a Hussite, the much-admired George of Poděbrady, was even elected king.

The First Prague Defenestration In 1419, a band of Hussites parading

Hus at the stake, 6 July 1415

through the city was pelted with stones from the windows of the New Town Hall. The furious crowd surged into the building and hurled the perpetrators through the windows to their deaths on the cobbles below, establishing a tradition of settling disputes unique to Prague.

■ The embers of Hussite radicalism smoldered away in the Czech Lands, helping to fire the flames of Lutheranism and other assorted forms of Protestantism in the 16th century. There was a measure of open-mindedness and tolerance in these early Renaissance times; questing spirits were drawn to the court of Habsburg Rudolf II (1552–1612), an avid collector whose esoteric interests encompassed alchemy, astrology, and astronomy, as well as some of the less-traveled byways of eroticism (see page 22)....■

The Second Prague Defenestration

By the start of the 17th century, most Czechs had turned away from Catholicism, their right to dissent apparently guaranteed by imperial edict. Unbeknownst to them, the Church was working closely with the Habsburgs to restore its hegemony. The Protestants were deliberately and continually provoked, until one day, in 1618, enraged by the acts of a pair of Catholic councilors, a band of noblemen stormed into the castle and hurled the two wretches and their secretary from a window.

This Second Prague Defenestration is generally regarded as the incident which precipitated the outbreak of the Thirty Years' War (1618–48), this in turn resulting in the downfall of the Bohemian nobility and the Czech nation as a whole. By 1621, the Czechs' elected Winter King, Frederick, had fled, his Protestant army easily overcome by imperial forces at the Battle of the White Mountain. Twenty-seven of the leading Defenestrators were executed on Staroměstské náměstí (Old Town Square), some of their heads being displayed on pikes on the Karlův most (Charles Bridge).

"Recant or go!" then became the catchword, and many went—clerics, academics, noblemen—in one of those emigrations that mark Czech history. Into their place surged the Jesuits, those clever commissars of the Counter-Reformation, together with a newly minted nobility from all over Europe, loyal to the Habsburgs.

The 1618 Defenestration

Destruction and construction The war went on, devastating Bohemia as much as any part of Central Europe. Great men made their careers out of it; the ambitious General Wallenstein (Valdštejn in Czech), who led the imperial armies, amassed a fortune in loot and property and went so far as to challenge the power of the emperor himself. For this offense he was assassinated in the frontier town of Cheb (Eger) by an Englishman, an Irishman, and a Scotsman, but not before he had built himself one of the grandest residences Prague had ever seen. Completed in 1630, the

Top: view of Prague, 1574

Wallenstein Palace in Malá Strana is essentially the prototype of all the city's palaces.

All the parvenus, as well as what was left of old Bohemian blood, had to have their place in town, and over the next century or so the city was given the smiling Baroque face that so much of it wears today. This great rebuilding affected not just palaces (mostly in Malá Strana), but also humbler burghers' houses and, above all, churches; Baroque was the conviction architecture of the Counter-Reformation, the message of the True Faith conveyed through sublime architectural theatrics. The greatest of Prague's Baroque churches is the Chrám svatého Mikuláše (St. Nicholas) in Malá Strana, but splendid spires and domes punctuate the streetscape everywhere, and everywhere there

The assassination of Wallenstein

are ecclesiastical interiors of the utmost sumptuousness.

Czech out All this architectural splendor was sugar to the bitter pill of religious, political, and linguistic suppression. Czech was made to cede to German as the language of the land. No longer a literary language, eventually it became the comic-seeming dialect of peasants, coachmen and washerwomen. Denied other forms of expression, the people's talent surged into music: *"Co Čech, to muzikant!"* ("Scratch a Czech and find a musician").

General Wallenstein's Malá Strana palace, the Valdštejnský palác

■ For two centuries or so after the Battle of the White Mountain (1621), Prague fell into a kind of slumber. The Kingdom of Bohemia still existed, but only on paper. The Court removed itself to Vienna, and the city led the life of a provincial town. The castle's countless rooms lay empty, and Rudolf II's amazing collection of paintings, sculpture, and manuscripts—albeit somewhat reduced after looting by Swedish soldiers during the Thirty Years' War—was auctioned off at bargain prices....■

A nation rediscovered Toward the end of the 18th century, Emperor Joseph II tried to turn his far-flung, and still largely feudal, realm into an up-to-date state by centralizing the administration, abolishing serfdom, formalizing religious freedom, and dissolving the monasteries. His idea of progress also included the vigorous imposition of the German language, and as the 19th century began, Prague would have seemed an almost entirely Germanic town to the outsider, with the use of Czech confined to the lower orders. This was also the moment when the Czech Lands started their upward climb as the industrial powerhouse of the Austrian Empire. As the economy developed, so did national consciousness. The Czech language was revived and codified by intellectuals, such as

The Habsburg reformer, Emperor Joseph II

Secession sirens on Široká street

Josef Dobrovský and Josef Jungmann, while historian-turned-politician František Palacký presented the nation with its rediscovered history in a text that took him 46 years to write.

Societies sprang up everywhere to promote Czech poetry, prose, and drama. Austria was able to tolerate all this, but the attempt to translate national awareness into political action was not acceptable; in 1848, the "Year of Revolutions," a popular uprising was ruthlessly put down by General Windischgrätz. Thereafter, all Czech attempts to claim some kind of autonomy for their ancient kingdom went unregarded in Vienna.

A nation on the move In the end, the swelling tide of nationalism could not be stopped. Denied political outlets, it flowed in other channels—artistic, literary, architectural, and entrepreneurial. In the latter part of

the 19th century, Prague grew rapidly, sucking in the rural Czech population and bursting out beyond its walls in the form of industrial and residential suburbs.

Battle was joined on the city council between a diminishing number of German speakers and the increasingly triumphant Czechs. Street names became one symbol of the struggle. At first, Czech was allowed to appear below the German name; in 1861 the order was reversed and by 1894 German street names were made to disappear altogether.

National feeling pervaded the music of Smetana and Dvořák, painters presented their bombastic vision of a glorious past, and writers such as Božena Němcová and Jan Neruda laid the foundations of modern Czech literature. Great cultural institutions, including the Národní muzeum (National Museum) and the Národní divadlo (National Theater), were established and given the most prestigious architectural expression possible. To bring an end to German domination of commercial life, banks such as the famous Živnostenská on Na Příkopě were brought into being to help found and finance specifically Czech-owned enterprises.

Secession city There was no slackening of energy as the 20th century dawned. Increasingly confident that they would one day control their own destiny, Czechs saw their capital become one of the great European centers of Art Nouveau. The jewel-like buildings of the Secession era (as it is known in Prague) stud the streetscape of the city center, foremost among them being the Obecní dům (Municipal House).

The Secession-era Obecní dům

PRAGUE WAS *Czechoslovak*

■ **The Czechs were dragged unwillingly into World War I by their Habsburg masters. The Austrian police reported "disgraceful scenes" in Prague as shambling conscripts were herded into the troop trains, flowers and beer bottles sticking from their rifle barrels. In no mood to slaughter the Russians, their Slav cousins, Czech troops went over to the enemy in large numbers, eventually forming a famous legion which fought its way home via the Trans-Siberian railroad....■**

The creation of Czechoslovakia
Other Czech and Slovak legionnaires battled alongside the French and Italians, lending more power to Tomáš Masaryk's elbow as he sought the Allies' support for the foundation of a Czechoslovak state. As Austria—Hungary crumbled in 1918, this vision came true; the new country was proclaimed in Prague on October 28. Like Habsburg Austria, it was a multiracial entity, inhabited not only by Czechs and Slovaks, but also by Hungarians, Poles, Ruthenes and 3 million Sudetan Germans.

Good times and adversity For the Czechs, the First Republic seemed a dream come true. Democracy prevailed, the economy prospered, and the arts flourished even more than they had in the period of the Secession. Prague's city center took on its present shape, some of its crisp new buildings a generation ahead of their time. Foreign Minister Beneš, who had shared Masaryk's exile in World War I, secured the country's frontiers with an impressive set of alliances.
    Then came the Great Depression. The Sudeten German areas were

Top: Independence Day, 1918

worst affected, and their inhabitants not unnaturally blamed the Czechs for the demise of their industries and the resulting hardship. Rumblings came from a backward Slovakia, denied autonomy and ruled insensitively from far-away Prague. The charismatic leader of the Slovaks, Štefánik, a committed Czechoslovlak and loyal collaborator of Masaryk, had been killed in an air crash in the early days of the new state; the loudest voice now was that of a Roman Catholic priest, Andrej Hlinka, whose nationalist and separatist outpourings were seen as treasonous in Prague.

Betrayed at Munich As economic ills persisted, more and more Sudeten Germans looked longingly across the frontier, hoping that redemption would come from Nazi Germany. Anxious to appease Hitler, and culpably ignorant of local circumstances, Britain and France put intolerable pressure on Czechoslovakia to yield to German demands. At Munich, in September 1938, the Western

President Masaryk in his coach (right) and on an interwar banknote (below)

democracies did a deal with the dictators; the country was carved up, Germany being given virtually all the territory it had demanded.

Czechoslovakia lost much of its industry and communications network as well as the whole of its modern border fortifications. The Wehrmacht moved into the Sudetenland, followed closely by the Gestapo, pleased at being able to pounce on large numbers of Jews and democratic Germans who had not been able to make good their

Above: Edvard Beneš
Left: the progressive architecture of the interwar Baba estate

escape, or who had been sent back into their clutches by the trainload by embittered Czechs.

Unlucky Beneš Edvard Beneš had been made president on Masaryk's resignation in 1935. Deserted at Munich by his supposed allies, Britain and France, he now resigned and left the country. This second period of exile came to a triumphant conclusion in 1945, when the Czechoslovak Republic was re-established and Beneš became president again, but his triumph was to last only until 1948: once again he was outwitted by opponents whose ruthlessness proved more than a match for his cleverness—the Communists.

PRAGUE WAS *"Protected"*

■ **The post-Munich Czecho-Slovak state soon fell apart. In March 1939, Hitler instructed the Slovak separatists to secede, then summoned aging and infirm Czech President Hácha to Berlin where, faced with Goering's threat to bomb Prague into ruins, he agreed to put the fate of the Czechs into the hands of the Führer....■**

The Protektorat When poor Hácha got home, he found the German army was already driving through the snowbound streets of Prague, the city's citizens shaking their fists impotently at the helmeted heads. Hitler saluted a carefully drilled crowd from a window in the Hradčany district, and the country was renamed Bohemia-Moravia, a Protectorate of the German Reich. Another haul of political prisoners was made, and the Wehrmacht received the bonus of the Czech army's up-to-date equipment; a year later they would be rolling through France aboard solidly built tanks from the famous Škoda works. Predictably, German guarantees of Czech autonomy proved worthless; within months the universities had been closed down, the population cowed and the Czech economy ruthlessly integrated into the Nazi war machine.

Second exile In his London exile, Beneš was supported by a new generation of legionnaires; Czech and Slovak airmen gave a particularly good account of themselves in the Battle of Britain. In 1942, disturbed by the lack of resistance at home, he sent in parachutists to assassinate acting Reichsprotektor Heydrich. The Germans were provoked into a frenzy of reprisals, including murder on a grand scale and the razing to the ground of two villages, Lidice and Ležáky. The parachutists were eventually tracked down to Prague; discovered hiding in the crypt of the Kostel svatého Cyrila a Metoděje

The Sudetenland ceded to Hitler

WIR DANKEN UNSERM FÜHRER

(Church of Saints Cyril and Methodius), their heroic struggle ended in death and suicide.

Czech hearts were hardened; though opportunities for overt resistance were few, sabotage was common and a bitter resentment built up against all things German. In 1944, the Slovaks showed their mettle in a magnificent uprising in their mountain stronghold, which was put down only after two months of hard fighting. Meanwhile, Beneš came to an agreement with the Soviet Union and with the Czechoslovak Communists in exile there, which was to guarantee them a disproportionate influence in postwar affairs.

Self-help In May 1945, with the Red Army approaching from the north and the east and the Americans from the west, Prague rose against its oppressors. Barricades were formed, and hidden arms distributed. Most of the German forces were only too anxious to escape westwards from Russian wrath, but others in the SS and the Gestapo relished the opportunity to settle old scores and hundreds of Praguers were killed even after the war was officially declared over. As the tide turned, however, a terrible revenge was exacted on those Germans who had not been prudent enough to make themselves scarce. The lucky ones found themselves doing forced labor, beaten and spat at by the population; the unlucky

Top: liberation celebrations

ones hung from lampposts or drifted lifelessly down the Vltava.

Impatient Patton American forces had pushed into the west of the country, liberating Carlsbad, Plzeň and České Budějovice. Here, by agreement with the Soviet Union, they were instructed to halt, even though nothing stood between them and Prague except for a few German stragglers eager to surrender. Impetuous General

41

Soviet troops entering the Czechoslovak capital on May 9, 1945

Patton strained at the leash, but was firmly held back by the Allied High Command, thus handing the Red Army the credit for "liberating" Prague (the last European capital to be freed), and with it a propaganda victory of incalculable proportions.

■ A restored Czechoslovak government followed the Red Army's tanks into Prague at the end of World War II. Beneš was still president, though it soon became clear that this would be a very different regime from the one established by Masaryk in 1918. The Communists were the largest party, enjoying considerable public support. Accused of collaboration with the Nazis, even moderately right-wing groups were thoroughly discredited and not allowed to participate in political life....■

Auf Wiedersehen As well as carrying out a sweeping programme of nationalization, the new government implemented a final solution to the problem of Czechs and Germans sharing the same country: apart from a handful of "anti-fascists" and workers with indispensable skills, the whole Sudeten German population—more than 3 million in total—was expelled, often in conditions of extreme brutality.

Prague had already lost its German-speaking inhabitants, most of whom were Jews, but the country now had to cope with an empty borderland, much of which had been inhabited by Germans since the Middle Ages. The abandoned areas attracted displaced people of all kinds, as well as an army of opportunists led by the Communists, who made use of the operation to consolidate their power.

Klement Gottwald

❑ By 1947 the overwhelming majority of Sudeten Germans had been forced to leave their homes, allowed to take with them only what they could carry. Estimates of those who perished in the process vary between 100,000 and 200,000. Although one of President Havel's first (and most controversial) acts on taking office was to apologize for this expulsion, there is at present no question of compensation; "restitution" only applies to injustices carried out after the Communists took over Czechoslovakia in 1948. ❑

"Victorious February" In early 1948, the Communists were ready to strike. With near total control of the police and army, and able to deploy tens of thousands of militiamen and demonstrators, they squeezed out their democratic coalition partners. On the cold and snowy morning of February 21, a huge gathering in Staroměstské náměstí (the Old Town Square) was addressed in triumphant tones by Communist Prime Minister Gottwald; with the democratic forces in complete disarray, an enfeebled Beneš was obliged to accept Gottwald's demands.

A few days later, the Red *coup d'état* was consolidated by yet another defenestration; the popular Foreign Minister Jan Masaryk, son of the former president and the sole

Top: youth parade in the late 1940s

surviving non-Communist member of the government, was found dead in the courtyard below the open window of his apartment.

Prague purged There now followed a classic example of totalitarian takeover. Public life was purged of all "unreliable elements" and of all those potentially contaminated with "Western ideas," such as the soldiers and airmen who had served with the Allies. Another emigration took place comparable to that of 1938.

The battle to build Socialism was joined. Many sincerely believed a new and more just age had dawned, and they toiled all hours on Soviet-style industrial projects designed to link the economy firmly to the Eastern bloc. But the revolution ended by eating its own children: in 1951, at the height of the Cold War and of Stalinist paranoia, Gottwald's lieutenant, Rudolf Slánský, who had overseen the first wave of arrests, was himself arrested along with a number of other old Communists.

Subjected to physical torture and brainwashing by a Soviet-trained

Foreign Minister Jan Masaryk

secret police, these faithful Party men all confessed to being imperialist agents, Trotskyites, Zionists, or Titoists, guilty of an array of improbable crimes against the People. Most were executed. Thousands of other political prisoners served out their sentences in labor camps, the unluckiest of them in appalling conditions in the uranium mines of Jáchymov.

President Beneš yields power to Gottwald on February 29, 1948

■   **Despite its excesses, Czech Communism was to some extent a home-grown product. The Communists had gathered the biggest vote in the last free elections, and for a while the Party kept the loyalty of many genuine believers. Czechoslovakia avoided the disturbances that rocked Poland and tore Hungary apart in the mid-1950s. By the 1960s, however, it had become clear that all was far from well....■**

The Prague Spring The country that had inherited most of the industrial wealth and skills of the Habsburg Empire, and which had been relatively untouched by war, was now much poorer than its neighbor Austria, a land with little industry and no natural resources. Pressure for change built up until it became irresistible: by early 1968, President Antonín Novotný was forced to resign, his place taken by a little-known Slovak, Alexander Dubček.

In April, Dubček and his colleagues proposed an Action Program for reform; this caught the public's imagination and the Prague Spring was born, a joyous flowering of enthusiasm for civic and political life. Suddenly, everything seemed possible: journals and newspapers explored hitherto forbidden questions, the censor abolished himself and people went on vacations abroad for the first time in 20 years. Foreign wellwishers flocked to Prague to see "Socialism with a human face."

August invasion Not everybody was happy with these developments. Hardline Communists at home mostly kept quiet, but the Russian bear growled menacingly, then sent troops into Czechoslovakia for "summer maneuvers," where they were subjected to unprecedented pestering by the Western journalists thronging the country.

Dubček's utterly sincere protestations of loyalty were not enough, and on the night of August 20 Czechoslovakia was invaded by 400,000

Dubček greets crowds celebrating the Prague Spring of 1968

troops from the Warsaw Pact—Poles, Hungarians, Bulgarians, and East Germans, as well as Russians. Prague woke to the menacing sound of tanks roaring over the cobblestones; leading members of the government were arrested and flown to Moscow where, like President Hácha summoned to meet Hitler in 1939, they were forced to sign documents legitimizing the Russian invasion.

Thousands gathered in the streets of Prague, building barricades and taunting the often bewildered soldiers who thought they had come to save their allies from imperialist invasion. Some panicked, one machine-gunner raking the façade of the Národní muzeum (National

Top: Soviet troops enter Prague

Museum). Many soldiers were so demoralized that they had to be withdrawn after only a few days.

Normalization For a while an intense feeling of national solidarity sustained the Czechs. Even after a shattered Dubček returned and spoke in a choking voice about the need to put "temporary restrictions" on freedom, many felt something could be saved from the wreckage. It was not to be. As 1968 gave way to 1969, one reform after the other was withdrawn; the leading instigators of the Prague Spring were cut down to size: Dubček himself was demoted to the role of ambassador to Turkey and finally sent back to his home town of Bratislava, condemned to ending his days as a Forestry Commission clerk.

Stranded Soviet tank in a suburban side-street

Yet another emigration then took place, the country losing tens of thousands of its best and brightest spirits. Many of those who remained were subjected to a ruthless process of "normalization," forced to give an account of their activities during 1968, and losing job or Party membership if the answers were not satisfactory. Even the police force was deprived of its cheerful blue uniforms and put into intimidating khaki.

Memorial to Jan Palach, the student who committed suicide in protest of the Soviet invasion

■ **Throughout the 1970s and 1980s the citizens of Czechoslovakia lived in the gloomy world of the "real existing socialism" created by normalization. Political life was conducted according to slogans about the building of socialism and of fraternity with the Soviet Union which no one believed, least of all those responsible for them. In retrospect, it seems the last chance for Communism to revitalize itself was lost in 1968, when the Russian tanks revealed it to be little more than a system for exercising power....■**

Protesters and survivors

Arbitrary rule extinguished all hopes of political change. Those who refused to conform suffered the loss of their jobs, police harassment and reprisals against their families, such as the exclusion of their children from higher education. This was a sufficient deterrent to ensure that all but a few played the rulers' game; the few included the signatories of Charta 77, a document demanding respect for the human rights guaranteed by the constitution. Among them was the playwright and future president, Václav Havel, unpublished and unperformed in his own country, and a seasoned jailbird and brewery worker.

Gottwald graces Communism's last Czech banknote (1989)

The majority of people simply kept their heads down, paying lip-service to whatever the Party demanded in the way of mouthing slogans or signing petitions for peace. At the same time, the system was milked for whatever could be got out of it. Offices and factories were treated as sources of supply rather than as places of work—rarely would a telephone be answered on a Friday afternoon once the exodus to the country cottage had begun. The government engineered a ramshackle consumer revolution, ensuring that the shelves in the stores were full of goods, albeit not in great variety or any quality.

The Velvet Revolution Gorbachev's Soviet Union encouraged the process of *přestavba*, an unconvincing Czechoslovak imitation of *perestroika* (reform). The country's rulers

Students celebrate the end of Communism in 1989

46

seemed blissfully unaware of the abyss opening underneath them as the "year of miracles," 1989, wore on and the Communist house of cards began to collapse all over Eastern Europe. But even this most rigid of regimes could not remain unaffected. On November 17, an officially approved demonstration—held to mark the anniversary of the Nazis' closure of the Czech universities—was viciously attacked by riot police. The event acted as a catalyst. The spot where a student was supposed to have died became an instant shrine; striking students were joined by actors, and colleges and theaters all over the country became the nodes from which popular protest spread.

❏ Some say the events of November 17 were stage-managed by the KGB and a group of home-grown Communists, anxious to discredit the rigid and incompetent regime and replace it by one more congenial to Gorbachev's Soviet Union. In this scenario, the corpse of the "student" felled by the police on Na Národní managed to get into the ambulance on its own legs, which were those of the secret agent who had led the demonstration. Happily, the events gathered their own momentum and meaning, independently of any manipulation. ❏

With Havel at its head, Civic Forum was set up in Prague to coordinate protest activity. Some massive demonstrations took place; one in Václavské náměstí (Wenceslas Square) was addressed by both Havel and a joyful Alexander Dubček,

Newly chosen President Havel and his wife on the castle balcony

who had been whisked back from obscure retirement in Bratislava. The regime offered concessions which soon became irrelevant. A new government was formed, and the crowd's cry of *"Havel na Hrad!"* ("Havel to the castle!") was heeded; on December 29 the former dissident was installed as president of what was still formally called the Czechoslovak Socialist Republic. Forty-one years of Communism had been brought to an end virtually without violence in what came to be known as the "Velvet Revolution."

Special delivery
The Loretto shrine, in Hradčany, incorporates a replica of the Virgin Mary's highly mobile home, the Santa Casa (Holy House). The original house was transported by angels from Nazareth; after a three-year stopover in Dalmatia, it finally reached Italy in 1294. Its sudden appearance in a laurel-grove (*loreto* in Italian) near Ancona on the Adriatic caused a sensation, resulting in any number of copies; there are no less than 50 in Bohemia alone.

Right: Karlův most (Charles Bridge) in the early morning light

Below: building detail, Staroměstské náměstí (Old Town Square)

With a population of about 1¼ million, metropolitan Prague can still be grasped as a whole, its outermost suburbs visible from the viewpoints which are such a feature of the city. The historic center is easy to understand too, although it is more correct to speak of several centers, for Prague used to be not one, but four towns. Each of these historic districts—Hradčany, Malá Strana, Staré Město (Old Town) and Nové Město (New Town)—is still a recognizable entity, and treated as such in this guide.

Hradčany The castle quarter spreads over the heights on the west bank of the River Vltava. Within the walls of the castle complex are the seat of the president, the old royal palace, the great Gothic cathedral and several galleries and museums, old streets and lanes, gardens, and belvederes. Beyond the castle gates are fine palaces and humbler dwellings, the famous Loretánská kaple (Loretto shrine) and, topping the Petřín hill, the twin spires of Strahovský klášter (Strahov Monastery).

Malá Strana Set in the limited space between the castle and the river, this is the city's most charming quarter. The name (literally "the Small Side") is usually translated in English as the "Lesser Town." Centered on the great Baroque Chram svatého Mikuláše (Church of St. Nicholas), its intimate squares and steeply climbing streets are lined with Baroque palaces and splendid townhouses.

Staré Město The Old Town is linked to Malá Strana by the superb Gothic Karlův most (Charles Bridge), one of the city's most important viewpoints and meeting places. Beyond the eastern bridge tower, the Old Town's maze of medieval streets repays leisurely exploration, while the popular Royal Way leads into Staroměstké náměstí, the Old Town Square. With the medieval town hall and its astronomical clock, the Hus monument, palaces, and arcaded burghers' houses, this is where the city's essence is most densely concentrated. Just off the square is Josefov, the ancient Jewish ghetto, with the Gothic Staronová synagoga (the Old-New Synagogue) and the Starý židovský hřbitov (Old Jewish Cemetery).

Nové Město The New Town is linked to the Old Town by the broad streets of Narodní and Na Příkopě. Together with Václavské náměstí (Wenceslas Square), they form the Golden Cross, the epicenter of Prague's contemporary life. Wenceslas Square is one of three laid out in the 14th century as focal points for Emperor Charles IV's New Town, much of which was redeveloped again when Prague grew rapidly in the late-19th and early 20th centuries.

Suburbs Beyond the four historic districts is a ring of suburbs, some unrelievedly dull, but most with attractions of their own. To the north are the Národní technické muzeum (National Technical Museum), the Expo grounds, and Trojský zámek (Troja Château). Overlooking the city from high up on Na Vrchu Žižkově (Žižkov Hill) to the east is the Národní památnik (National Memorial). To the south is the ancient, legend-encrusted fortress of Vyšehrad, while to the west is the 1,000-year-old monastery of Břevnov.

Prague in a weekend

This is Praha...

Day 1 Begin at the top end of Václavské náměstí (Wenceslas Square) and take in the view from the steps of the Národní muzeum (National Museum). Go down the square and into Staré Město (the Old Town) via Na Můstku. Turn right past the Stavovské divadlo (Estates Theater), continue along Ovocný trh, then turn right to pass under the Prašná brána (Powder Tower) and into the Obecní dům (Municipal House) for coffee.

Retrace your steps through the Powder Tower then head west along Celetná and into Staroměstské náměstí (Old Town Square). Here you can visit the Kostel Panny Marie před Týnem (known simply as the Týn Church). From the square, head north into the old ghetto district of Josefov, to see the Staronová synagoga (Old-New Synagogue) and the Starý židovský hřbitov (Old Jewish Cemetery).

Return to the Old Town Square area for lunch and a climb up the tower of the Staroměstská radnice (Old Town Hall). After this, you can plunge into the maze of streets to the west, making sure you take in Husova street and Betlémské náměstí (Bethlehem Square) and Betlémské kaple (Bethlehem Chapel).

Continue your wanderings southwards and emerge on to the Vltava embankment by the Národní divadlo (National Theater). Go along Smetanovo nábřeží (Smetana Quay) and finish the walk with a drink by the composer's statue on the tip of Novotného lávka. Enjoy dinner in the Old Town and an evening stroll around Wenceslas Square.

Walkers' Prague

With its major sights all crammed comfortably into the historic center, Prague is an ideal city to explore on foot. Traffic-free streets and squares complement charming courtyards and alleyways, and many pedestrianized areas have been attractively repaved. If you do plan to tour the city in this way, however, do be wary of traffic elsewhere and obey the lights at controlled crosswalks in particular. One notorious black spot is at the eastern end of the Karlův most (Charles Bridge), where the stream of pedestrians coming off the bridge meets the equally continuous tide of vehicles speeding through the tunnel that runs alongside the Vltava. Survival here depends on keeping your eye on the lights, rather than following your fellow sightseers as they stroll blithely across the road into oncoming traffic.

The Prasná brana (Powder Tower—left) and Obecní dům (Municipal House—right), Staré Město

Day 2 Start where you left off yesterday, at the eastern end of Karlův most (Charles Bridge). Walk across the Vltava on the bridge, then descend the steps on to Kampa island to explore the streets and squares in the southern part of Malá Strana.

Have coffee in Malostranské náměstí (Malá Strana Square), then walk up Nerudova street. At the end of this street is the stairway called Radnické schody, which will take you to the Loretánská kaple (Loretto Shrine). From there you can continue to Strahovský klášter (Strahov Monastery) for lunch and a fine view over the city.

Now walk down to Nový Svět (New World) and on to Hradčanské náměstí (Hradčany Square) for Pražský hrad (Prague Castle). Make sure you see the Vladislavský sál (Vladislav Hall) and, if possible, the Bohemian Art Collection in Jiřský klášter (St. George's Convent). From here it is not far to Malostranská metro station, or you can walk along Valdštejnská street and work your way back across Karlův most (Charles Bridge).

The stupendous view from the castle of Hradčany and the city beyond is well worth the steep climb

HRADČANY

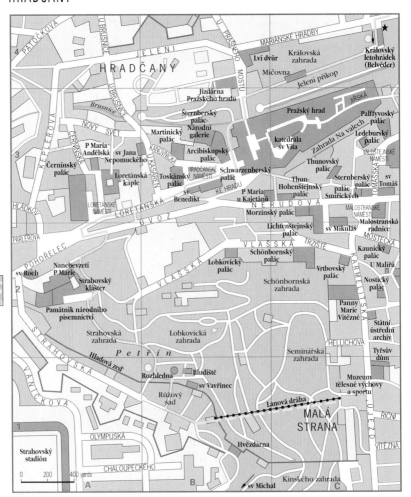

52

Blue-uniformed guards and large crowds at Pražský hrad (Prague Castle)

Hradčany A city within a city, Prague's acropolis spreads along the easily defended rock spur above Malá Strana, the spires and towers of the cathedral crowning the secular buildings which have housed offices of state for a thousand years. This is the symbolic heart of the nation, its unmistakable silhouette reproduced over and over again in paintings and prints, on stamps and currency, and in the photographs of the visitors who climb the hill and crowd its courtyards.

The castle Nowadays the castle is the seat of the president, and has been so since the declaration of the Czechoslovak Republic in 1918. Before that it tended to be shunned by the city's Habsburg rulers, most of whom felt more at home in Vienna than in a Prague known for its tendency to throw unpopular representatives of power out of the window.

The early Czech princes held sway here, though for a while during the 10th and 11th centuries some of them preferred to sojourn southward atop the city's other castle rock, Vyšehrad. However, the natural advantages of the Hradčany site prevailed, and it was here that the power of the Czech state was consolidated.

In the 14th century, wise Emperor Charles IV ruled from here, starting work on the great Gothic cathedral of St. Vitus and making the castle his base while turning Prague into a cosmopolitan capital of high medieval Europe. Some of Charles's successors preferred to live downtown, in the royal palace near Náměstí Republicky (Republic Square) which has long since disappeared, but in the 15th century Hradčany was popular again, a period marked by the construction of the extraordinary Vladislav Hall, a wonderful marriage of the Gothic spirit with that of the dawning Renaissance.

Perhaps the castle's greatest days came before the so-called Second Prague Defenestration of 1618 (see page 34), which provoked the Thirty Years' War; in the 16th century, under the rule of the eccentric Emperor Rudolf II, the place seethed with alchemists and necromancers, mathematicians and astronomers, as well as artists of all kinds.

Master builders
Charles IV (1316–78) patronized the best architects of his day. Matthew of Arras was working at the papal court in Avignon for Charles's old tutor, Pope Clement VI, when the emperor summoned him to Prague. His work seems smoothly conventional when set beside that of his successor, Petr Parléř, one of a dynasty of master masons who originally came from Cologne. Parléř's imaginative inventiveness is best seen in the bold vaulting of the cathedral's sacristy, in the south porch, and in the Wenceslas Chapel, prototypes for Benedict Ried's even more extravagant work in the castle's Vladislav Hall (see page 88).

Cobbled streets draw visitors up towards the castle

Theresa tidies up
In the classic view of Prague's castle from Karlův most (Charles Bridge), an immensely long line of plain-looking buildings marches along the hilltop, the continuous roofline broken only by the spires and roof of the cathedral and the twin towers of St. George's church. This homogenous appearance is the result of the rebuilding which took place in the reign of Empress Maria Theresa (1717–80); before this the castle's outline was much more picturesque, not to say ramshackle, consisting of a medieval jumble of turrets, balconies, dormer windows, and oddly shaped projections.

The early citadel The Hradčany district formed a natural site for the stronghold built by Prince Bořivoj toward the end of the 9th century. The limestone heights descend from Bílá Hora (the White Mountain) to the west, ending in a bluff which forces the broad and easily fordable Vltava to turn 90 degrees eastward in the great bend which forms the northern limit of the Old Town. The ground drops away abruptly to the north and south of the spur, while the eastern end tapers to a point. Only the western approach lacked strong natural defences, and even here a little valley was easily converted into a deep moat.

Hradčany Square Beyond the moat to the west of the castle a settlement grew up around a long, irregularly shaped open space, now called **Hradčanské náměstí** (Hradčany Square). Although markets were held here at an early date, this quarter was never a rival to commercially-minded Malá Strana far below; instead the square became the domain of those who, for one reason or another, found no space within the crowded castle walls.

In 1541 a great fire raged, burning down much of the district. When rebuilding took place, Hradčany Square took on a more aristocratic appearance than before; great magnates established themselves in the prestigious palaces (such as the **Schwarzenberský palác**, or **Schwarzenberg Palace**), which helped introduce the architecture of the Italian Renaissance to Central Europe. The Baroque age added a sumptuous façade to the **Arcibiskupský palác (Archbishop's Palace)** opposite, leaving too little space on the square itself for the Šternbergs to build their Šternberský palác, which is tucked in behind the Archbishop's Palace. The Šternberg Palace is now home to the superb **European Art Collection of the National Gallery**; the even more fascinating **Bohemian Art Collection** is found within the castle precincts, in the Jiřský klášter (St. George's Convent).

Other sights Two roads straggle westwards from the castle. One passes more palaces as it rises, including the **Černínský palác**, the grandest of them all, the great pile built by Count Černín in 1669. Opposite this palace is the **Loretánská kaple (Loretto Shrine)**, a far more joyful exercise in the Baroque and one of the country's most famous places of pilgrimage. The fire of 1541 is commemorated in the cobbled square of Pohořelec, the "place of burning," while the top of the rise is crowned by the twin steeples of the ancient **Strahovský klášter (Strahov Monastery)**, its bookish treasures on display in libraries of stunning sumptuousness.

The other road starts out with similar pretensions to grandeur, but after passing a palace or two soon settles down among the picturesque houses of **Nový Svět (New World)**; this intriguingly named little area of crooked streets and hidden gardens was once the castle slum, the abode of servants and scullery maids, now replaced by artists and other Bohemian types.

Hradčany has visual delights aplenty, from this old-fashioned lamp...

55

Sgraffito rules OK
The Renaissance Italian technique of sgraffito work consisted of applying two layers of plaster, one dark, one light, to the façade of a building. Patterns were then incised through the lighter layer to reveal the darker undercoating. Designs could be geometric (such as the diamond quoins of the Schwarzenberg Palace) or figurative (such as the biblical scenes of the Martinic Palace). The technique enjoyed a revival in the late 19th century, as did Czech neo-Renaissance architecture, and it is still practiced today by expert restorers.

...to the interesting patterns of the Staré zámecké schody (Old Castle Steps)

HRADČANY

▶ Černínský palác (Černín Palace) *52A3*

Loretánské náměstí (Loretto Square)

Metro: Malostranská, then Tram 22 to Památník písemnictví

Nowadays home to the Ministry for Foreign Affairs, the biggest of all Prague's aristocratic palaces was begun in 1669 by Humprecht Jan, Count Černín. Its colossal façade, over 400 ft. in length, seems to stare haughtily into space, oblivious of the far more appealing buildings of the Loretánská kaple (Loretto Shrine) fronting the lower half of the same square.

The Černíns had made their fortune as war profiteers during the Thirty Years' War. Humprecht Jan became the emperor's Ambassador to the Venetian Republic, returning from Italy with a bride, a substantial picture collection, and a fair measure of social ambition, all of which required a suitable home to set them off. The Valdštejnské palác (Wallenstein Palace), down in Malá Strana, was considered as one possibility, but in the end the count preferred to build anew, choosing a site a few discreet meters above the level of the castle, on what was then the edge of town.

The count's architect was, of course, an Italian—the fashionable Francesco Caratti—but both architect and patron died before the work was completed. Subsequent Černíns, burdened with an equally elaborate edifice in Vienna, eventually managed to complete what Emperor Leopold referred to as their "big barn," but they spent all their money in the process. Over the years the palace suffered the indignity of being vandalized by French soldiers (in the 1740s) and bombarded by the Prussians (in the 1750s). In the end the Černíns were glad to get rid of it to the Austrian Exchequer, which turned the building into a cavalry barracks and its beautiful Baroque garden into a parade ground.

On the night of March 9, 1948, the Černín Palace was the scene of an infamous Prague defenestration. In despair at the Communist takeover of the country that his father had created, and aware that the new government was cynically using him as a figurehead, Foreign Minister Jan Masaryk jumped from the window of his official apartment. Or was he pushed?

Unhappy occupants
Count Černín died long before the palace he had commissioned was completed, and the building seems to have brought bad luck to others as well as to the melancholy Jan Masaryk, who ended up dead in one of its courtyards. Of the Nazis who strutted here, Reichsprotektor Heydrich was assassinated and the repulsive Karl Hermann Frank was hanged in public, while Masaryk's Communist successor as Foreign Minister, Vladimir Vlado Clementis, was one of the victims of the Stalinist show-trials of the early 1950s.

Count Černín's immense 17th-century palace makes an opulent base for the Czech Republic's Ministry for Foreign Affairs

►► Hradčanské náměstí
(Hradčany Square)
52B3

Metro: Malostranská, then Tram 22 to Pražsky hrad
From the gates of Pražský hrad (Prague Castle) the cobbles of this splendid square sweep gently uphill, dividing just to make space for a plague memorial column embedded in greenery. The square was originally lined with modest burghers' houses but, after a great fire in 1541, the nobility moved into the square, building themselves the grand palaces that stand here today. Traffic is restricted, making the square an attractive esplanade for the masses of tourists on their way to or from the castle. One of the classic views over the city, usually crowded with visitors leaning over the wall, is from the point where the steep ramp known as Ke Hradu joins the square.

57

Cannons line the corridors of the Vojenské muzeum (Military Museum)

The Schwarzenberg Palace The most distinctive of the prestigious residences that surround this square is, without doubt, this splendidly gabled palace with its decoration of sgraffito (plaster-incised) designs. It was built in 1563 by the Lobkovic family, but is now known as the **Schwarzenberský palác** (Schwarzenberg Palace)►► after its later owners.

The palace is now home to the pre-World War II collections of the **Vojenské muzeum (Military Museum)**. A stroll through the airy rooms and stairways of what is one of the city's grandest buildings is well worth doing, even for the most committed pacifist. Many of the exhibits are wonderful creations in their own right.

There are models of sieges and battles, as well as maps, paintings, guns, and uniforms, few of the latter as dandyfied as the attire of the Landsknecht of the Thirty Years' War, complete with extravagant headgear and ornamental codpiece. The exploits of the Czechoslovak legionnaires in World War I are commemorated in the endearing figurines made by the outstanding sculptor of the 1920s, Otto Gutfreund.

Above and below: the beautifully restored façade of the Rococo Archbishop's Palace; the interior is only open on the Thursday before Easter

The Archbishop's Palace A flamboyant contrast to Schwarzenberg magnificence, on the opposite side of Hradčany Square, is the Arcibiskupský palác (Archbishop's Palace). This, too, dates from the time of the Early Renaissance, when Florian Gryspek, from Bavaria, decided to build himself a place in town to complement his country home down the Vltava at Nelahozeves. The change to church ownership was accompanied by a Baroque rebuilding, followed by a Rococo restyling that resulted in the present, deliciously restored façade. The rarely accessible interior is one of the best preserved of its kind, with superb and specially commissioned Lyons tapestries. Sharing an entrance with the archbishop's, but tucked away out of sight from the square, is the most visited of all these palaces, the **Šternberský palác (Šternberg Palace)**, the wonderful setting for the European Art Collection of the Národní galerie (National Gallery—see page 76).

The Martinic Palace The upper, western end of Hradčany Square is dominated by the massive Thun-Hohenstein Palace of 1691, but more appealing is the building on the corner facing out into Kanovnická street. The **Martinický palác (Martinic Palace)**▶, originally a cluster of burghers' houses, is named after Jiří of Martinice, one of the famous pair of Catholic councilors thrown into the dungheaps of the castle moat in the second of Prague's defenestrations (see page 34). Converted long ago into cramped apartments for the poor, the palace has since been painstakingly restored to make enviable offices for the staff of the City Architect's Department. Inside are Renaissance painted ceilings, while outside there are droll scenes of Old Testament goings-on executed in sgraffito. The courtyard has an elegant, modern fountainhead.

▶ ▶ ▶ Katedrála svatého Víta (St. Vitus's Cathedral)

82C1

Pražský hrad (Prague Castle)
Metro: Malostranská, then Tram 22 to Pražsky hrad

The towers and pinnacles of one of Europe's great Gothic cathedrals rise triumphantly over the sober skyline of the castle. Begun by Charles IV in 1344, it was the keystone of the emperor's ambitious plan to transform Prague into a magnificent medieval metropolis, but its completion had to wait for the nationalist enthusiasms of modern times. The cathedral is the spiritual heart of the nation, the mausoleum of the Bohemian kings, the treasure house of the crown jewels, and the city's greatest landmark.

An integral part of most panoramas of Prague, the cathedral is visible from far away across the rolling fields of Central Bohemia. But close up, as you approach it through the castle courtyards, it vanishes, only for its cliff-like west front to spring almost frighteningly skywards as you emerge from the passageway leading into the Third Courtyard.

This, surprisingly, is the cathedral's modern face; its original 14th-century architects were only able to complete the eastern end before the troubles of the 15th century brought building operations to a halt. The whole of the nave, the twin western towers and much else besides all stem from the commitment of the founders and followers of the 1843 "Association for the Completion of the Cathedral."

Decades of devoted work were brought to a conclusion by the celebrations attending the cathedral's final consecration on May 12, 1929, the millennium of the assassination of Prince Wenceslas, the country's patron saint. The west front is a sculptural record of these years, with depictions of the architects as well as the more conventional figures of saints.

St. Vitus
Why this early Christian martyr, a 3rd-century Sicilian, should have become so popular in Bohemia remains a little unclear, though his name in Czech is Svatý Vít, confusingly but conveniently close to Svetovit, a pagan god held in high esteem by the 10th-century Slavs whom Prince Wenceslas hoped to convert to Christianity: consecrating the first church on this site to Vitus may have been a ploy to win them over. Wenceslas had been given one of the saint's arms as a present; centuries later, that enthusiastic collector of relics, Charles IV, added other bits of the saint's body, whose partly complete remains are now tucked away safely in his tomb at the east end of the cathedral.

St. Vitus's Cathedral and Prague Castle rise majestically over the red roofs of Malá Strana

St. Wenceslas' Chapel
The bronze door-knocker at the main entrance to St. Wenceslas' Chapel is supposed (erroneously) to have been the one grasped by Wenceslas when he was cut down by his assassins. Beyond the chapel is the chamber containing the crown jewels; all seven keyholders must be present to unlock the door to this chamber.

History Wenceslas built the first church on the site of today's cathedral. His church, probably consecrated after his death in 929, was a rotunda, of more impressive dimensions than those of the several round churches that still exist in Prague today. He was buried here, and, as his cult grew, the rotunda was replaced by a Romanesque basilica, not unlike the Bazilika svatého Jiří (St. George's Basilica—see page 90), but more grand altogether. This in turn was pulled down to make way for Charles IV's even more ambitious project, though remains of both these early churches can be seen in the crypt and in the castle's Third Courtyard.

Exterior For many years the cathedral was entered through the magnificent south portal, sometimes called the Golden Gate, completed around 1367. High above, the great Gothic south tower is crowned with a gloriously elaborate Baroque cupola, 288 ft. above the paving. The portal is the work of the cathedral's second architect, Petr Parléř; its interior vaulting is a typical example of his eagerness to experiment. Outside, the *Last Judgment* mosaic is Venetian, of about 1370, while the grille showing the *Labors of the Months* was completed in 1954, evidence that even the Communists dared not interfere with the work of completing the cathedral.

The cathedral's magnificent south tower, Gothic below and Baroque above

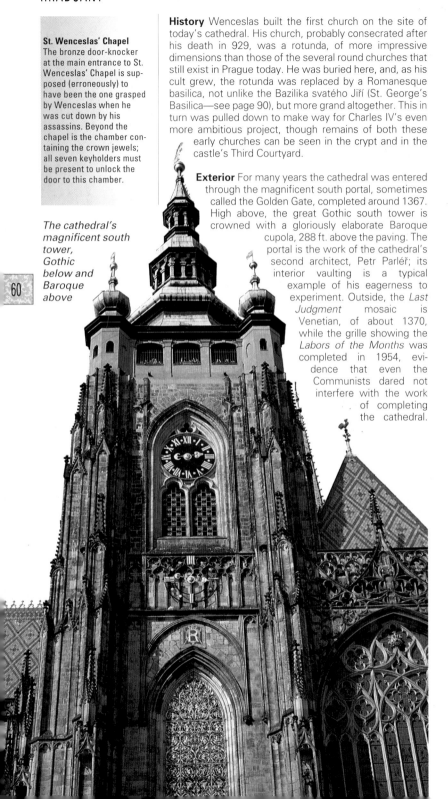

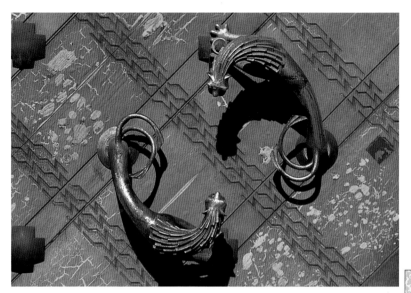

Interior Though invariably swarming with visitors, the cathedral's soaring interior imposes an atmosphere of order and calm, its essentially simple structure a superb container for the wealth of decorative features accumulated over the centuries. The crowds of visitors usually press most thickly around the two little entrances to the Chapel of St. Wenceslas.

Before joining them, look east into the chancel, the first part of the great building to be completed. The Frenchman Matthew of Arras designed and supervised the work between 1344 and his death in 1352, living long enough to see the semicircle of chapels completed around the ambulatory at the east end. Matthew's inspiration came from the great new churches of his native country, in particular the cathedral at Narbonne.

After Matthew's death, Petr Parléř took over, flinging an airy vault over the completed chancel. He was followed in turn by his sons; by the end of the 14th century the chancel had been finished, together with the stump of the south tower. A temporary wall was erected at the west end of the chancel in anticipation of construction of the nave. It stood for 500 years.

St. Wenceslas' Chapel Charles IV was concerned to promote the cult of his predecessor, Prince (subsequently Saint) Wenceslas, the "Good King." The **Kaple svatého Václav (St. Wenceslas' Chapel)►►**, beneath the vault designed by Petr Parléř, is consequently the most richly ornamented component of the whole cathedral, its sumptuous decoration an echo of the equally lavish Chapel of the Holy Rood at Karlštejn (see page 227).

Semi-precious stones stud the lower part of the chapel walls, which are completely covered with paintings of Christ's Passion and scenes from the life of St. Wenceslas. An appealingly posed statue of Wenceslas stands with shield and spear in hand, overlooking his tomb, a 19th-century copy of the original.

Strange creatures adorn the cathedral's south portal

Mystical light illuminates the sumptuous interior of the Kaple svatého Václav (St. Wenceslas' Chapel)

The Royal Mausoleum In a central spot within the cathedral stands the huge white marble slab of the Royal Mausoleum, the work of the Dutch Renaissance sculptor Alexander Collin. Stretched out on its expansive upper surface are relief figures of Emperor Ferdinand and his wife and son, while the sides carry representations of other rulers, such as Charles IV and George of Poděbrady. The actual tombs lie deep below, in the confined spaces of the crypt of the Romanesque church which preceded the cathedral. Here are sinister cylinders of polished granite containing all that remains of Emperor Charles and many others.

The Royal Oratory Above ground again, in complete contrast to all this solemnity, is the late 15th-century Royal Oratory, its balcony overloaded with heraldic emblems, supported by rustic ribs carved to look like gnarled branches. Linked to the Royal Palace by an underground passageway, the Oratory allowed the ruler to attend church services while remaining free of any contact with the lesser orders. Its designer was Benedict Ried, architect of the even more fantastic Vladislav Hall in the Royal Palace (see page 88). The figures of miners with their lamps are later Baroque additions, reminders of Bohemia's mineral wealth, which made all this extravagance possible.

The solid silver statue of Nepomuk atop his tomb

Portraits in stone
The greatest monument to the architects of the cathedral is, of course, the building itself. Both Matthew of Arras and Petr Parléř are buried here, their tombs close together. High above, in niches in the triforium, their likenesses accompany the busts of the great and the good which the emperor ordered to be placed here. Best viewed through binoculars, these are some of the earliest sculptures in Europe to attempt to portray their subjects in a realistic manner.

The Tomb of St. Jan Nepomuk Nothing could be more lavish than this sumptuous silver tomb, which far outdoes the Oratory for flamboyance. The ultimate in Baroque bad taste, it shows Nepomuk kneeling on top of a coffin borne up by bigger-than-life angels, while other members of the heavenly host hover high above, bearing a red velvet baldachin (canopy) in their hands.

The east end The chapels of the east end of the cathedral contain many treasures, among them the tombstones of the Přemyslid kings Otakar I and II, the work of Petr Parléř and his pupils. Set into the walls of the chancel enclosure are carved oak relief panels. The one on the south wall depicts the Calvinists indulging in some image-breaking in the course of the raid on the cathedral in 1619, while to the north is a fine depiction of Prague at the time of the Battle of the White Mountain a year later, its streets full of the fleeing minions of Frederick of the Palatinate, the unfortunate "Winter King." Almost opposite is Parléř's splendid sacristy, its vault held in place by a keystone suspended in mid-air. Close by is the massive presence of the kneeling Cardinal Schwarzenberg, a late 19th-century masterpiece by the great sculptor Myslbek.

The nave and aisles A burst of artistic activity accompanied the final stages of the cathedral's construction in the 1920s, the results of which can mostly be seen in the nave. At the same time, the Renaissance organ loft, which had enclosed the choir, was moved to its present position against the wall of the north transept. The nave is a bleak attempt by the 19th-century architect, Mocker, to re-create the work of Matthew of Arras rather than follow in the more inspiring footsteps of Petr Parléř.

More appealing than the architecture is the stained glass. A number of the most prominent and patriotically-minded artists of the time provided designs for windows, including the colorful example in the Archbishop's Chapel in the north aisle. This tells the story of Saints Cyril and Methodius, Apostles to the Slavs, and is the work of Alfons Mucha, better known for the languid ladies of his Art Nouveau posters published in pre-war Paris. Contrasting essays in stained glass include Max Švabinský's *Descent of the Holy Ghost* and the dancing figures of K. Svolinsky's *Acts of Mercy* (first and second chapels of the south aisle).

Perhaps the most remarkable work of art that can be found in the nave is the altar, carved by František Bílek. Its figure of Christ crucified is a powerful statement by this highly individual artist.

The tower The cathedral tower is open to the public. The reward for an interminable climb up its 287 steps is one of the most magnificent all-round views of the city in its setting, plus intriguing close-ups of the intricate exterior structure of the great cathedral itself, with its bristling buttresses, its steep-pitched and diamond-tiled roofs and its bronze cockerels, which appear to crow atop their spiky perches.

Matthew of Arras' medieval chapel is lit by modern glass

Big bells
A quartet of bells boom out from the cathedral's great south tower, kept company by an elaborate timepiece from the days of Rudolf II. The biggest of these bells bears the name of Sigismund, and is a splendid 18-tonner cast by the Brno bell-founder, Jaroš, in 1549.

The Slavia Bank sponsored Alfons Mucha's stained-glass window in the Archbishop's Chapel

■ **The most visually appealing of all cities, Prague constantly presents itself from new points of view. Even the most casual or hurried of visitors will sooner rather than later find themselves escaping from the confines of the streets to emerge at a point that offers a heart-stopping prospect of river and city. With a little more time and patience—and a willingness to climb—Prague's panoramas can be savored to the full....■**

Top: the view over the city from Prague Castle should not be missed

64

Private view I
Enthusiasts of early Modernist architecture finding their way to the pioneering Baba villa colony (see page 191) will be rewarded not just by the city's finest collection of cuboid houses but also by an unusual panorama of the city's northern flank. A short walk along the footpath that continues the little road called Nad Patánkou northwards is well worth while.

An unusual panorama of Hradčany from Nové Město's Town Hall

Looking up The classic Prague view is that of the long silhouette of the castle and Malá Strana seen from the eastern side of the Vltava or from the Karlův most (Charles Bridge). The long curve of the bridge makes a westward walk past its procession of saints a particularly fascinating experience, as the towers and domes of Malá Strana rearrange themselves in ever-changing compositions in relation to the blank walls of the castle and the spires of the cathedral. A climb up either of the bridge towers will give a new angle on this prospect. Alternatively, this view can be enjoyed from the café tables and balustrade by the statue of Smetana outside the composer's museum at the tip of Novotného lávka, or by walking along the riverside embankments thoughtfully provided by Count Chotek in the mid-19th century.

Looking down The outlook from the top is equally fascinating. There is always a crowd leaning over the wall by the western entrance to the castle in Hradčanské náměstí (Hradčany Square), drinking in the view as well as recovering their breath after the long climb up Staré zámecké schody (New Castle Steps). Once inside the castle complex, it is worth going into the Starý Královský palác (Old Royal Palace) or the Lobkowický palác (Lobkovic Palace) for the view from their terraces. Best of all, despite the 287 steps, is the superb panorama from the top of the cathedral tower. From here the city can best be appreciated in its Central Bohemian setting, astride the Vltava and ringed by suburbs packed with *paneláky* (prefab apartment complexes—see page 192).

Viewpoints and towers A change of emphasis, with the castle featuring in the view once more, comes with a walk up to Petřín hill and along the ridge (see walk on page 66). Here, the most impressive viewpoint is from the footpath leading up to Strahov from the steeply climbing street called Úvoz. The Petřín itself is crowned with a man-made viewpoint, the Petřín rozhledna (Observation Tower), a miniature Eiffel Tower.

Across the river is the city's biggest 20th-century visual intrusion, the immensely tall Žižkov television tower, from whose gallery there is an unusual view westward, best enjoyed early on in the day. The same advice applies to the terrace of the Národní památnik (National Memorial) near by, with its big statue of Jan Žižka. This was meant

to be seen from all over town, as was the monstrous statue of Stalin on Letenské sady (Letná Plain), long since demolished.

A walk along the western rim of this public park, up above the Vltava, gives an interesting and changing vista of Staré Město (the Old Town), as well as the best view of the succession of bridges upstream. A giant metronome now stands on Stalin's vacant plinth, from which the eye goes straight down Pařížská street right into the heart of the Old Town. Here the tower of the Staroměstská radnice (Old Town Hall) offers more steps and stairways with the reward of a dizzying view of all the activity in the square and the ancient rooftops all around. A more modest prospect of the Old Town is from the Prašná brána (Powder Tower) at the end of Celetná street.

The Nové Město (New Town) is perhaps less easy to grasp in its entirety than the rest of this historic city. Everyone should, of course, peep over the shoulder of Good King Wenceslas from the steps in front of the Národní muzeum (National Museum); alternatively, there is the terrace outside the huge Palace of Culture which looks across the Nusle valley to the edge of the New Town and beyond.

An excursion to Vyšehrad is worth while for its own sake, and for good northward views as well as a fine prospect of the Vltava southwards. The river itself makes an excellent standpoint: even if you do not venture out in a boat, at least make your way to one of the Vltava's islands to see the city from this different perspective.

Private view II
Don't forget to look out of windows wherever you are. Some of the upper windows of the Národní muzeum (National Museum) look out on to Václavské náměstí (Wenceslas Square)—but don't try to open them! For an unusual glimpse of the Starý židovský hřbitov (Old Jewish Cemetery) nothing could be bettered than the view from the upper floor of the Umělecko-průmyslové muzeum (the Decorative Arts Museum, or UPM).

A quartet of copper cupolas seen from the western Charles Bridge tower

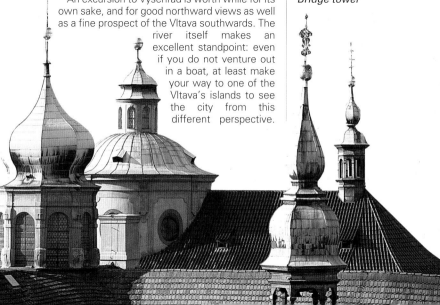

Walk Along the heights

This half- or whole-day walk takes you in a great half-circle around the Hradčany heights overlooking Malá Strana, revealing some stunning views over the city.

See map on page 52.

Start at **Malostranská** metro station. Tram 22 mounts the hairpin turns above the station with great ease, saving you a lot of breath and depositing you at the Marianské hradby stop near the **Královský letohrádek** (the **Royal Summer Palace**, or **Belvedere**). It is worth the entrance fee to go up the stairs to the Belvedere's upper terrace for the unusual view of the eastern end of the castle, looking like some

Above: Strahov Monastery detail
Below: gardens of the Belvedere

forgotten fortress buried in the forest (if you ignore the city below).

You should linger for a few moments in the formal garden around the Belvedere's Singing Fountain, then stroll through the **Královská zahrada (Royal Gardens)**. Until recently these were the strictly guarded private preserve of the president, who alone was permitted to enjoy the views of the castle through the trees.

The charmingly informal **U Prašného mostu (Powder Bridge Street)** crosses the ravine protecting the north flank of the castle. Blue-uniformed sentries guard the passageway leading directly into the castle's

west, **Pohořelec náměstí (Pohořelec Square)** doesn't quite have the class of Hradčany Square, but there are some fine Baroque and Rococo houses nevertheless. Tucked away on the left-hand side is an entranceway leading steeply up to **Strahovský klášter (Strahov Monastery)**, but for one of the best views over the city turn almost 180 degrees left as you come into the square, go a short way down Úvoz, then follow the path up towards the monastery. The ground here drops away steeply through

Petřín hill's funicular railroad

Druhé nádvoři (Second Courtyard). This could be your starting point for a tour of the castle, but to continue with the walk, turn to the right after crossing the bridge, passing through the **Zahrada Na Baště (Bastion Garden)**, and out into **Hradčanské náměstí (Hradčany Square)**. Here, if you choose, there is a whole day's worth of sightseeing (see pages 57–8); to your left, the Schwarzenberský palác (Schwarzenberg Palace) with the Military Museum, to your right; past the Arcibiskupský palác (Archbishop's Palace), the Šternberský palác (Šternberg Palace) with its superb collection of European art.

From the square, head for the narrow gap in the upper left-hand corner (southwest) and make your way up Loretánská street. On the right is the crushing bulk of the **Černínský palác (Černín Palace)** doing its best to outface the cheerful buildings of the Loretto chapel opposite. Further

orchards and meadows down to Malá Strana.

Continue uphill into the rustic courtyard of the monastery and visit its ornate library halls, or follow the curving panoramic pathway around towards the **Petřín rozhledna (Observation Tower)**, the little brother of the Eiffel Tower that pokes above the treetops of Petřín hill. If you are not yet sated with city views, climb to the top of this tower for an incomparable panorama, then recover in the rose gardens further along.

You can descend to Malá Strana on foot or take the **Lanová dráha (Funicular Railroad)**. The best views are from the front of the carriage. The lower station is just a step from busy Újezd with its trams (including the ubiquitous Tram 22). You can return to Nové Město (the New Town) via most Legií (the Bridge of the Legions) or to Staré Město (the Old Town) via Kampa island and Karlův most (Charles Bridge).

►► Královský Letohrádek (Royal Summer Palace, or Belvedere) 52C4

Pražský hrad (Prague Castle)
Metro: Malostranská, then Tram 22 to Belvéder
This exquisite pleasure pavilion, the earliest and most elegant of Prague's Renaissance buildings, stands in its own little formal garden on the far side of the castle's Stag Moat.

History In 1535, when Ferdinand I decided to build a summer palace for his queen, Anna, the only suitable site lay beyond the constricted castle bounds, on the flat land on the far side of the moat. Here, as well as space to spare, there was fresh air and a wonderful view over river and city. Ferdinand employed Italians to design the delicate building, which looks like some fairy craft wafted over the Alps by warm southern breezes. It is surrounded by an arcade carried on slim columns, with ornamental relief panels contributing to the general sense of lightness and elegance. Paolo della Stella supervised its construction from 1535 until his death in 1552, when Bonifác Wohlmut took over, completing the upper story with its distinctive roof resembling the upturned hull of a ship.

The Singing Fountain The Belvéder (Belvedere), as the palace is also known, is now used for temporary exhibitions. The gravel paths and low clipped hedges of its garden are centered on the famous **Singing Fountain►►**, so called because of the subtle sound made by the water falling into its basin. Cast by the maker of the cathedral's Sigismund Bell, the fountain was installed as the palace was completed; it features an endearing bagpiper, four sphinxes and a wealth of other ornamentation. Jan Štursa's modern sculpture of a skinny youth (*Victory*) seems completely at home in these refined surroundings.

The king's beasts
At the far end of the Royal Gardens from the Summer Palace is the Lví dvůr (Lion Court). Lions, Bohemia's emblematic beasts, had been kept in the castle as early as the Middle Ages, but in the 1570s eccentric Emperor Rudolf II's love of the exotic led him to establish a more comprehensive menagerie. Aside from lions, and the stags browsing peacefully in the moat, there were bears, wolves, and a whole array of big cats, some of them kept in heated cages to combat the city's winter chill.

68

►►► Loretánská kaple (Loretto Shrine) 52A3

Loretánské náměstí (Loretto Square)
Metro: Malostranská, then Tram 22 to Památník písemnictví
The Loretto's west front, alive with statuary and topped by a tall bell-tower with a cheerful carillon, turns a welcoming face to its great gloomy neighbor, the Černínský palác (Černín Palace) brooding over the esplanade on the far side of the square. To enter the courtyard beyond is to experience the essence of the Counter-Reformation, a world of cults, miracles and mysteries, and bizarre beliefs pushed beyond the boundaries of the credible in the cause of the forced re-Catholicization of the Czech Lands.

The kernel of the complex is the Santa Casa, a reproduction of the home of the Virgin Mary, miraculously flown by angels from the Holy Land to Loreto in Italy. This copy of her "Holy Hut" is housed in a windowless, relief-encrusted Renaissance pavilion, built

The jewel-box interior of the Loretto's Church of the Nativity

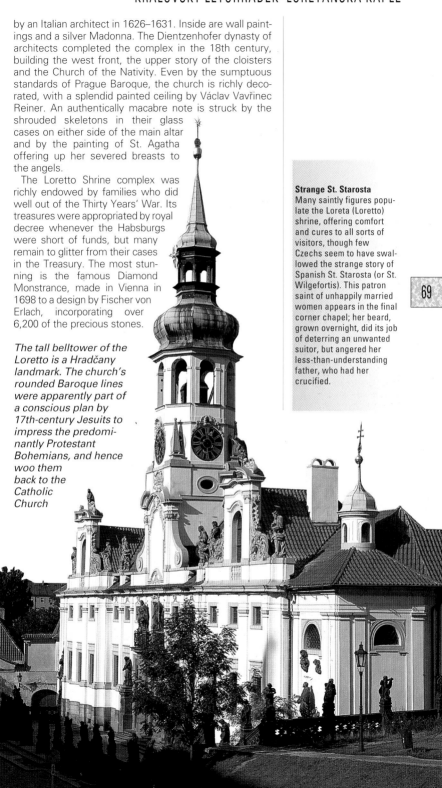

by an Italian architect in 1626–1631. Inside are wall paintings and a silver Madonna. The Dientzenhofer dynasty of architects completed the complex in the 18th century, building the west front, the upper story of the cloisters and the Church of the Nativity. Even by the sumptuous standards of Prague Baroque, the church is richly decorated, with a splendid painted ceiling by Václav Vavřinec Reiner. An authentically macabre note is struck by the shrouded skeletons in their glass cases on either side of the main altar and by the painting of St. Agatha offering up her severed breasts to the angels.

The Loretto Shrine complex was richly endowed by families who did well out of the Thirty Years' War. Its treasures were appropriated by royal decree whenever the Habsburgs were short of funds, but many remain to glitter from their cases in the Treasury. The most stunning is the famous Diamond Monstrance, made in Vienna in 1698 to a design by Fischer von Erlach, incorporating over 6,200 of the precious stones.

The tall belltower of the Loretto is a Hradčany landmark. The church's rounded Baroque lines were apparently part of a conscious plan by 17th-century Jesuits to impress the predominantly Protestant Bohemians, and hence woo them back to the Catholic Church

Strange St. Starosta
Many saintly figures populate the Loreta (Loretto) shrine, offering comfort and cures to all sorts of visitors, though few Czechs seem to have swallowed the strange story of Spanish St. Starosta (or St. Wilgefortis). This patron saint of unhappily married women appears in the final corner chapel; her beard, grown overnight, did its job of deterring an unwanted suitor, but angered her less-than-understanding father, who had her crucified.

■ **The earliest known depiction of Prague is a colored woodcut dating from 1493. It shows a stylized panorama of the whole city, with Vyšehrad and Nové Město (the New Town) in the foreground, the Vltava and Malá Strana in the middle, then Hradčany rising dramatically above the ridge in the background. The picturesque appeal of the city and its setting is already apparent, a magical mixture of river, hills and valleys, buildings and open land, with a skyline punctuated by towers and spires....■**

Top: engraving of Prague, 1648

Photographer Plicka
The most successful photographer of Prague was undoubtedly the long-lived Karel Plicka (1894–1987). Plicka was a true Czechoslovak, a Praguer who fell in love with Slovakia and spent much of his life there, collecting folk-songs (some 20,000 in all) and photographing the people, sometimes using the big camera which was given to him as a present by President Masaryk. Forced to quit Slovakia when the country was broken up in 1939, he returned to Prague, devoting himself to photographing the whole city in meticulous detail, often climbing into dusty attics or shimmying up church spires in pursuit of the perfect picture. A gallery entirely dedicated to his work lies in his home village of Blatnica, which lies some distance from Prague in the Tatra Mountains of the Slovak Republic.

Early views Since that anonymous 15th-century wood engraver gave his impression of late-medieval Prague, topographical artists have found the city endlessly fascinating, and they have left a more or less complete record of the changing townscape over the centuries. By the mid-16th century the printers Kozel and Peterle were selling what was described as a "Most Accurate Expression of the Metropolis of Bohemia, Prague" which crams an extraordinary amount of detail into its distorted perspective of the whole city, including target practice on Střelecký ostrov (Shooters' Island), the half-completed roof of Panny Marie Sněžné (Our Lady of the Snows) and crowds going up and down the Staré zámecké schody (New Castle Steps).

A far greater degree of accuracy appears in the meticulously drawn views by Václav Hollar, who worked in the mid-17th century. Hollar spent most of his life in England where, known as Wenceslas Hollar, he is regarded as the founder of English landscape drawing. His 1636 panorama takes in the city from that favorite viewpoint of topographers and tourists alike, the peak of Petřín hill. Even today, with its "Index of Several Places" his panorama can be used to anatomize the city in its setting.

The appeal of Hollar's work is cerebral; a much more vivid depiction of the city is given in the big relief woodcarving in the cathedral (see page 62) showing the *Flight of the Winter King after Defeat in the Battle of the White Mountain.* The vanquished monarch's enormously long baggage train is shown winding through the streets of Malá Strana, over Karlův most (Charles Bridge) and through Staré Město (the Old Town), heading eastwards and away from the enemy.

Photography and painting Later generations of draftsmen, such as Dietzler, Huber and Sembera, brought Hollar's great and accurate work up to date, making it possible to reconstruct the city's evolution in detail. Crowning these efforts, and more of a sublime hobby than a work of art, was Antonin Langweil's huge model which brings the Prague of the early-19th century back to life (see page 165).

Artists of the period were more captivated by feeling and atmosphere than by strict exactitude, though Vincenc

Morstadt's Biedermeier promenaders gaze down at a very accurately rendered (but treeless) Václavské náměstí (Wenceslas Square) of the 1830s. Most atmospheric of all is the work of Jakub Schikaneder, painter of twilight winter scenes, where horse-drawn cabs stand quietly in the street and gaslights illuminate the snowbound gloom.

In the 20th century, art, here as everywhere, moves away from the representational. The distorted geometry of the 1911 view of Karlův most (Charles Bridge) and Staré Město (Old Town) from Kampa island by Bohumil Kubišta shows this aptly named artist to have thoroughly learned the lessons of Parisian Cubism. The best-known modern paintings of Prague are the intense and colorful panoramas by the Austrian Expressionist Oskar Kokoschka, who found temporary refuge here in the mid-1930s as the shadow of Nazism fell on his native country.

Schikaneder's Winter Evening in the City

Where to see the pictures
The best collection of pictures of Prague is in the Muzeum hlavního města (City Museum—see page 165). Works by Shikaneder can be seen in the Anežský klášter (St. Agnes' Convent—see page 122) and works by Kokoschka can be seen in the Národní galerie (National Gallery—see page 78).

▶▶▶ **Národní Galerie, Jiřský Klášter (National Gallery, St. George's Convent)** 83D1

Pražský hrad (Prague Castle)
Metro: Malostranská, then Tram 22 to Pražsky hrad
No visitor with even a minimal interest in Czech art should miss this gallery, installed in the luxuriously restored buildings of the country's oldest convent. The collection ranges over painting and sculpture from the Middle Ages to the Baroque era. The works of the Gothic period in particular are outstanding in their sheer beauty and intensity of religious expression, a reminder that, until the devastation brought about by the Hussite Wars of the 15th century, Czech art led the way in Central Europe.

St. George's The convent itself was founded in 973 by Abbess Mlada, the sister of King Boleslav II, at the same time that Prague was proclaimed a bishopric by the pope. It was the most prestigious of all such institutions, the place where young ladies of noble birth received their education and where many of Mlada's successors as abbess were princesses as well. This privileged past was no deterrent to Emperor Joseph II, who shut the convent down in 1782 along with virtually all the religious dwellings within his realm. Used for a variety of unsuitable purposes, the convent then had to await the coming of Communism for more appropriate treatment (see panel).

The art collections are displayed in the rooms flanking the cloister, where early building foundations have been exposed. The medieval objects benefit from being shown in the basement and first floor of the oldest part of the building, while the Baroque works are housed in the more spacious surroundings of upper floors dating from a 17th-century rebuilding.

Sculpture Among the Gothic sculptures is an uncharacteristic piece, the original carving of the *St. George and Dragon*, a replica of which now stands in the castle's Third Courtyard. This is an opportunity to examine closely the fascinating details of the craggy wooded landscape that forms the base of the statue, and the way in which the tormented dragon tries to grip George's elegantly armored foot with its long prehensile snout.

More typical is the blissful *Krumlov Madonna* (circa 1400), the epitome of what came to be called the "Beautiful Style," gently swaying as she restrains the struggling Christ child in her arms. The gallery also has the imposing tympanum from the north portal of the Týn church (see page 138), a masterpiece from the workshop of Petr Parléř, the central *Crucifixion* scene probably being the work of the master himself.

Painting The Gothic painting is even more compelling than the sculpture. From the Cistercian monastery of Vyšší Brod, deep in the forests of southern Bohemia, comes a series of panels on the theme of Christ's Life and Passion, painted by an anonymous master and his

72

Master Theodorik's portraits rank among the National Gallery's greatest treasures

Medieval masterpiece in the cloisters of St. George's Convent

pupils, with animals that smile endearingly as they attend the Nativity and delightfully stylized landscapes forming the background to many of the scenes.

The court painter of Charles IV, Master Theodorik, is represented by a fraction of the work he produced for the now inaccessible Chapel of the Holy Cross at Karlštejn castle; though their gaze seems turned heavenward, his vividly painted portraits of saints almost burst from their frames with vitality. Much more ethereal are the figures of the Master of the Třeboň Altarpiece; in one painting, Christ is shown praying on the Mount of Olives as Judas and the rough soldiers crouch behind a wattle fence; in another, the slim Savior rises from his tomb as his guardians recline in disarray.

Baroque art Medieval mysticism is left far behind on the upper floor, where fascination with the power and sensuality of the human body predominates, wonderfully exemplified by Adriaen de Vries' muscular Hercules wielding his club. This part of the gallery is the best place to enjoy close-up views of the work of the master sculptors of the Prague Baroque, such as Braun and Brokoff. Here, too, are paintings by Karel Škréta, Václav Vavřinec Reiner, and Petr Brandl. The portraits of Jan Kupecký are worth more than a glance—particularly that of the sardonically smiling miniaturist Karl Brun—and there are some charming scenes of courtly life by Norbert Grund.

Lusty Rudy
Many of the Mannerist painters of Emperor Rudolf's court seem to have pandered to the bachelor emperor's enjoyment of erotic byways. Josef Hertz's *Last Judgment* looks more like an orgy than the end of the world, while the focal point of Hans von Aachen's painting of Lucretia contemplating suicide is her superbly swelling bosom, rather than her dire dilemma. Rudolf's restless mind was also drawn to the peaks, clefts, and forested chasms of the Alps, a taste satisfied by the Flemish painter, Roelant Savary.

Czechs and Slovaks

■ **At the end of 1992, Czechoslovakia broke up into its component parts—Slovakia and the Czech Republic—putting to rest the idea of a common Czechoslovak nationality cherished by the creators of the new state in the early part of the century. Since the split, the differences between the two nations have become more apparent, and no one is willing to predict that they will come together again in any forseeable future....■**

Good riddance!
Initially, some Czechs found the Slovak desire for independence incomprehensible. As the split approached, however, this turned in some cases to relief. The thought of not having to send vast subsidies eastwards had its own attraction. The huge Danube dam downstream from Bratislava, which had caused so much bad blood with Hungary and so much despair among environmentalists, now became a Slovak problem, as did the status of the big Hungarian minority in the southern part of the country.

An uncomfortable marriage The relationship between Czechs and Slovaks has been compared to that between the English and the Scots: A lot of mutual resentment, and jokes made at each other's expense. But in the post-war years the sense of common interests and a common background made the thought of separation, if not unthinkable, then at least unlikely.

Particularly under the interwar First Republic, Slovaks considered themselves to be the underdog, sending taxes to a capital that ruled them from a very long way away. True Slavs, with a way of life that had endured centuries of Hungarian rule, they felt the Czechs to be tinged with Germanism: officious, arrogant and irritatingly efficient. To the Czechs, Slovakia was a backward country which they had rescued and were doing their best to bring into the modern world. They were surprised when their efforts were resented, and considered the Slovaks ungrateful, especially in view of the massive subsidies that flowed from the richer partner to the poorer.

The war and Communism The Czechs' strong sense of nationhood was confirmed when Czechoslovakia was created and reinforced, rather than diminished, by the German occupation and Nazi persecution, just as Slovak nationalism simmered away until it found unexpected expression in the so-called Slovak State, called into being on Hitler's orders in 1939. Euphoria at having their own country at last made some of them overlook the dark side of Father Tiso's authoritarian regime, such as its collaboration with the Nazis and its persecution of Jewish citizens. Slovak honor was saved by the Uprising of 1944, an act of anti-Nazi resistance equal to that of the Warsaw Poles; although the Uprising was defeated, it paved the way for the re-establishment of the Czechoslovak state at the end of the war.

74

Under Communism, great efforts were made to reduce inequalities. Slovakia, previously a peasant country, was "proletarianized," receiving the lion's share of industrial investment, and the *panelák* (high-rise) became a more prominent feature of the landscape than the traditional timber farmhouse. "Bourgeois Slovak nationalism" was regularly denounced by the Communists, but under their regime the republic was federalized, with parliaments set up in both Prague and Bratislava.

After 1989, some of the most bitter struggles in parliament concerned not just the structure of the state, but its very name. After threats to resign were made by President Havel over what seemed to him to be utter pettiness, the country became "The Czech and Slovak Federative Republic', for which no better short form was found than ČSFR. Even this was not enough; sensing that separation would serve their interests more than attempting to settle the real differences between them, the politicians of both nations closed their deal without ever seeking a mandate from the electors, and thus the mutual life led by Czechs and Slovaks for most of the 20th century came to a sad end.

Czechs desert Communism

Czech and Slovak
The Czech and Slovak languages are much more similar than they are different. Each has its own idiosyncrasies, special words and ways of saying things, but each can usually be understood by the other. For Czechs, Slovak has an exotic tinge, with a number of words taken from Hungarian or Turkish, while a Czech's *"Jo, jo!"* ("yeah!") reminds Slovaks of how close their western neighbors are to Germany.

Czechoslovakia unzipped

Magnanimous magnates
The use of the Šternberg Palace as a setting for the National Gallery seems entirely appropriate. The gallery's origins go back to 1796, when a Patriotic Association of Friends of Art was formed. The Friends bought some paintings of their own, but to begin with the bulk of their collection consisted of works on loan from the Šternbergs. Over the years the collection has had a number of homes, including the Černín Palace and the Rudolfinium, as well as the Šternberg Palace—twice: first from 1814 to 1871, then from 1945 onwards.

Let's bag a Picasso!
The collapse of the Communist police state in 1989 encouraged all kinds of crooks to become over-confident. In 1991, two thieves broke into the poorly guarded Šternberg Palace and stole $2.6 million worth of paintings by Picasso. Although the pictures were recovered and the thieves convicted, lax security arrangements in many of the country's galleries remain a temptation to the light-fingered.

Entrance to the National Gallery's collection of European art at the Šternberg Palace

▶▶▶ **Národní Galerie, Šternbersky Palác**
(National Gallery, Šternberg Palace) 82A2
Hradčanské náměstí (Hradčany Square)
Metro: Malostranská, then Tram 22 to Pražsky hrad
The national collection of European (that is, non-Czech) art is housed in the somewhat somber palace built for the Šternberg family at the very beginning of the 18th century. Most schools and periods are covered, and there are enough individual masterpieces to detain an art lover for at least an afternoon. One of the gallery's great strengths is its array of late 19th- and early 20th-century French works.

History The Šternbergs' town house is tucked away discreetly to the left of the Arcibiskupsý palác (Archbishop's Palace), but is none the less pretentious for that, with imposing proportions and a splendid oval pavilion as the centerpiece of its west wing. The palace was commissioned in 1698 as an urban counterpart to his out-of-town residence, at Trója, by Václav Vojtěch Šternberg, the richest man in Prague after Count Černín. Designed by Domenico Martinelli, it was realized by Giovanni Alliprandi, whose other major work was the Lobkovic Palace in Malá Strana. The interiors still retain much of the original frescos and plasterwork.

Second floor The bulk of the collection is hung on the second and third floors of the main building, while the later French work is displayed in the rooms on the far side of the courtyard. On the second floor are a number of early Italian paintings, mostly from the collection inherited by Archduke Franz Ferdinand when he became Duke of Modena in 1875 and subsequently displayed at Konopiště Castle. Their delicate intricacy compares interestingly to the exquisite Greek and Russian icons displayed in an adjoining room. Here, too, are portraits of dark-eyed beauties from 2nd-century BC Egypt.

Most of the space on this floor is, however, given over to masters from the Low Countries. The highly stylized late-Gothic figures of Dieric Bouts contrast with the much more fully realized human beings who populate the triptych of the *Adoration of the Magi* by Giertgen tot Sint Jans. The huge canvas of *St. Luke Drawing the Virgin* by Mabuse (also known as Gossaert) once graced the altar of the cathedral, and depicts the Gothic-looking pair situated in a nightmarishly complicated classical building.

Third floor Works by della Robbia and Donatello enliven the stairway leading up to the second floor. This part of the collection begins with major German works of the 15th and 16th centuries. The darker side of the

German psyche is evoked by a number of painters, including Schucklin, Baldung Grien, and Altdorfer, who are able to extract the maximum of horror from various beheadings and martyrdoms; the executioner's ax swishes through the air above St. Barbara's head, while St. Florian is dispatched during the course of a particularly nasty mugging.

The great Lukas Cranach the Elder is well represented, with an *Adam and Eve*, a glamorous *Madonna* and an exceptionally silly *Old Fool* playing around with a none-too-unwilling maiden.

Adam and Eve, *by the German artist Lukas Cranach the Elder*

Albrecht Dürer's Feast of the Rosary *(1506)*

Renaissance works The dominant canvas of the second floor is Dürer's superb *Feast of the Rosary*, painted for the German merchants' church in Venice in 1506. A huge group portrait, and a wonderful synthesis of Italian and northern art, the painting shows the Virgin crowning Emperor Maximilian, and the Infant Jesus performing the same ceremony for the pope. Dürer himself appears among the other prominent 16th-century personalities, modestly presenting his signature.

Among the other works on this floor are a Tintoretto, an El Greco, and a wonderful *St. Jerome* by Ribera, the saint's manuscript bright against a somber background. In his depiction of *The Thames*, Canaletto shows London's river as a northern version of the Venetian Grand Canal. There are pictures by Ruysdael and Rubens, and a fine Rembrandt of a *Scholar in his Study*, none too certain of the purpose of his research.

Roses for Rudolf
Dürer's *Feast of the Rosary* held a particular fascination for Emperor Rudolf II. After arranging for its purchase, he had it laboriously transported across the Alps from Venice to Prague, securely wrapped in rugs and held upright the whole way by a quartet of stalwart carters to keep it from coming to any harm. The huge picture somehow survived the notorious sale of castle treasures in 1782, and after a spell in the Strahovský klášter (Strahov Monastery), was returned to the state in the 1930s.

Art of the 20th century A sudden leap from the muted art of the Low Countries takes visitors to the bold experimentation and expressiveness of early 20th-century Central Europe. The gallery has a selection of works by the likes of Klimt, Klee, Schiele, and Kokoschka. Egon Schiele was a Bohemian in both senses: his mother came from Český Krumlov (Krummau) in Southern Bohemia, and he turned this most picturesque of medieval towns into a place of brooding menace in a number of his paintings.

By contrast, Kokoschka's panoramas of Prague are bright, dynamic, and joyful, not least because the city seemed to offer a sanctuary from the growing threat of fascism in the artist's native Austria. Gustav Klimt's sensuous response to femininity is seen in his *Virgin*, and his equivalent love of landscape in his *Water* (in other words, moated) *Castle*. As well as works by these and other German and Austrian artists, there are a number of Russian and Italian moderns, and an ecstatic but sinister *Dancers on the Shore* by Edvard Munch.

French collection Across the palace courtyard, an oval entrance hall introduces the modern French collection with a characteristically robust bust by Rodin of *Balzac*, in total contrast to the sleek and curvaceous Maillol near by. Beyond are rooms full of paintings by the French masters who dominated the artistic scene in the early part of the 20th century. The pictures are all the more stimulating because of their relative unfamiliarity, few having been shown or reproduced outside Czechoslovakia in recent decades.

There are canvases by Rousseau (his only self-portrait), Derain, Dufy, Utrillo, and Vlaminck, and a flagrant, lazy nude by Van Dongen. Gauguin is represented by his *Good-day Mr. Gauguin*, Cézanne by the *House in Aïx*, and Monet by an *Orchard in Blossom*, reminiscent of the springtime scene on nearby Petřín hill. Renoir's lovers nestle picturesquely in a natural green bower, quite unlike the tormented Nature depicted in Van Gogh's *Green Rye*, and there are any number of other Impressionists, including Pisarro and Manet, as well as the Pointillistes Signac and Seurat.

The furthermost rooms show earlier French works, by Corot, Courbet, Delacroix, and Daumier, but the centerpiece of this part of the collection is formed by the exceptional array of Cubist paintings. The early careers of both Picasso and Braque can be traced better here than in most other places outside France; this is thanks largely to the foresight of a gallery director who bought up works by these two artists well before they had become fashionable. The presence of these works in Prague at an early date had an incalculable influence on the development of Czech Cubism, a movement that encompassed not just painting and sculpture but the decorative arts and architecture as well.

Oskar OK
Oskar Kokoschka loved both Prague and President Masaryk, painting many landscapes of the one and the portrait of the other. But his refuge in the city was a temporary one: after the Munich crisis of 1938, he no longer felt safe here, and got away to England before the Gestapo could knock at his door. His feelings about fascism are expressed in the splendidly satirical painting called *Red Egg*, featuring a Humpty Dumpty Mussolini and dunce-capped Hitler. This painting is on display in the National Gallery.

Oskar Kokoschka's Charles Bridge and Hradčany, Prague, *a typically vibrant Expressionist panorama of the city*

HRADČANY

The rustic charm of Nový Svět

80

Švankmajer's world
Using a unique combination of live action, collage, puppets, and drawn animation, Jan Švankmajer creates a surreal universe where heads explode and swelling organs take on a life of their own. His film, *The Death of Stalinism in Bohemia*, is a visceral evocation of the irrationality of Communism, closer to the inner truth than any political tract.

► **Nový Svět** 52A3

Metro: Malostranská, then Tram 22 to Brusnice
Meaning "New World," this is the name given to the village-like district to the north of Loretánské náměstí (Loretto Square) as well as to its picturesque main street, whose crooked course is brought abruptly to a halt by a great brick wall, part of Hradčany's remaining Baroque fortifications. The road once rambled on to Střešovice, and the buildings on either side once housed the castle servants in appalling conditions. Now Nový Svět is a cul-de-sac, a quiet quarter of charming houses, trees, and secret walls, somewhat removed from the main tourist trail, spreading westwards from the castle and northwards from Strahovsky klášter (Strahov Monastery). Artists have tended to settle here in recent years, among them the animator Švankmajer, master of the surreal cartoon.

The stepped alleyway of Na nápsu leads down from the tramlines along Keplerova (Kepler street) into cobbled Černínská street, where the smiling little stone figure of St. John Nepomuk seems to beam a welcome. House No. 7 ("The Golden Pheasant"), with its bright new sign,

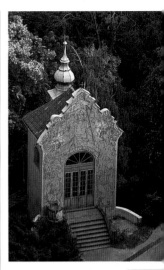

has been immaculately restored, in contrast to some of its more run-down neighbors. At the junction where Černínská curves charmingly into Nový Svět itself, an incongruously rustic-looking timber house stands, now a luxury pensione. Nový Svět staggers off eastward, barely able to maintain a constant distance between the houses to one side and the high wall to the other. The birthplace of violin virtuoso František Ondříček is marked by a bust at No. 25, while the painter's studio at No. 19 is full of voluptuous girls and leering dwarves. The most famous residents of Nový Svět, the astronomers Tycho de Brahe and Johannes Kepler, lived at No. 1, next door to a what is now a fashionable restaurant.

Marking the beginning of Kanovnická street, the Baroque palace residence of the Austrian ambassador faces the Kostel svatého Jana Nepomuckého (Church of St. John Nepomuk); this was the first building in Prague designed by the architect Kilián Ignác Dientzenhofer. Begun in 1720, it seems permanently shrouded in scaffolding, but has an interior of unusual dynamism, with ceiling paintings by the prolific Václav Vavřinec Reiner.

▶▶   **Petřín**   52A2

Metro: Malostranská, Tram 12 or 22 to Hellichova, then Lanovka (funicular railway)

The woods, orchards, and gardened slopes of the Petřín form a glorious counterpoint to the castle area and its crowded streets, contributing to the pleasant illusion of a city still contained within its historic boundaries.

The hill is made from the same limestone as the White Mountain to the west, and over the centuries its quarries have supplied the city with much of its building material. The vineyards covering the south-facing slopes never recovered from the ravages of the Thirty Years' War, and much of the area was later fenced off to furnish private villas with extensive gardens. In the early 19th century, thanks in part to the pioneering efforts of the public-spirited Count Chotek, virtually the whole of the hill became a public park. Through the park wanders the Hladová zed' (Hunger Wall), part of the new fortifications thrown around the city by Emperor Charles IV in 1360, given this name because it was intended to provide employment for an undernourished populace.

Footpaths penetrate all parts of the park, offering splendid views whenever they emerge from the often scrubby woodland. A climb on foot can be avoided by taking the Lanová dráha, the rack-and-pinion railroad which runs up from Újezd in Malá Strana. Recently renovated, the railroad was built for the Provincial Jubilee Exhibition of 1891, along with the 180-ft. imitation Eiffel Tower, the Petřín rozhledna, from whose viewing platform the panorama ostensibly extends from the Giant Mountains to the Alps. At its foot is another contemporary attraction, the Bludiště, or Mirror Maze (containing both a maze and a painted diorama of a battle that took place in 1648), while near by stands Kostel svatého Vavřinec (the Church of St. Lawrence), a little Baroque church built on Romanesque foundations. The flat land at the top of the slope is intensively gardened; the city's Hvězdárna (Astronomical Observatory) is set among roses, and there is also a delightful alpine garden.

The Calvary Chapel of the Kostel svatého Vavřinc na Petříne (Church of St. Lawrence on Petřín), seen here from the Petřín rozhledna (Petřín Tower), has fine 19th-century sgraffito decoration by Mikuláš Aleš

Carpathian construction
Utterly unlike any other building in Prague, the timber Kostel svatého Michal (Church of St. Michael) stands in the southern part of Petřín. Its sophisticated rusticity is a reminder that in the days of the First Czechoslovak Republic, Prague's rule extended eastwards to the Ukraine; the building was brought here in 1928 from Medvedovce—"the place of bears"—among the forests and mountains of the far-off province that used to be known as Ruthenia.

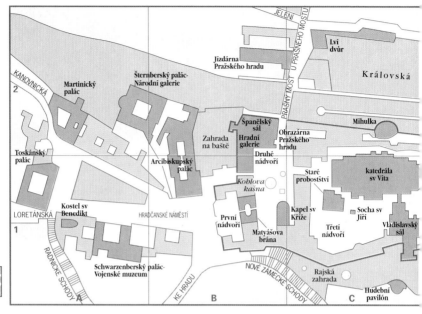

►►► Pražský hrad (Prague Castle)   52C3

Metro: Malostranská, then Tram 22 to Pražsky hrad

The Přemyslid princes of the 9th century were the first to build on this site, and almost every subsequent ruler has added something in adapting the castle to his or her needs. Their legacy is a complex, tightly packed assemblage consisting not only of a royal palace and cathedral, but also of offices, courtiers' quarters, lesser churches, and minor palaces. All these are linked by streets, courtyards, and stairways, and are set off by the lawns, terraces, trees, and pleasure pavilions of extensive gardens. Every age of building is represented, from the outline of the Přemyslids' first church, which can still be traced in the north range of the Second Courtyard, to the sensitive but highly original adaptations to the ancient structure carried out by Josip Plečnik, President Masaryk's personal architect, in the 1920s.

Getting there The castle is linked to the city in a number of ways. The cobbled ramps and steps of two stairways—Nové zámecké schody (New Castle Steps) and Staré zámecké schody (Old Castle Steps)—climb up from Malostranské náměstí (Malá Strana Square) and Malostranská metro station respectively. A longer, though popular, route from the square is up picturesque Nerudova street and the steep ramp known as Ke hradu. The climb can be avoided or even turned into a descent by judicious use of Tram 22, with its choice of stops: you can get off at Královský Letohrádek (the Royal Summer Palace) and walk to the castle through the Královská zahrada (Royal Gardens); you can get off at the stop called Pražský hrad and walk across the Stag Moat into the castle's Second Courtyard; or you can continue right up to Strahov then stroll gently downhill to reach the castle through the Hradčany quarter.

Map

MARIÁNSKÉ HRADBY

Herkulova kašna

zahrada

Mičovna

Královský letohrádek

Zpívající fontána

Jelení příkop

VIKÁŘSKÁ

Bílá věž

Daliborka věž

Jiřský klášter-Sbirka starého českého umění (Národní galerie)

ZLATÁ ULIČKA

NÁMĚSTÍ U SV JIŘÍ

Bazilika sv Jiří

JIŘSKÁ

Černá věž

NA OPYŠI

Starý Královský palác

Kostel Všech svatých

Lobkovický palác (Národní muzeum)

STARÉ ZÁMECKÉ SCHODY

Zahrada

Na valech

D

E

83

The approach The usual spot to start a tour of the castle is from the ceremonial entrance facing Hradčanské náměstí (Hradčany Square). The square's broad sweep of cobbles cover what was once a deep moat dug to defend this most vulnerable approach to the original fortress; it was filled in in the 18th century. The president's blue-uniformed guards stand to either side of the gateway, dwarfed by the battling giants above them, 20th-century copies of the Baroque originals. Beyond are the bland buildings of the **První nádvoří (First Courtyard)**, part of the 18th-century reconstruction carried out by Empress Maria Theresa. Set into the main façade is the outline of the 17th-century **Matyášova brána (Matthias Gate)**, a reminder of the days when it formed the western entrance to the castle.

PRAŽSKÝ HRAD ❖ VSTUPENKA

The boys in blue—the castle guards march back to barracks

The First Courtyard Major, but subtle modifications took place at the castle in the 1920s. Conscious of the need to make the castle the dignified yet welcoming focal point of his new, democratic republic, President Masaryk employed Professor Plečnik to redesign many rooms and outside spaces. As well as repaving the První nádvoří (First Courtyard) and providing it with two fine flagpoles of Moravian pine, Plečnik restored the presidential apartments and reception rooms, located to the right of the Matyašova brána (Matthias Gate). To the left of the gate he created a lofty columned hall, only occasionally open to the public. Named after its creator, the Plečnik Hall has a grand staircase and copper-covered ceiling; it forms a monumental antechamber to the Španělský sál (Spanish Hall) to the north, once the locale for meetings of the Central Committee of the Czechoslovak Communist Party.

The Second Courtyard The monotonous appearance of the spacious Druhé nádvoří (Second Courtyard) is partly due to the extensive reconstructions carried out during the reign of Empress Maria Theresa (1717–80), when much of the castle was "homogenized" in a cool late-Baroque style. The courtyard focuses on the Baroque fountain at its center, while a modern lion fountain stands next to the Kapel svatého Kříže (Chapel of the Holy Rood), which protrudes from the range of buildings to the south. Baroque in origin, the chapel was remodeled in the 1850s to serve as the court chapel of the retired Habsburg Emperor Ferdinand, who chose to spend his declining years in Prague. Until recently, it housed the dazzling objects now located in the cathedral Treasury.

Pierced by the passageway leading to the causeway over the Stag Moat, the north side of the courtyard is closed by the Španělský sál (Spanish Hall) and the Rudolfova galerie (Rudolf Gallery). An avid collector of just about everything, Emperor Rudolf amassed an array of paintings, some in what might be delicately described as dubious taste. Most have been dispersed, but among those that remain are paintings by Tintoretto, Titian, Veronese, and Rubens, as well as

Bargain basement
The fate of Emperor Rudolf's amazing art collection exemplifies the castle's decline during the later years of Habsburg rule. Imperial cash-flow was often aided by selling off a picture here, a statue there. In 1782, the still very substantial remains of the collection were discovered gathering dust in the cellars by army officers engaged in converting this part of the castle into an artillery barracks. Carelessly packed up into oddly assorted lots, antique statuary, medieval charters, and Renaissance paintings were auctioned off at reduced prices to make space for the storage of ammunition.

A statue of St. George and Plečnik's obelisk stand in the spacious surroundings of the Third Courtyard

PRAZSKÝ HRAD

10 Kčs

* 091727

numerous canvases by Rudolf's Bohemian contemporaries and an unstimulating array of Habsburg portraits.

The Third Courtyard A passageway tunnels through the Second Courtyard's eastern range into the Třetí nádvoří (Third Courtyard), which is utterly dominated by the Katedrála svatého Víta (St. Vitus's Cathedral—see page 59). Narrow Vikářská (Vicars' Street) squeezes along the northern flank of the cathedral. Here is a café and an entranceway through to the drum-like Mihulka (Powder Tower), part of the 15th-century fortifications. Exhibits on each of its floors recall its highly diverse history as a gunpowder store (accidentally blown up in 1649), an alchemists' den, and the foundry of the famous metalworker Jaroš.

To the south, the Third Courtyard opens out expansively, allowing the soaring lines of the cathedral to be appreciated more fully. Here, too, late 18th-century blandness predominates, though the long southern range is broken up by a balcony from which the president traditionally receives the cheers of the crowd after his election. The previously sloping courtyard was ingeniously leveled by Plečnik in the 1920s to expose the foundations of the churches predating the cathedral. Plečnik also designed the great obelisk as a war memorial, and in addition created a stairway through to the gardens far below on the southern side of the castle.

From the courtyard, this splendid staircase is entered through a beautiful ornamented canopy borne on the backs of bronze bulls. Its six flights of stairs are interrupted by balconies giving some of the most carefully composed views of the city. A far older feature is the Gothic statue of St. George, elegantly spearing a somewhat small dragon; he is the work of 14th-century sculptors from far-off Cluj (then Klausenburg) in Transylvania (though you will have to visit the National Gallery in St. George's Convent—see page 72—to see the original).

The building at the southwestern corner of the cathedral is the Staré proboštsví (Old Provost's House), Baroque outside but containing the far older Romanesque core of what was once the Bishop's Palace.

Continued on page 88.

85

Above: gilt, glitter, and gorgeous painting in the Kaple svatého Kříže (Chapel of the Holy Rood), also home to the castle complex's information center

Philosopher presidents

■ **Two presidents stand out in the 20th-century history of the Czech Lands, not least because their early careers gave little hint that each of them would one day lead the nation out of the bonds of oppressive regimes. In their work as thinkers and writers, both Tomáš Masaryk and Václav Havel gave primacy to the notion of philosophical truth as the underlying principle of human affairs, an apt starting point for a nation whose motto is *Pravda vítězí!* (Truth will prevail!)....■**

Top: President Masaryk returning to Prague in December 1918; note the car he used in preference to the old imperial coach

Fit to be president

Masaryk seems to have taken a modest pride in his appearance and physique. A tall man, he dressed simply and elegantly in the way that might be expected of "a slightly idiosyncratic country gentleman" (Z. Zeman), in jodhpurs, a jacket buttoned up to the neck and a cap or broad-brimmed hat. He enjoyed riding at his country residences at Lány in Bohemia or Topolčianky in Slovakia. A visitor who remarked on the quality of the president's carpet was amazed to find that the 80-year-old immediately bent down to examine the truth of what had been said.

Right: President Masaryk, founder of the First Republic

Tomáš Masaryk Masaryk emerged from humble origins in the Moravian countryside to become Professor of Philosophy at Prague University in 1882. Never conventional, he sought contact with students (unheard of in those days) while refining his vision of a just future for the Czech nation. Narrow-minded nationalists heaped abuse on him for his involvement in unpopular causes; in the 1880s he helped prove that supposedly ancient Czech manuscripts were in fact chauvinistic forgeries, and in 1899 he defended a Jew against a trumped-up charge of ritual killing. Truth prevailed, but it took a while for its defender to overcome his subsequent isolation.

In World War I, Masaryk worked for the Czech cause without respite, spending most of his time abroad arguing persuasively with the Allies to support the establishment of a free Czechoslovakia. He returned to Prague in triumph in December 1918, but balked at using the old imperial coach for the procession from the station, choosing instead to ride in a car.

Elected president three times in a row Masaryk played an active role in the often-stormy politics of the First Republic, refusing to become a mere figurehead. Having reviewed his troops on horseback for the last time at the age of 83, he resigned in 1935 in favor of his protégé, Edvard Beneš. He died two years later, just before the tragic dismemberment of the country which, through his wise and energetic leadership, he had done so much to create.

Václav Havel Havel came from a grand background compared with his predecessor. Grandfather Havel, another Václav, had been a successful builder and developer; his grandson was made to suffer for his bourgeois origins by the Communists, who denied him

From passportless dissident to international statesman—President Havel

access to higher education. Havel educated himself anyway, working as a stage-hand while establishing himself as a playwright.

After the Prague Spring a long winter began for Havel. Refused permission to publish, he sent his manuscripts abroad, where his plays enjoyed consistent acclaim for their exposure of the absurdity of life led under a regime which had no philosophical foundation. Despite its shaky moral basis, or perhaps because of it, the regime hounded the obstinate writer, setting up permanent police posts outside his Prague apartment and his country cottage.

Havel spent a total of five years in prison, where he nearly died on one occasion through lack of proper medical treatment, otherwise working in manual jobs (such as the stint at the brewery where the management, at a loss for words of their own, asked him to write the confidential reports on him required by the secret police).

Since being catapulted into a presidency which he never sought, Havel has attempted to put state life on to the ethical basis advocated by Masaryk. Despite the fact that this has not always pleased his countrymen, it seems likely that he will continue to offer them a broader vision of themselves than the one put forward by many more conventional politicians.

Along the corridors of power
President Havel presents as distinct an image of himself as did Masaryk. Informality rules when possible. Suits are worn and banquets attended when required, but the president really prefers to hang around in the bar in sweater and jeans, chain-smoking the cigarettes which seem likely to give him a shorter lifespan than that of octogenarian Masaryk. To speed his progress along the endless corridors of the castle, Havel used a child's scooter, a habit which had to stop when the cleaners complained about skidmarks on the parquet floors.

Continued from page 85.

Now you see him...
The Old Provost's House is featured in a famous photograph showing prominent Party men standing outside the cathedral's Golden Gate following the election of President Svoboda in 1968. Among them is a beaming Alexander Dubček. Reissued a year or so later, the photo bears no trace of the former First Secretary, by then in disgrace. Close inspection of the print reveals the subtle art of the retoucher; not only has Dubček been airbrushed out of history, but the Old Provost's House has been shifted eastward to compensate for the changed composition of the picture.

Final flowering of Gothic genius— Benedict Ried's magnificent Vladislav Hall, completed in 1493. Used in the past for banquets, jousts, and tournaments, the hall is also the setting for presidential inaugurations, from Gottwald's in 1948 to Havel's in 1990

The Old Royal Palace The eastern end of the Third Courtyard is closed off by the **Starý Královský palác (Old Royal Palace)**▶▶▶. This is a layer cake of Bohemian history, beginning at foundation level with Soběslav's 12th-century palace and rising through successive levels of early- and late-Gothic construction to the unique Vladislavský sál (Vladislav Hall) built at the precise moment when the first rays of the Renaissance sparked a final flare of medieval inventiveness and extravagance.

The Vladislav Hall The palace entrance is past the delightful little Eagle Fountain. To the right, in the antechamber, is stonework from the keep of Soběslav's castle. To the left is the Green Chamber, with a Baroque fresco depicting the judgement of Solomon, then the Vladislav Bedroom with a colorful late-Gothic vault.

Next, with the Vladislav Hall, comes the apotheosis of medieval vaulting, created in the 1490s by the versatile architect, Benedict Ried. Ried's walls and windows are pure early Renaissance, square and solid, but the ribs of

his vault writhe weightlessly into space, escaping earthly constraints to create one of the most stunningly original spaces in Central Europe. Often compared to floral forms, the ribs divide the vault into taut sections of membrane, the result having as much in common with a Leonardo da Vinci flying machine as with any design of Nature.

Rooms of state Ried also built the Ludvik (Louis) wing, leading south from the hall. This once housed the Bohemian Chancellery, and is best known for the spectacular defenestration of the Catholic councilors in 1621, the event which heralded the outbreak of the Thirty Years' War (see page 34). The broad steps of a spiral staircase lead up to the Court Chancellery, where the second act of the defenestration drama was played out, the condemning to death of its Protestant perpetrators three years later. Its windows provide a wonderful view, but the south side of the palace is best appreciated from the terrace, entered from the far (eastern) end of the hall. The modern helical staircase was designed, very much in the spirit of Plečnik, by his pupil, Otto Rottmayer.

Kostel Všech svatých (All Saints' Chapel), originally built by Petr Parléř for Charles IV but much altered since, is also approached from this end of the hall, through a Renaissance portico. A doorway on the north side of the hall leads into the Diet Hall, originally built by Ried but rebuilt after the great fire of 1541 by Boniface Wohlmuth, with vaulting in pale imitation of his predecessor's virtuosity. The room is laid out as if for a meeting of the Diet, with the monarch's throne, proper places for the Church and nobility, and standing-room-only for the townsfolk.

Another doorway gives access to the Riders' Staircase, also by Ried, with vaults whose ribs are heavier but even more convulsed than those in the hall; this ramped entrance was used by horsemen making their way to and from tournaments in the Vladislav Hall.

Sumptuous decoration in the Bohemian Chancellery

Out you go!
Prague's Second Defenestration was plotted by Protestant nobles in one of the palaces in Malá Strana. Accompanied by an enthusiastic mob, they burst into the castle's Chancellery where the fanatical Catholics, Martinic and Slavata, were in conference. The unfortunate pair were manhandled through the open window. Cruel blows rained down on their knuckles as they clung to the sill and they fell into the moat far below, accompanied by their secretary. Was it divine intervention that put in place the deep dung-heap which broke their fall? Or merely the unhygienic habits of the age? With no bones broken, but with their fine clothes ruined forever, they scrambled to their feet and fled, continuing the bitter struggle against their religious opponents from abroad.

St. George's Basilica In medieval times the castle's center of gravity was formed by Jiřské náměstí (St. George's Square), dominated by the radiating chapels and spectacularly buttressed choir of the cathedral. Confronted with this Gothic splendor, the **Bazilika svatého Jiří (St. George's Basilica)▶▶** puts on a brave Baroque face, heavily made up with paint the color of bull's blood. Beyond rise twin towers in sober white stone, built, like most of this austerely beautiful Romanesque church, in the mid-12th century, following the fire which destroyed the original building begun in AD 920 by Vratislav I. For centuries the basilica served the adjacent convent which, lavishly rebuilt, now houses the National Gallery's magnificent collection of Bohemian art (see page 72). The church itself has been deconsecrated and functions as a concert hall. It is the grandest Romanesque building in the whole country, its austere interior a reminder of the great antiquity of the castle complex.

Among the tombs of Přemyslid princes is one looking like a Gothic dollhouse. The semi-circular apse, with remains of Romanesque painting in its vault, is approached by a charming Baroque staircase. St. Ludmila's Chapel is Gothic, St. John Nepomuk's Baroque, while Benedict Ried added a lively St. George slaying the dragon in the Renaissance tympanum of the south door.

The eastern precinct From the square, narrow Jiřská (George Street) is one of the very few Prague thoroughfares to

LOBKOVICKÝ PALÁC
NÁRODNÍ MUZEUM V PRAZE
VSTUPENKA 25,-
* 079827
HISTORICKÁ EXPOZICE

The palace basements
After the Vladislav Hall, visitors can continue downwards to the lower depths, with their arcaded passages, vaulted Gothic chambers, and the mysterious spaces of the Romanesque palace. At present sparsely furnished with building models and sculptural oddities, this part of the palace may well become the home of the precious objects of the Castle Treasury.

Stylish contrasts—the Baroque façade and Romanesque towers of St. George's Basilica

91

Pretty Zlatá ulička is popular with tourists

retain a bilingual Czech and German street sign; it descends towards the Černá věž (Black Tower) overlooking the castle's eastern entrance. For many years this tower was used as a debtors' prison. Just beyond the gateway is an observation terrace, laid out on the site of an old gate-tower, as well as the eastern entrance to the castle's terraced gardens (see page 92).

On the south side of Jiřská stands the Lobkovický palác (Lobkovic Palace), a Baroque building which contains the collections of the History Museum. Its few foreign visitors soon give up trying to translate the Czech captions of the objects on display (though a leaflet with translations is available) in favor of enjoying a fine city view from the balcony. There is also much of interest in the richly decorated interiors, from accurate reproductions of the inaccessible Crown Jewels, to a delightful Chinese Room with early musical instruments and the earliest extant example of a Czech marionette (18th century).

The museum is a good place to while away a quiet hour waiting for the crowds to disperse from the over-popular Zlatá ulička (Golden Lane) to the north. Reputedly the residences of alchemists, its toy-sized dwellings were originally the quarters of the castle guard, later attracting an unsavory population of artisans who, for one reason or another, had been excluded from the city guilds. The noise, smells, and general boisterousness of the artisans upset the nearby nuns, who closed their bar and eventually had them evicted. Other residents continued to live here right up to the advent of Communism, since which souvenir sharks have taken over.

At one end of the alley is the Bílá věž (White Tower), at the other the Daliborka věž (Dalibor's Tower). Both served as prisons, the latter being named after Dalibor, the medieval knight, promoted over the years as a sort of Robin Hood figure and celebrated in Smetana's opera of the same name.

The Golden guys
Two of Prague's greatest literary figures are associated with Golden Lane. The Nobel-prize-winning poet, Jaroslav Seifert, lived in a now-demolished house, while Franz Kafka often spent his evenings at No. 22 where he found an atmosphere congenial to the writing of his short stories. The house was the home of his sister Otla, who long outlived her tubercular brother, only to perish in a Nazi concentration camp.

Sunshine sign in Golden Lane

Castle gardens

■ **Beyond the castle walls is an array of green spaces making a perfect foil to the citadel's tightly packed buildings and crowded courtyards. Overlooking the city to the south, the old ramparts are linked to gardens climbing up from the aristocratic palaces of Malá Strana, while on the spacious plateau to the north are the Královská zahrada (Royal Gardens), whose delightful Summer Palace is only one of a number of fascinating garden buildings....■**

Pineapple present
The Royal Garden was damaged in the course of the Thirty Years' War when uncouth Swedish soldiers felled the trees and burned down buildings. A hundred or so years later a Prussian bombardment had much the same effect. In 1743, French fury was averted when a timely gift of 30 pineapples was made to the commander of the occupying army, who agreed to discipline his men who, once more, were threatening to reduce the garden to ruin.

The Royal Gardens First laid out in Renaissance style by Ferdinand I, in 1534, these gardens replaced the vineyards that had previously existed to the north of the Stag Moat. The south-facing slopes on which the vines had grown made an excellent site for exotic shrubs and for fig and almond trees, while greenhouses were built for oranges, lemons, and apricots. The Královský Letohrádek (Summer Palace) was provided with a little formal garden of its own, where Europe's first tulips, a present from the Sultan of Turkey, were cultivated long before they became a Dutch specialty. The famous Singing Fountain was placed here in 1568.

Further west along the plateau the **Ball Game Hall (Míčovna)** was built with big windows and fine sgraffito (incised plasterwork) decoration. In the 18th century, avenues were planted in accord with Baroque taste, and at the same time sculptures were added, such as the statue of *Night* by Braun. Open since 1989, these gardens now make a most attractive approach to the castle, with superb specimen trees and enticing glimpses of walls, towers, and spires to the south. To the west of the entrance to the Royal Garden is the grand and simple building of the Jízdárna (Riding School), designed by Mathey in 1694. It now forms a setting for temporary art exhibitions.

The Ramparts Garden The castle originally presented a formidable face to the city below, its stark walls and ramparts overlooking Malá Strana. These fortifications became obsolete at about the same time as the Royal Garden was being created, and ever since have served as (mostly private) gardens for the residents of the castle. In the 1920s they were renovated with great care and sensitivity by the architect Josip Plečnik, who linked them to Hradčanské náměstí (Hradčany Square) to the west and, by means of a bold staircase tunneled through the very substance of the castle, to the Third Courtyard high above. The private spaces where President Masaryk meditated, and where the Communists thought their own thoughts, have now been comprehensively renovated, and since 1993 have been open (though not all the time) to the public.

Relax and enjoy the view from the Ramparts Garden

The Royal Palace, as seen from the Ramparts Garden

93

Post-modern Plečnik
While Czechoslovakia's progressive architects, working in the 1920s and 1930s, experimented with glass, steel, and concrete, and the stark forms of Modernism, Josip Plečnik contented himself with subtle reinterpretations of classical motifs: columns with capitals, obelisks, and urns. No detail was too trivial to escape his attention (look at the dog-head handles to the doors off the Third Courtyard staircase) and for preference he would use the rarest and most expensive materials. Driven to resign from his post as castle architect by the resentment of lesser artists, he is acclaimed today as a precursor of Post-modernism and as a link with the long-standing traditions which Modernism rejected.

To create a route to the gardens, Plečnik pierced the wall at the top of the Nové zámecké schody (New Castle Steps), thus making an opening into the terraces. He then designed a wonderful flight of stairs rippling down into the Rajská zahrada (Paradise Garden), beyond which the Zahrada Na valech (Ramparts Garden) stretches its immense length eastward. After much calculation, Plečnik placed a pyramid in the garden, which links the Third Courtyard and St. Nicholas's Church to far-off Vyšehrad on a single visual axis. All along the garden balustrade are marvelous views down into the secret gardens of Malá Strana.

Ceiling fresco of The Banquet of King Balthasar *by the monk Siard Nosecký (1753); it can be found in the former Abbot's Dining Room at Strahov Monastery*

▶▶ **Strahovský Klášter (Strahov Monastery)** 52A2

Strahovské nádvoří

Metro: Malostranská, then Tram 22 to Památník písemnictví

The buildings of this ancient foundation crest the hilltop to the west of the castle, their twin towers an indispensable element of the Prague skyline. Recently returned to its original owner, the Premonstratensian Order, the monastery is famous for its magnificent libraries.

History Strahov was founded by Bishop Zdik of Olomouc in 1140. Royal support for the venture had been gained by the bishop's flattering comparison of Prague to Jerusalem, and the establishment's first name was Zion. Continual fires and occasional sackings and plunderings led to periodic rebuilding, though the walls of the church still contain original Romanesque masonry.

The greatest threat to the monastery came in the late 18th century. In his ambition to construct a secular, centralized state, Emperor Joseph II closed down religious establishments wholesale. Crafty Abbot Meyer saved Strahov by an emergency expansion of its already highly reputed library (libraries were considered by the Emperor to be "useful" institutions). Books were brought in by the wagonload from the dissolved monastery of Louka, in Moravia, and accommodated in the splendid Philosophical Hall, built specially to house them.

The buildings The monastery once stood on the very edge of town, and a breath of country air still pervades the somewhat unkempt courtyard, with its trees and cobblestones. The main entrance is guarded by a Baroque portal bearing a statue of St. Norbert, the founder of the Premonstratensian Order. To the left of the entrance is the Kostel svatého

Flattery pays
While Abbot Zdik's unctuous comparison of Prague to Jerusalem may have helped to sway King Vratislav II's decision to support the construction of the new monastery in 1140, Abbot Meyer too saw no shame in playing up to the right people; he had a gilded figure of Joseph II, the greatest persecutor the monasteries had ever known, mounted over the entrance to the establishment's new library.

Rocha (St. Roch's Chapel), completed in 1611 and a curious mixture of Gothic and Renaissance. Across the courtyard is the west front of the Kostel Nanebevzetí Panny Marie (Church of the Assumption). The layout of the building reflects its origins as a Romanesque basilica, but successive rebuildings and reconstructions have given it an overwhelmingly Baroque character, with altars of stately black and gold lining the nave, while elaborate stucco work provides sumptuous frames for wall and ceiling paintings. Beyond the church lies another courtyard with the former entrance to the Pamatnik Narodniho Pisemnictví (Czech Literature Museum), where you may find a temporary exhibition on some literary theme.

The main attraction of the complex consists of the two great library halls in the western part of the monastery. The Filosofický sál (Philosophical Hall) of 1782 is a barn for books, not inappropriately, since it was built on the site of a grain warehouse. The elaborately carved walnut shelves rise a sheer 45 ft. from the floor, interrupted by a single balcony. The ceiling is covered with a huge painting, one of the last works by the great Viennese painter Maulpertsch; its theme is the *History of Philosophy*, beginning with Adam and Eve, and ending with "heretical" writers of the French Enlightenment, such as Voltaire and Diderot, being cast into hell.

Museum of Czech Literature
When the Communists closed Strahov monastery they respected the bookish traditions of the place. The confiscated libraries of other religious foundations suppressed by the atheistic state were brought here, and the monastery buildings became the Museum of Czech Literature, an unusual institution, of interest mainly to native speakers, but subject to an uncertain future since the return of the monks.

95

The Teologický sál (Theological Hall), completed in 1679, is even more atmospheric. The low ceiling is decorated with rich stucco and with paintings on the theme of *True Wisdom*, complete with pious captions in Latin. The walls are lined with the original bookcases, while the central space is kept clear for a parade of venerable globes and bookstands holding some of the libraries' greatest treasures, including the 9th-century Strahov Gospels.

The 17th-century library of the Teologický sál (Theological Hall); Nosecký's frescos illustrate humanity's struggle to acquire wisdom

MALÁ STRANA

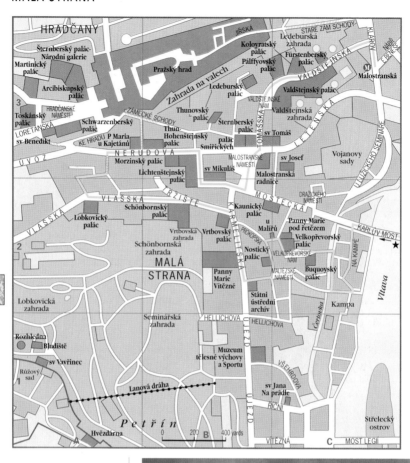

HRADČANY

Šternberský palác-Národní galerie
Martinický palác
Arcibiskupský palác
Toskánský palác
sv Benedikt
Schwarzenberský palác
Hradčanské Náměstí
Loretánská
Ke Hradu
P Maria u Kajetánů
Zámecké Schody
Neruda
Vlašská
Morzinský palác
Lichtenštejnský palác
Vlašská
Schönbornský palác
Lobkovický palác
Vrtbovská zahrada
Vrtbovský palác
Schönbornská zahrada
MALÁ STRANA
Panny Marie Vítězné
Lobkovická zahrada
Seminářská zahrada
Rozhledna
Bludiště
sv Vavřinec
Růžový sad
Lanová dráha
Muzeum tělesné výchovy a Sportu
Hellichova
Hvězdárna
Petřín

Jirská
Staré Zam Schody
Koloyratský palác
Ledeburská zahrada
Pražský hrad
Pálffyovský palác
Fürstenberský palác
Valdštejnská
Zahrada na valech
Ledeburský palác
Valdštejnské Nám
Valdštejnský palác
Malostranská
Thunovský palác
Valdštejnská zahrada
Šternberský palác
Tomášská
Thun-Hohenštejnský palác
sv Tomáš
Smiřických
Malostranské Náměstí
sv Mikuláš
sv Josef
Vojanovy sady
Malostranská radnice
Dražického Náměstí
Karmelitská
Mostecká
Kaunický palác
u Malířů
Panny Marie pod řetězem
Prokopská
Nostický palác
Velkopřevorský palác
Karlův Most
Velkopřevorské Nám
Na Kampě
Maltézské Náměstí
Buquoyský palác
Státní ústřední archív
Čertovka
Kampa
Hellichova
Vltava
Uluzického Seminaře
Nabř Edvard Beneše
Všehrdova
Klárov
sv Jana Na prádle
Říční
Střelecký ostrov
Vítězná
Most Legii
0   200   400 yards
B   C

96

The dome and belltower of Chrám svatého Mikuláše (St. Nicholas' Church) dominate the Malá Strana skyline

Malá Strana Seen from Karlův most (Charles Bridge), Prague's Lesser Town seems to crouch at the foot of the castle heights, its towers, domes, spires and red roofs, giving way to terraced gardens and the orchards and woodlands of Petřín hill. This is the most picturesque quarter of a picturesque city, its townscape almost exactly as it was 200 years ago, though restoration has not always kept pace with the aging process affecting all its buildings.

A feature of the district is the Royal Way. After crossing the Charles Bridge, this runs through Malá Strana, winding around the city's greatest Baroque building, Chrám svatého Mikuláše (St. Nicholas' Church), then climbing delightful Nerudova street before rounding the final hairpin turn up to the castle. Many visitors follow this route—pausing to window-shop in Mostecká street or to down a drink beneath the arcades around Malostranské náměstí (Malá Strana Square)—but many of Malá Strana's delights lie off this main tourist axis, down quiet streets and passageways, along the old millstream by Kampa island, and behind high garden walls.

Malá Strana wears an aristocratic air, with its unique Baroque palaces and patrician houses. But it was once a workaday sort of place, laid out on planned lines by a 12th-century Přemyslid king to accommodate a population of traders to help support the economy of the castle high above. Once Hradčany had filled up with aristocratic residences, courtiers found it convenient to live in Malá Strana—hence the plethora of palaces. Courtiers needed attending to just as much as kings, and soon servants, dressmakers and tailors, coachmen and washerwomen moved in too. Even today, the residents are a mixed bunch, with ambassadors sharing the same streets as the humblest tenants of the city corporation. This intriguing amalgam may, however, give way to more monied social groupings as Malá Stran's uniquely attractive ambience brings in expensive restaurants and prestige offices.

MALÁ STRANA

Modernity comes to Malá Strana
The Lesser Town will eventually be completely bypassed by a tunnel under Petřín hill. In the mean time, through-traffic consists mostly of the trams gliding up Karmelitská street and through Malá Strana Square. The southern corner of the square is now occupied by one of Malá Strana's rare modern buildings, a Cubist structure designed by Ludvík Kysela.

Travel through time by tram in Malá Strana

History Malá Strana's fortunes were tied to those of the Hradčany district from the earliest times. Soon after the castle's foundation, at the end of the 9th century, a series of straggling settlements grew up along the routes linking the Hradčany heights to the riverside, and to the ford which was later replaced by a timber bridge.

In the 1250s, King Otakar II decided to impose his idea of order on the area; he cleared out most of the inhabitants, replaced them with industrious German immigrants, laid out a spacious marketplace around the new parish church of St. Nicholas and built a ring of protective walls. With only a few changes, the charmingly intimate street pattern of Malá Strana dates from this time, though most of the medieval houses burned down in the great fire of 1541 which started here and raged through the castle quarter, too.

Rebuilding soon began, but only really took off after the Battle of the White Mountain in 1620, when those savvy enough to have chosen the right side acquired the confiscated properties of the expelled or executed Protestant aristocracy. It was this wave of Counter-Reformationary reconstruction of palaces, churches and townhouses that gave Malá Strana its present delightful Baroque face. Even though the Habsburg court left Prague for Vienna,

Bohemia itself remained a kingdom with an aristocracy and they found it convenient to maintain a palace in town as well as one in the country; as a result, there is no quarter of Prague where the palaces are so tightly packed together.

Since the last great wave of rebuilding, which took place in the 17th and 18th centuries, little has changed in Malá Strana. Here students of urban history can find a living example of the pre-industrial city, where busy streets and squares coexist with quiet squares and courtyards, and parks and gardens come down to an unspoiled riverside. No wonder this is a filmmaker's favorite location, a ready-made Baroque background against which Miloš Forman was able to shoot most of *Amadeus*, his film about the life of Mozart.

View over Malá Strana from Petřín hill

MALÁ STRANA

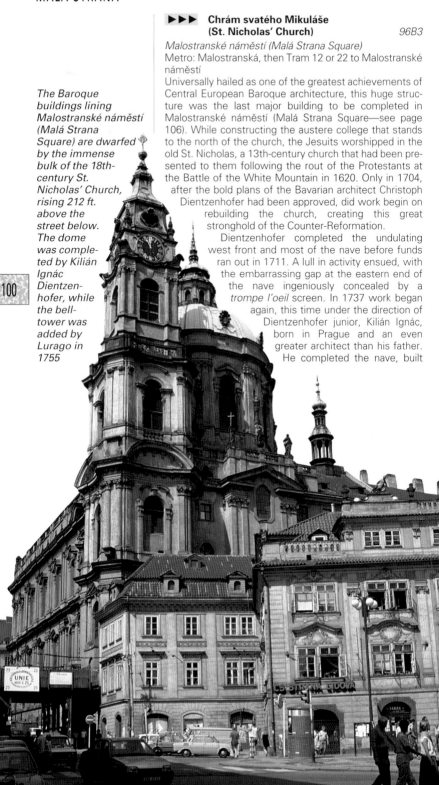

The Baroque buildings lining Malostranské náměstí (Malá Strana Square) are dwarfed by the immense bulk of the 18th-century St. Nicholas' Church, rising 212 ft. above the street below. The dome was completed by Kilián Ignác Dientzenhofer, while the bell-tower was added by Lurago in 1755

► ► ► **Chrám svatého Mikuláše
(St. Nicholas' Church)**   *96B3*

Malostranské náměstí (Malá Strana Square)
Metro: Malostranská, then Tram 12 or 22 to Malostranské náměstí

Universally hailed as one of the greatest achievements of Central European Baroque architecture, this huge structure was the last major building to be completed in Malostranské náměstí (Malá Strana Square—see page 106). While constructing the austere college that stands to the north of the church, the Jesuits worshipped in the old St. Nicholas, a 13th-century church that had been presented to them following the rout of the Protestants at the Battle of the White Mountain in 1620. Only in 1704, after the bold plans of the Bavarian architect Christoph Dientzenhofer had been approved, did work begin on rebuilding the church, creating this great stronghold of the Counter-Reformation.

Dientzenhofer completed the undulating west front and most of the nave before funds ran out in 1711. A lull in activity ensued, with the embarrassing gap at the eastern end of the nave ingeniously concealed by a *trompe l'oeil* screen. In 1737 work began again, this time under the direction of Dientzenhofer junior, Kilián Ignác, born in Prague and an even greater architect than his father. He completed the nave, built

the chancel, and crowned it all with a superb dome, rising 212 ft. above the ground.

Gazing up into Dientzenhofer's colossal dome in St. Nicholas' Church

The exterior The west front of the church faces uphill towards the Lichtenstein Palace; the slope of the square is compensated for by the steps leading up to its trio of doorways (the south door opens into a souvenir shop). The imposing façade is unusual in that it undulates, in a satisfying series of convex and concave curves. The statues adorning it proclaim the triumph of the Jesuit Order under the patronage of the House of Habsburg, whose double-headed eagle is, however, positioned in an inferior position beneath the central figure of St. Nicholas himself.

The interior Inside the vast nave, there is an almost overpowering impression of light and movement. Gilt, ceiling paintings and altarpieces combine in the glorious colors of a celestial coral reef, while gesticulating saints beckon towards the even greater space beneath the dome.

To the left of the entrance is the Chapel of St. Barbara, with a painting of the *Crucifixion* by Karel Škréta. Almost obscuring the intricate structure of the nave vault, the great fresco by the Viennese, Kracker, depicts miraculous scenes from the *Life of St. Nicholas*, while beneath the dome is a representation by Palko of the *Holy Trinity*. Most of the statuary, including the large figures of the Fathers of the Church around the crossing, is from the workshop of the sculptor Franz Platzer.

Perhaps the most extraordinary feature of the interior is the pulpit, a fantastic Rococo spacecraft ready to spirit its occupant into the celestial realm. St. Nicholas appears again, above the high altar, crafted in gilded bronze, with mirrors to accentuate the effect. The Baroque organ, with 2,500 pipes, was played by Mozart on several occasions. The southern counterpart to the Chapel of St. Barbara is the Chapel of St. Anne, built over the tombs of the Kolovrat family, whose munificence helped the Jesuits build and decorate this resource-consuming project.

Two towers
Towers often come in pairs, frequently as identical twins. This is emphatically not the case with the towers of St. Nicholas: Dientzenhofer's colossal dome is accompanied by a municipal belltower, of exactly the same height, but of completely different design. The odd couple nevertheless seem to harmonize perfectly well; an indispensable element in Prague's townscape which, over the years, have become "the pivot on which silently the city turns" (Brian Knox).

Barricade the bridge!
Barricades went up by the Old Town Bridge Tower in May 1945 in the confused fighting that characterized the very last days of World War II. A century earlier, in the Prague Rebellion of 1848, a motley crowd of students, printers, and brewery men had fought here, defying the overwhelming power of the Austrian artillery. But the most bitter struggle for the bridge was in 1648, when the ancestors of the 19th-century students, helped by Jews from the ghetto, held the bridge for months against the marauding Swedes who were holed up on the far bank of the river, an event depicted in a diorama in the Bludiště (Hall of Mirrors) on Petřín hill (see page 81).

The first strollers enjoy the early morning sunshine on Charles Bridge

Whose bridge?
Charles Bridge was named in honor of its founder only in the 19th century; prior to that it had been known simply as "Prague Bridge," or the "Stone Bridge." For hundreds of years it formed the city's only river crossing, and only when its unique status ended with the construction of other bridges did it become necessary to give it a more specific name.

▶▶▶ Karlův most (Charles Bridge)   96C2
Metro: Staroměstská

For hundreds of years the city's sole river crossing, this marvel of Gothic engineering, linking Staré Město (the Old Town) to Malá Strana, formed a central part of Emperor Charles IV's ambitious mid-14th-century program of civic improvements. Today its cobblestoned traffic-free surface is trod by every tourist enjoying the incomparable panorama it offers of the city in its river setting. A vital link in the Royal Way followed by the monarch's coronation procession, the bridge has carried carts and wagons, cars and trams, and it has served as the setting for tournaments, legal hearings, executions and punishments—even the occasional battle. The hawkers and souvenir sellers of today are the descendants of the wheeler-dealers and shopkeepers of earlier times, while friends have long met, and lovers cuddled, beneath the bridge's stone saints; added in the 17th century, these have made the bridge a glorious procession of outdoor sculpture in addition to all its other attractions.

History The bridge is the successor to an earlier crossing, the Judith Bridge, destroyed in 1342 by one of the river's frequent tantrums. The emperor appointed the cathedral architect, Petr Parléř, to design and supervise the work, and the great structure's grace and poise lift it far above the realm of ordinary engineering. Between the towers guarding both approaches, the bridge's 16 sandstone arches and piers span the extraordinary distance of more than 1,500 ft. It is laid out on a slightly curving alignment, partly because of re-use of some of the foundations of the older bridge. In 1378, though still awaiting its finishing touches, the bridge was sufficiently complete for Charles IV's funeral procession to pass over it.

The bridge is protected by stout timber cutwaters on its upstream side. It has survived the worst the temperamental Vltava could hurl at it, though the great flood of September 3, 1890 swept away three of its arches, as well as assorted statuary.

The towers At its western end, the bridge slices through Kampa island and part of Malá Strana with all the confidence of an elevated urban highway, giving its users the chance to eavesdrop at windows or peer down into the streets below. The archway framing the view up into the heart of Malá Strana dates from 1410, but the smaller of the two towers is much older; part of the fortified approach to the Judith Bridge, it was built in 1166, though its chisel cap was added in Renaissance times.

The taller tower, well worth climbing

103

for the view from its parapet, dates from the 15th century. Attractive enough in its own right, it doesn't quite have the panache of Staroměstská mostní věž (the Old Town Bridge Tower) at the eastern end. This superb structure was completed in 1390 to a design by Petr Parléř, and served ceremonial and symbolic as well as defensive functions. Its richly ornamented eastern face has sculptures of the two monarchs who presided over the bridge's construction, Charles IV and Wenceslas IV, while above them is the bridge's patron saint, St. Vitus.

An antidote to excessive solemnity is provided by the couple holding up one of the brackets, usually referred to as "Lovers," though "The Groper" might be a more appropriate title. Wenceslas's symbol, a kingfisher, also appears.

The western face of the tower lost its decoration when vandalized by Swedish troops towards the end of the Thirty Years' War. The tower stands on a foundation formed by a hidden pier of the bridge; on its townward side, similarly hidden, is the bridge's first arch, an ancient and legally protected structure which makes impossible any radical solution to the acute traffic problem of Křížovnické náměstí (Knights of the Cross Square).

The western end of the Charles Bridge; the central archway leading to Malá Strana dates from 1410

■ **Beautification of the bridge began in earnest in 1683. Always on the lookout for new and dramatic ways of getting the message of the Counter-Reformation across, the Jesuits installed a statue of St. Jan Nepomuk, carved by Johann Brokov, close to the point from which he was flung to his watery martyrdom (see panel) ....■**

Ill-starred saint

Jan Nepomuk, the patron saint of bridges and those that cross them, was a Vicar General of Prague. As confessor to the queen, the conscientious cleric displeased the suspicious King Wenceslas IV, allegedly for refusing to betray her confessional secrets. For this lack of co-operation he was tortured, trussed up in a sack and thrown off the bridge. His body bobbed around on the surface for an uncannily long time, accompanied by a quintet of dancing stars. To the Jesuits, he made a far more satisfactory martyr than the radical Jan Hus, and his cult succeeded to the extent that he was canonized in 1729. Nepomuk statues grace bridges all over Roman Catholic Central Europe, but his most spectacular monument is his sumptuous silvery tomb in St. Vitus's Cathedral (see page 62).

Something about the dynamism of Johann Brokov's sculpture and its positioning high above the broad river, where it is seen against the background of city and castle, gave it instant appeal. Other statues were soon in place, sculpted by Baroque masters such as Jäckel and Braun, as well as by Brokov and his son Ferdinand. In the 19th century, the Max brothers contributed further figures, while the final addition was made by Karel Dvořák in 1938 with his figures of Saints Cyril and Methodius.

Most of the statues on the bridge today are copies, the originals having been removed to protect them from attack by acid rain. The oldest work is the *Crucifixion*, a bronze placed on the third pedestal on the right to the west of the Old Town Bridge Tower. Dating from 1657, it was given additional figures in the 19th century by the Max brothers. The Hebrew inscription was put here by the city magistrates in 1696, paid for by the fine levied on a Jew who had blasphemed while walking past.

The spot where Nepomuk last felt terra firma is marked by a plaque; his bronze statue, with its starry halo, is still the most popular of all the bridge sculptures.

One of the more dynamic groups portrays Saints Vincent and Procopius; the former is shown reviving a dead man, the latter stamping on a devil. The duo's other feats are celebrated in an inscription which notes that St. Vincent performed his act of resuscitation 40 times; in his spare time he redeemed sinners (100,000) and converted Jews (2,500) and Saracens (8,000). St. Procopius's tally of 70 devils crushed seems modest by comparison.

Below the bridge is a 19th-century statue of Bruncvík, a knightly figure who, like Roland, was a guardian of civil liberties; according to legend he will one day return, when a real crisis threatens, with St. Wenceslas and his army. Early in 1989 he was given a new

Patron saint of bridges—St. Jan Nepomuk (1684)

The bronze Crucifixion is the oldest statue on the bridge, dating from 1657

sword, and some people enjoy linking this with the outbreak of the Velvet Revolution later that year.

The intensely emotional depiction of St. Luitgarde succoring the Savior is generally held to be Braun's most perfect work, while F. Brokov's characteristic realism is seen to good effect in his celebration of the Trinitarian Order, where a bored and beer-bellied Turk stands guard over an infidel prison.

Below: St. Anthony of Padua (1707)

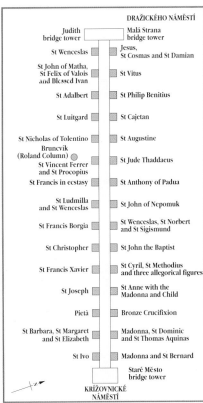

DRAŽICKÉHO NÁMĚSTÍ

Judith bridge tower	Malá Strana bridge tower
St Wenceslas	Jesus, St Cosmas and St Damian
St John of Matha, St Felix of Valois and Blessed Ivan	St Vitus
St Adalbert	St Philip Benitius
St Luitgard	St Cajetan
St Nicholas of Tolentino	St Augustine
Bruncvík (Roland Column)	
St Vincent Ferrer and St Procopius	St Jude Thaddaeus
St Francis in ecstasy	St Anthony of Padua
St Ludmilla and St Wenceslas	St John of Nepomuk
St Francis Borgia	St Wenceslas, St Norbert and St Sigismund
St Christopher	St John the Baptist
St Francis Xavier	St Cyril, St Methodius and three allegorical figures
St Joseph	St Anne with the Madonna and Child
Pietà	Bronze Crucifixion
St Barbara, St Margaret and St Elizabeth	Madonna, St Dominic and St Thomas Aquinas
St Ivo	Madonna and St Bernard
	Staré Město bridge tower

KŘIŽOVNICKÉ NÁMĚSTÍ

MALÁ STRANA

The "Bloody Governor"
This was the name given to Karl von Lichtenstein, who dealt with political rivals with the same ruthlessness with which he had wiped out the whole west side of Malá Strana Square. In 1621, it was he who presided with relish over the trial and gruesome execution of the rebel Protestant noblemen who had carried out the Second Defenestration three years earlier after hatching their plot at No. 18, just round the corner from their vengeful neighbor.

Baroque grandeur in Malá Strana Square—the former town hall

The Lichtenstein Palace
In the Thirty Years' War the Swedish set up house here, as did Austrian General Windischgrätz while squashing the Prague rebellion of 1848. In the square in front of the palace, the Holy Trinity plague column, topped by a baleful eye, dates from 1715, and commemorates the ending of the epidemic which had ravaged the city two years previously.

►► **Malostranské náměstí (Malá Strana Square)**   *96B3*

Metro: Malostranská, then Tram 12 or 22
Almost overwhelmed by the great Baroque bastion of the Chrám svatého Mikuláše (St. Nicholas's Church) planted uncompromisingly at its center, Malá Strana Square seems too small for its many users: tourists on the trek from Karlův most (Charles Bridge) to the castle and commuters waiting for the trams that squeal in and out. The sloping square has been the heart of the Lesser Town since the late-13th century, when King Otakar II laid out a new square of imposing dimensions lined with burghers' dwellings and focused on a little Gothic church, the modest predecessor of today's St. Nicholas. While some medieval features, such as the arcades, have survived, the square is predominantly Baroque in character.

A cluster of lesser structures clings to the monumental bulk of St. Nicholas (see page 100). Facing Mostecká (Bridge Street) at an odd angle is the Rococo building known as the "House at the Stone Table," once a famous café frequented by the city's literary set. Beyond is the bland façade of the college built by the Jesuits in 1691; the great Hungarian patriot Ferenc Rakoczi studied here in the 1690s before raising the flag of anti-Habsburg revolt in his native land. Who knows what plans today's math and physics students have in mind?

The northern side of this lower part of the square is mostly taken up by a fine pair of Baroque palaces, built over the arcades which run around three sides of the square. The Smiřický family built No. 18 in Renaissance style in 1612, giving it a Baroque façade in 1763. It was here that the Protestant nobles met on the night of May 22, 1618, to hatch the plot put into effect the following day, when they stormed the castle and threw the Catholic councilors into the moat. The massively buttressed Šternberský palác (Šternberg palace) at No. 19 was rebuilt in 1720. Even though it was on this site that the great fire of 1541 broke out, the later palace enjoyed a more peacable history: cultured Kašpar Šternberg kept open house here for the international intellectual élite of the day, and it was here, in 1796, that the Society for Patriotic Friends of the Arts started to assemble the works that now fill the Národní galerie (National Gallery). At the corner with Tomášská street is a multi-story oriel (bay) window, a feature much repeated around the square.

No. 21 is Malá Strana's former town hall, an early-Renaissance building abandoned when the different parts

The *pavlač*
Meaning "gallery" in Czech, *pavlač* has come to signify the courtyards around which so many older residential buildings are laid out, with access to individual dwellings via a series of balconies. It is always worth casting a glance into these semi-secret places, many of which have considerable, if somewhat tarnished, charm.

of the city were amalgamated in 1784 and the councilors made to commute to municipal meetings in the Staroměstská radnice (Old Town Hall) across the river. The arcades continue around the square, whose southern side was subject to less attention from ambitious palace builders, so that it retains a more domestic character. Nos. 1 and 2 are both of Gothic origin, the former with a particulary fine *pavlač* (courtyard).

Uphill from the trams surging round the S-bend out of Karmelitská (Carmelites' Street) is No. 10, the Dům U zlatého Lva (House at the Golden Lion), with a well-preserved Renaissance façade. The western side of the square is dominated by the classical façade of the Lichtenstein Palace, built in 1620 when Karl von Lichtenstein summarily demolished a row of medieval houses.

Tram 22 squeezes through the crowd in Malá Strana Square

Malá Strana palaces

■ **Near the castle and close to the bridge, the Lesser Town had long been a favored residential location for the Bohemian nobility, but it was only after the Battle of the White Mountain, in 1620, that a real building boom began. War profiteers and other nouveaux riches then assiduously bought up the property of the dispossessed or executed Protestant aristocracy, building themselves the fine palaces in the Renaissance and, later, Baroque styles which give this part of the city so much of its present character ....■**

Embassy exit
In summer 1989, the Lobkovický palác (Lobkovic Palace) was the setting for the incredible scenes which marked the beginning of the end for the German Democratic Republic. Thousands of East German tourists dumped their Trabants and Wartburgs in the street, climbed over the embassy gates and squatted in the grounds; eventually it was agreed that they could be given exit visas and they were taken to West Germany by train, a terminal humiliation for their government, which collapsed within months. Go up the street and around to the rear of the garden to see the tongue-in-cheek memorial to these events, a Trabant perched on seven-league legs by the Czech sculptor Černý.

The first, and greatest, of these palaces was the complex of buildings, courtyards, pavilions and gardens built at the northeastern end of Malá Strana by General Albrecht von Wallenstein (or Valdštejn), the most ambitious and (temporarily) successful of all those who profited from the Thirty Years' War (see page 113). His dynamism is reflected in the sheer extent of the redevelopment which took place to make way for his sumptuous residence; large tracts of land were acquired and dozens of houses demolished, though his plan to enlarge Valdštejnské náměstí (Wallenstein Square), by pushing its south side almost to Malá Strana Square, fell through.

Ambassadorial residences At the other end of the scale from Wallenstein's overweening edifice, and built over a century later in charming Rococo style, is the Kaunický palác (Kounic Palace) at No. 15 Mostecká (Bridge Street), grander than its townhouse neighbors, but still unassumingly integrated with them. Like so many of Malá Strana's more sumptuous residences, it now houses an embassy.

Among the grandest of the foreign embassies is Germany's, splendidly housed in the Lobkovický palác (Lobkovic Palace) on Vlašská street. Built by the architect Giovanni Alliprandi at the very beginning of the 18th century, it has a south front which curves inwards to make space for a great oval vestibule giving on to the garden. In Tržiště, a little way down the hill, is a hardly less imposing edifice, the Schörnbornský palác (Schönborn-Colloredo palace), now the home of the American Embassy. For a while it provided a substandard apartment for, among others, Franz Kafka. Its extensive gardens rise up to the summerhouse where Old Glory flutters from the flagpole.

A number of other embassies cling to the steep slopes below the castle, among them that of the United Kingdom, housed in one of the several palaces bearing the name of the Thun family. Approached from Thunovská (Thun Street) up a little cul-de-sac with a bust of Winston Churchill set in the wall, it has British connections going back to 1630, when it was presented by the emperor to Walter Leslie, the Scottish mercenary who had helped assassinate General Wallenstein.

Described as Britain's "most beautiful ambassadorial residence" by a former occupant, it has an unusual layout as a result of being built into the hillside, with a terrace garden reached from the third floor. In the 1920s, President Masaryk is supposed to have climbed down the castle wall on a private ladder for his regular tête-à-têtes with the ambassador.

Not in quite such close proximity to the castle, a row of palaces runs along Valdštejnská (Wallenstein Street), bearing the names of the Fürstenbergs, the Kolovrat-Černíns, the Pálffys, and the Ledebour-Trautmansdorffs. Fine buildings themselves, they are more than matched by the glorious terraced gardens which ornament the slopes behind them (see page 124).

A final cluster of palaces is tucked away among the intimate little streets and squares of the southern part of Malá Strana; these include such fine buildings as the Buquoy-Valdštejn palace (the French Embassy) and the Nostic palace (the Netherlands' Embassy).

Princes and paupers
Under Communism, many palaces were turned into apartments and occupied by anyone whose name happened to come up on the housing list. This gave Malá Strana a rich social structure, with ordinary folk mingling with diplomats and intellectuals. The new generation of owners seems more likely to convert their returned properties into luxury hotels or offices.

109

Thun Palace, home of the British Embassy

MALÁ STRANA

Quiet days on Kampa island

Little Venice
The part of Kampa that overlooks the Devil's Brook is sometimes given the rather complimentary name of "Little Venice," and the houses and trees along the old mill-race are undeniably picturesque. Among the people who plied their water-based trades here were many washerwomen, their presence recalled by the charmingly named little church of svatého Jana ne prádle (St. John at the Wash-House—see page 116).

► **Na Kampě (Kampa Square)**   *96C2*

Metro: Malostranská, then Tram 12 or 22 to Malostranské náměstí

Divided from the rest of Malá Strana by the mill-race called Čertovka (the Devil's Brook), Kampa island lives a dreamy life of its own, somewhat detached from the continuous stream of visitors on the Karlův most (Charles Bridge) which cuts across its northern end. From the bridge, which is joined to the island by a double staircase, there is a rustically charming view upstream of the big waterwheel of the Štěpanovský mill.

Mills were established here as far back as the 13th century. The millers were joined by boatmen, toll-keepers, ice merchants, and by potters, who held their market in the pretty, approximately oval-shaped square called Na Kampě. This was the first part of the island to be built up, though most of the buildings lining it have later Baroque or Rococo façades. Several of them have names and corresponding house-signs: there is a Golden Lion, a White Boot, a Golden Grape, and a Blue Fox.

An early attempt was made to stabilize the riverbank by dumping huge quantities of debris here from the great fire of 1541, but until its spring floods were finally brought under control in the 1950s, the Vltava regularly inundated the island, changing its outline more than once. Most of the southern part of the island remained free of building, being used for orchards and gardens until it was turned into a public park in 1940. This is an excellent spot in which to relax, with wonderful views of the river, the bridge, and the far bank.

Footbridges cross the Devil's Brook into the little labyrinth of streets and squares leading back into Malá Strana; near the northernmost of these bridges, indecipherable scribbles on the surrounding walls indicate that the John Lennon Wall is nearby (see page 114).

▶▶ Nerudova (Neruda Street) 96A3

Metro: Malostranská, then Tram 12 or 22 to Malostranské náměstí

Named after the novelist Jan Neruda, the "Dickens of Malá Strana," steeply climbing Nerudova forms part of an ancient route which led from the now defunct Judith Bridge up the flank of the castle hill, then on to Strahov and the west. Later it formed the final leg of the Royal Way followed by coronation processions as they climbed up to the cathedral. Several noble families built their palaces here, but most of the houses are relatively modest burghers' dwellings; though they stand on medieval foundations, many were rebuilt in Baroque or Rococo style to make the street one of the capital's most attractive thoroughfares. Here, more than anywhere else, the buildings have kept those charming house-signs which made life so difficult for deliverymen until the city authorities insisted on systematic numbering at the end of the 18th century.

Probably the most popular, if not the quickest, way up to the castle, Nerudova has its fair share of souvenir stores and the like, though it begins authentically enough at No. 1 with an old and famous drinking den, the U kocoura (Tomcat). House No. 6 is the U červeného orla (Red Eagle), No. 12 the U tří housliček (Three Little Fiddles), once lived in by a dynasty of violinists. The U zlaté číše (Golden Goblet) is at No. 16, and more precious metal is alluded to at No. 27, the U zlatého klíče (Golden Key) and at No. 34, the U zlaté podkovy (Golden Horseshoe).

Opposite No. 16 is an altogether more pretentious establishment, the Morzinský palác (Morzin Palace), built by the architect Santini. The splendid Moors sulkily holding up the balcony are a none-too-subtle play on the family name, and the façade is decorated with other fine sculptures of *Night* and *Day* and the *Continents*. The Morzins have long since given way to the diplomats of Romania, while the Thun-Hohensteins of No. 20 have been displaced from their home by the Italians; their equivalent of the Morzin Moors is a brace of monstrous eagles.

Beyond the narrow gap leading up to the castle steps is the Baroque Kostel Panny Marie ustavičné pomoci u Kajetánů (Church of Our Lady of Divine Providence), built by Santini for the Theatine Order in 1691–1717. House No. 25 is called Osel u kolébky (the Ass at the Cradle), while in the late-18th century No. 33 was the home of fun-loving Baron Bretfeld, host of many a glittering party (see panel). The stairway dropping down to the south, Jánský vršek, leads to a quiet little street between Nerudova and the old Italian quarter of Malá Strana.

To the castle At its upper end, Nerudova widens out into what is almost a square. The houses on the right are built into the cliff-like slope rising to the castle, reached by a hairpin bend and the ramp called Ke hradu. Here coronation processions would, no doubt, have extracted the maximum of effect while executing the turn,

Neruda and Neruda
Jan Neruda's *Prague Tales* celebrates the life of the little people of Malá Strana with wit and affection. He has been compared to Chekhov and Steinbeck as well as to Dickens, and such was the impact of one of his tales that his name was adopted by the Latin-American novelist, Pablo Neruda.

Bretfeld's bashes
Baron Bretfeld threw one of his famous parties in 1787 for the first performance of *Don Giovanni*. A famous Don Juan from another age turned up. The aging Casanova, now librarian to a Bohemian nobleman, came to the ball to meet his fellow Italian, Mozart's collaborator, Da Ponte.

111

Malá Strana citizens pass the time of day on Nerudova

The tourist train scales steeply sloping Nerudova

Spur Street
Nerudova's old German name was Sporngasse, or Spur Street. This was a reference not to a horseman's spurs but to the skid-like brake which a coachman would have to apply during the whole of the descent down this steeply sloping route.

with banners flying and horses' hooves striking sparks on the cobbles. On an unhappier occasion (March 15, 1939), the convoy bringing the German occupying army up to the castle stalled here in the snow while attempting the same maneuver. Ke hradu is relatively modern, having been built as recently as 1644. An alternative approach to Hradčany is via the flights of stairs known as Radnické schody (Council House Stairs), which lead into the upper end of Hradčanské náměstí (Hradčany Square).

The route heading on westwards now changes its name to Úvoz and provides a wonderful way to approach Strahovský klášter (Strahov Monastery), with a view of Malá Strana and the city as a whole opening up to the left as the road leaves the houses behind. Nearly the last house in Nerudova is No. 47, called U dvou slunců (the Two Suns). This is where the novelist Jan Neruda lived, from 1845 to 1857, as recorded in the somewhat over-ornate Art Nouveau plaque attached to the façade.

►► Valdštejnský palác (Wallenstein Palace)

96C3

Valdštejnské náměstí (Wallenstein Square)
Metro: Malostranská

This great palace and its formal garden proclaim the prestige of its builder, General Albrecht Wallenstein, the man whose power at one point rivaled that of the emperor.

Born in 1583, Wallenstein (or Valdštejn in Czech) worked his way into the favor of the emperor, soon becoming governor of Prague. After the Battle of the White Mountain in 1620, vast estates and whole towns fell into his hands. He was made a duke and built his own little capital city at Jičín in northeastern Bohemia. Further wealth came his way from contracts to supply the armies ranging over Central Europe in the course of the Thirty Years' War, a war in which he participated as his generation's most successful general.

Uneasy at his henchman's ambition, the emperor dismissed Wallenstein but then hurriedly reinstated him when military crisis threatened. Even so, well-founded rumors of collaboration with the emperor's enemies could not be ignored, and the greedy generalissimo was murdered in Cheb in Western Bohemia on February 25, 1634. His assassins included an Englishman, an Irishman, and a Scotsman.

The Wallenstein home Wallenstein's principal residence has a long main façade giving on to Valdštejnské náměstí (Wallenstein Square), and an immensely long perimeter wall enclosing a total of five courtyards, a barracks, a riding school, and an extensive garden. The most spectacular interior is that of the Great Hall. Here, concerts are viewed from the ceiling by Wallenstein himself, reincarnated by the painter B. Bianco as Mars, the god of War.

The most remarkable feature in all the great complex is the Sala Terrena, the loggia facing over the formal gardens which are approached from Letenská street.

Stolen statues
Wallenstein's garden is adorned with splendid statuary. They are convincing copies of the originals, designed by the great sculptor Adriaen de Vries but stolen by light-fingered Swedish soldiers in 1648 and carried off to grace the grounds of Stockholm's Drottningholm Palace.

The general's grotto
Strange, half-hidden faces stare out from the globulous material coating the walls of the grotto, a reminder of Wallenstein's characteristically Bohemian preoccupation with the mystical and occult.

113

The Wallenstein Palace and gardens rival the castle and cathedral in their magnificence

Walk Around Malá Strana

This half-day stroll through the Lesser Town takes in most of the sights of this fascinating quarter located at the foot of the castle.

See map on page 96.

Begin on **Karlův most (Charles Bridge)**, but instead of passing between the towers at the western end of the bridge, descend the steps on to Kampa island and into the attractive oval-shaped square known as **Na Kampě**. From the park to the south there are fine views across the Vltava to the far bank.

Cross the arm of the river called Čertovka (the Devil's Brook) into Velkopřevorské náměstí (Grand Prior Square). Linden trees grow defiantly from the road surface, giving the square an allure all of its own. To the left, the French Embassy occupies the lavish Baroque Buquoy-Valdštejn palace. To the right, looking rather dazed, the bearded face of a Beatle stares out from a graffiti-plastered wall. The **John Lennon Wall**, a shrine to an alternative way of life, was the scene of many a confrontation between police and would-be graffiti artists in the days before the Velvet Revolution, when to daub a wall was a daring gesture of defiance.

Continue through the labyrinth of this part of Malá Strana, past the

Rock icon Lennon

Intriguing Maltézské náměstí, near the Nostic Palace

charmingly named Panny Marie pod řetězem (Church of Our Lady under the Chain—see page 116), the Japanese Embassy in its Rococo palace, and the huge Nostic palace (the embassy of the Netherlands). The confident sweep of Karmelitská street and its trams seem to belong to another world. The church of Panny Marie Vítězné (Our Lady of Victory—see page 116) has the much-venerated figure known as the Bambino di Praga (the Little Child of Prague).

In Tržiště (Market Place) is the Schönborn-Colloredo palace (the U.S. Embassy). In Vlašská street is the Lobkovic palace (the embassy of Germany), in whose garden stands a famous sculpture of a Trabant on legs, a whimsical tribute to the hordes of East Germans who ditched their plastic-paneled two-stroke vehicles here before seeking refuge in the embassy during the summer of 1989.

Steps lead up to Nerudova street, possibly the most picturesque of all Prague thoroughfares (see page 111). Nerudova descends to Malá Strana's heart, the Malostranské náměstí (Lesser Town Square), utterly dominated by the great bulk of **Chrám svatého Mikuláše (St. Nicholas' Church**—see page 100). Take time to admire the palaces lining the square (see page 106), or pause in one of the cafés.

The trams heading into Letenská street seem to dive into the interior of the buildings adjoining Kostel svatého Tomáše (St. Thomas's Church—see page 117). Instead of following them, walk along Tomášská street, with its Baroque houses, into Valdštejnské náměstí, the square named after ambitious General Wallenstein. The long façade of his palace (see page 113) occupies the east side of the square. Now home to the Ministry of Culture, it has splendid formal gardens, reached from Letenská street.

Valdštejnská street skirts the foot of the steep terraced slope up to the castle, and is lined with yet more palaces bearing the names of their former owners—the Ledebour-Trauttmansdorffs, the Pálffys, the Kolovrat-Černíns. When restored, their delightful Baroque gardens will make an incomparable approach to the castle.

The walk ends at Malostranská metro station, but before descending the escalator you should spend a few minutes relaxing in the station's unique walled water garden.

■ **The towers and steeples of numerous churches rise over the pantiled roofs of Malá Strana, planets centered on the great sun of the dome of St. Nicholas. Most of the churches were built or remodeled in Baroque times, but there are intriguing traces of an earlier age when, in order to be close to the Bishop of Prague in his riverside palace, various religious orders founded monasteries nearby....■**

Below the chain
Among the first to settle within the protection of Malá Strana's walls were the Knights of St. John, later known as the Knights of Malta. In 1169 this crusading order founded a monastery at the western end of the old Judith Bridge, calling their church Panny Marie pod řetězem (Our Lady under the Chain) because one of their duties was to mount guard over the chain barring access to the river crossing.

Our Lady under the Chain The church of Panny Marie pod řetězem (Our Lady under the Chain), located in Lázeňská street) is one of Prague's oldest (see panel).

Beyond the massively buttressed Gothic towers of the church, only the evocative outline of the arcades of the first Romanesque basilica survives, this having been demolished to make way for a 14th-century rebuilding which was itself left unfinished when the monks were chased away by the Hussites. Beyond the roofless nave is the only usable part of the church, its chancel, "Baroqued" in the 17th century. Next door is the 18th-century palace of the Grand Prior of the Order, once the Museum of Musical Instruments, but now returned to its original owners.

St. John at the Wash-house Of equal antiquity to the Knights' establishment, but far more modest in structure, the charmingly named Kostel svatého Jana Na Prádle (Church of St. John at the Wash-house) is located near the southern tip of Kampa island. This was founded in the 12th century as the parish church of the community that lived beyond the Malá Strana walls in the Újezd area, but was rebuilt in early Gothic style in the following century. The interior was partly redone during the Baroque period, but it retains some 14th-century wall paintings.

Our Lady of Victory Located in Karmelitská street, this is one of the earliest Baroque churches built in Prague, designed for the German Lutherans who fled the city after the Battle of the White Mountain in 1620. Their building was then given to the Carmelites, who entered the conquered city along with the triumphant Catholic armies, hence the church's present name of Panny Marie Vítězné (Our Lady of Victory). Architecturally the building is unremarkable, but it is home to the celebrated wax-work figure of the Bambino di Praga (the Little Child of Prague), one of the city's most visited attractions (see panel opposite).

St. Joseph's A very different interpretation of what the Baroque style was all about can be seen in the Kostel svatého Josef (St. Joseph's Church) in Josefská street. Designed by a Carmelite monk from Leuven (Louvain) in what is now Belgium, it is unique in Prague in its Flemish look, with banded columns all over its façade and a cool dome dominating the interior. The church was flush with

Top: the sturdy stonework of the Church of Our Lady under the Chain

the street until the Lobkovic family next door complained at the loss of light to their palace.

St. Thomas's Just up the street from St. Joseph's is Kostel svatého Tomáše (St. Thomas's), founded in the 13th century by the Augustinians and extensively remodeled by Kilián Ignác Dientzenhofer in 1722–1731. The friars founded a brewery and beer cellar which still function, while their cloisters have become a home for the elderly. The church retains its medieval layout, but is covered in rich decoration throughout (its splendid Rubens altarpiece is now in the National Gallery, replaced here by a copy). Outside, Dientzenhofer overcame the constraints of the church's site with a wealth of overblown detail, including huge scrolls and chunky broken pediments.

The Little Child of Prague
A strong Iberian influence pervaded the compulsory re-Catholicization of the citizens of Prague. Descended from the Spanish branch of the Habsburgs, Polyexna of Lobkovic presented the Church of Our Lady of Victory in 1628 with the miracle-working waxwork of the Infant Jesus which later came to be known under the Italian name of the Bambino di Praga. Reclothed at regular intervals in a variety of sumptuous costumes, the diminutive figure continues to exert its fascination, particularly on tourists from Hispanic countries, who throng the church throughout the day.

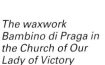

The waxwork Bambino di Praga in the Church of Our Lady of Victory

STARÉ MĚSTO

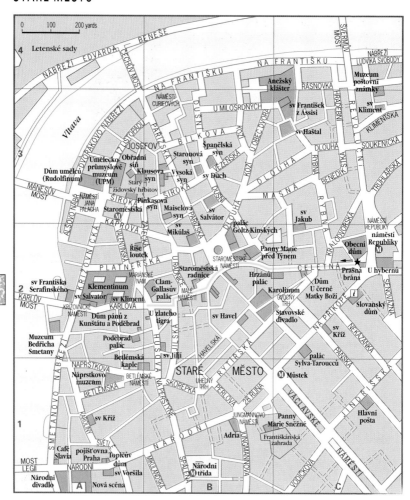

Opposite top: the Bedřich Smetana Museum (foreground)

Right: the gloriously crowded skyline of Staré Město

Staré Město Between the bend in the Vltava and the ring of boulevards where the city wall once stood, Prague's Old Town has kept its medieval layout almost intact, many of its apparently Baroque buildings rising over cellars which may be a thousand years old. Centered on the splendid Staroměstské náměstí (Old Town Square), this was the burghers' town, its population a mixture of merchants and craftspeople, priests and rabbis, monks and nuns, professors and students, the place where civic consciousness grew and flourished, often in opposition to the rulers from their castle height on the far side of the river.

STARÉ MĚSTO

The royal route

For most of the 15th century the Bohemian kings lived downtown. The site of their palace is now occupied by the Obecní dům (Municipal House). This palace is linked by a little bridge to the Prašná brána (Powder Tower), the most splendid of the gateways guarding the Old Town. The tower was the starting point for the monarch's coronation procession, which would wind through the Old Town, across Karlův most (Charles Bridge), then up to the castle and cathedral. The Royal Way, as it is known, makes an easily understandable axis for tourists trying to orient themselves, but leaves many secret parts of the Old Town unseen.

The symbol of the Old Town's sense of independence from their castle rulers is the Staroměstská radnice (Old Town Hall), its tall tower looking down on the great Pomník Jana Husa (Jan Hus Memorial) erected 500 years after his martyrdom. Many of the Old Town's churches were strongholds of those radical preachers who were Protestants long before the term was invented; Hus himself preached at the Betlémská kaple (Bethlehem Chapel), hidden away in the labyrinth of streets and little squares which makes much of the Old Town such a delightful confusion to explore.

The Bethlehem Chapel has been lovingly re-created in its 14th-century form in recent years, and most of the area's churches are built on medieval foundations, though their present character is overwhelmingly Baroque. All make their mark on the townscape, from svatého Salvátora (St. Savior) and svatého František (St. Francis) standing guard at the eastern end of Karlův most (Charles Bridge), or svatého Havel (St. Gall) embedded in its marketplace or svatého Jakuba (St. James), betraying its Gothic origins by its immense length, to svatého Mikuláše (St. Nicholas) on Old Town Square. The white towers and dome of St. Nicholas were never meant to dominate the north side of the square in the way they do, but were originally intended to remain half-hidden like the resolutely Gothic Panny Marie před Týnem (Týn Church), whose towers explode with spires and spikes above the townhouses at its base.

The Jewish quarter The most venerable place of worship in the Old Town is not a church, but rather the Gothic Staronová synagoga (Old-New Synagogue). Together with the 12,000 tumbled tombstones of the extraordinarily atmospheric Starý židovský hřbitov (Old Jewish Cemetery) and a little cluster of other synagogues, it is all that is left of the former ghetto, home of learned Rabbi Loew and his "man of mud," the Golem. As old as the Old Town itself, the ghetto had become a slum, deserted by most of its Jewish inhabitants, when it was obliterated at the turn of the century by well-meaning town planners.

In place of the ghetto there arose new streets and a grand boulevard, Pařížská, whose great width and ruler-straight alignment contrast strangely with the crooked roads and alleyways all around. This redevelopment plan was not the first attempt to try to straighten out the Old Town's irregularities—irregularities of thought as well as urban design: in the 17th century the Jesuits launched their attack on loose religious thinking from the great complex of the Klementinum (named after St. Clement), whose construction required the demolition of whole streets of houses.

Bohemian bounty—Czech porcelain and glass make excellent souvenirs; this shop is on Celetná

More recently, in the late-19th century, city fathers attempted to give Prague's riverside something of a Parisian air by erecting pompous institutional buildings, such as the UPM (Decorative Arts Museum) and the Rudolfinum, the former housing the national collection of arts and crafts. Today's equivalent, at the end of Pařížská, is the InterContinental Hotel, but further along is the Anežský klášter (St. Agnes' Convent), now the home of the National Gallery's 19th-century Czech Art Collection and an island of tranquility again after interminable years of restoration.

The Old Town Square, its stalls and open-air cafés over-looked by the twin towers of the Týn Church

▶▶   **Anežský Klášter (St. Agnes' Convent)** *118C4*
Anežská street
Metro: Staroměstská
Hidden away behind its walls in a quiet corner of the Old Town, the convent founded by St. Agnes of Bohemia in 1233 has recently become the impeccably restored home of the National Gallery's extensive collection of 19th-century Czech art.

History Agnes was the sister of King Wenceslas I. A sophisticated young woman, who wanted at all costs to avoid an arranged marriage, she escaped into religious life, inviting a community of Poor Clares here from Assisi and becoming their first abbess. The nuns were soon joined by their male equivalents, the Franciscans. With more or less unlimited funds available from the royal coffers, a splendid array of stone and brick buildings arose on the banks of the Vltava, Bohemia's first convent complex to be built in the new Gothic style.

The community flourished under royal patronage, housing for a while the mausoleum of the Přemyslid dynasty. In the 15th century the Hussites put an end to this golden age, melting down the convent's silver plate and turning parts of it into an armory and arsenal. A handful of nuns eventually returned, but in 1556 the place was taken over by the Dominicans, who seem to have managed their new estate strictly for profit, selling off land for speculative building, running a timber yard and brewing beer.

The nuns crept back again after the Battle of the White Mountain in 1620, but, like most such establishments, the convent was finally shut down by Emperor Joseph II in 1782. The buildings were sold off at auction, passing into the hands of slum landlords, who partitioned them up into poky dwellings for the poorest of the poor. The ruinous charm of the whole area attracted painterly devotees of the picturesque, and when, at the end of the 19th century, it was proposed to 'sanitize' the area along the lines of the redeveloped ghetto, there were loud protests.

What the city council had described as a 'jumble of evil-smelling yards' was saved, and a restoration process was set under way which lasted for the better part of the 20th century. The focal point of the convent today is the two-storied cloister, mostly medieval but with a Renaissance gallery added by the Dominicans. To the east is the empty and well-scrubbed Kostel svatého Salvátora (Church of the Holy Savior), with carved heads of Přemyslid rulers on the capitals, and the Kostel svatého František (St. Francis's Church), now used for chamber concerts.

Czech art The restorers' original and wholly appropriate intention was to use the atmospheric setting of the convent for the national collection of Czech Gothic art, but these wonderful works eventually found an equally suitable home in the Jiřský klašter (St. George's Convent) in the castle (see page 72). On show here instead is the

National Gallery's **Collection of 19th-century Czech Art▶▶**. The paintings and sculpture are interesting enough in their own right, though many of the works are suffused with a literalness and sentimentality which has yet to come back into fashion. Some of the big history paintings, such as the one showing the warrior Oldřich eyeing the peasant-maiden Božena, are of the type which cry out for irreverent captions.

Perhaps the gallery's most appealing theme is that of the discovery of the landscapes of Bohemia; here you will find the townscapes and rural scenes which have become the stuff of today's guidebooks: medieval Český Krumlov, the rock formations of the Central Bohemian uplands, the depths of the Šumava primeval forest, and, above all, the Prague of the turn-of-the-century painter Schikaneder, a mysterious city of hushed twilights and snowbound, gaslit streets.

One of the most appealing pictures is *Pod chalupou* (*Below the Cottage*), by Josef Mánes; it shows a 19th-century version of the pastoral weekend retreat so popular with Czechs today, complete with charming cottage, outside *hejzl* (privy), and mother and toddlers splashing in a pool.

Infinitely painstaking restoration has transformed St. Agnes' Convent into an almost too-immaculate setting for the National Gallery's 19th-century Czech art collection. This view of the interior looks east into the apse of the Church of the Holy Savior

Parks and gardens

■ **Late 18th-century maps show a Prague that had hardly grown since Charles IV laid out the New Town in the 14th century, still with the ring of defensive walls he built, albeit much improved by the military engineers of Baroque times. Most of the city at this time seemed densely built up, but a closer look reveals a wealth of green spaces—not only parks and gardens, but woodlands, orchards, and vegetable plots as well. Some of these city spaces disappeared as Prague expanded rapidly in the 19th century, but others remain, offering welcome retreats from the rigors of sightseeing....■**

Suburban pleasures
Like certain privileged people everywhere, the kings of Bohemia enjoyed the thrill of the hunt. The game-rich forests extending over much of Bohemia offered sporting opportunities aplenty, but for a casual afternoon's killing somewhere nearer at hand was needed; thus, in the 14th century, a great tract of woodland and pasture, enclosed by the bend of the Vltava and downstream from the city, was turned into the Royal Chase. The indefatigable Chotek had the Chase opened to the public, under the name of Stromovka, as early as 1802. In the 16th century another royal hunting ground was created, this time around the curious star-shaped summer palace, known as Hvězda, on the White Mountain to the west of Prague (see page 194).

Modern Prague can be an oppressive place, especially in the height of summer when the air thickens and there seems to be no escape from the heat and glare of buildings and sidewalks. This is the time to head away from right-bank Prague and to cross one of the bridges to Malá Strana, perhaps pausing on the way beneath the big trees of Střelecký ostrov (Shooters' Island) to enjoy the cool of the waterside and admire an unusual view of the city. Another shady spot is on Kampa island, where, in spite of wartime preoccupations, another attractive riverside park was laid out in 1940.

Romantic rambles Away from the banks of the Vltava, on the slopes leading up to the castle and Petřín hill, is where the most enchanting gardens are still to be found. As long ago as the early Middle Ages these sunny slopes were much in favor for growing vines. The vineyards have long since gone, succeeded in Renaissance and Baroque times by an almost continuous strip of Italianate gardens, their terraces ornamented with belvederes, pavilions, and the best statuary the city's sculptors could supply. Most of Petřín has now become a huge public park, its fruit trees glorious with blossom in spring, and with paths winding romantically through the woodland.

Other formal gardens were re-landscaped in the English style in the late-18th century, like those belonging to the Lobkovic and Schönborn-Colloredo palaces, now the German and U.S. embassies. Even so, a number of Baroque gardens have kept their original character, among them the superb **Vrtbovská zahrada (Vrtba Garden)►►** tucked away behind nondescript buildings at the junction of Karmelistská and Vlašská streets (closed for many years, this garden will eventually reopen), or the incomparable chain of gardens that rises from the row of palaces along Valdštejnská street to the very walls of the castle.

Here, architects such as Santini and Palliardi excelled themselves, turning the once-bare slopes into a paradise which is neither architecture nor garden but a wonderful fusion of the two. The army of dedicated gardeners who once maintained these, the **Ledebour, Pálffy and**

Kolovrat Gardens►►, have long since retired, and both these and the Vrtba Garden pose complicated problems for today's restorers; check whether they have yet been reopened to the public.

The castle gardens are described elsewhere (see page 92). They were immeasurably enriched in the 1920s by the work of the castle architect, Josip Plečnik, whose 19th-century predecessor, in spirit if not in title, was the castle burgrave (monarch's representative), Count Chotek. It was the count who turned the Petřín slopes into a public park, laid out the embankments and promenades along the Vltava, and, just to the east of the Royal Summer Palace, designed the fine park which bears his name, Chotkovy sady (Chotek Park). Later landscapers continued his work in an eastward direction along the slopes leading down from the Letná plain. Chotek was also instrumental in saving the New Town's Cattle Market (now Karlovo náměstí, or Charles Square) from building development, promoting its use as yet another public open space.

Amid the rocks and trees of romantic Stromovka Park in the district of Holešovice, west of the Výstaviště Exhibition Grounds

Top: traffic conditions in Prague drive cyclists into the parks

125

Floral Franciscans
The secluded Františkan-ská zahrada (Franciscan Garden) belonging to the church of Panny Marie Sněžné (Our Lady of the Snows—see page 184) was long ago turned into a small public park, a wel-come oasis for office workers munching their lunchtime sausages. In 1992 the garden was com-pletely redesigned in an imaginative contemporary style by the Prague Parks Department, making it even more popular.

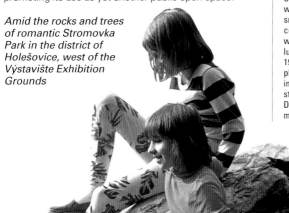

Statue of the composer Bedřich Smetana

▶ **Bedřicha Smetany Muzeum (Bedřich Smetana Museum)**   *118A2*

Novotného lávka
Metro: Staroměstská

This museum, dedicated to the memory of the composer of the symphonic poem *Má vlast* (*My Country*), is housed in a splendid neo-Renaissance structure which once formed part of the municipal waterworks.

As well as a museum, part of the Vltava embankment, Smetanovo nábřeží, is named after the composer. Until the mid-19th century, this part of the town met the waterside in a sloppy way, its old parish church being referred to as "St. John on the Garbage Dump," since much of the city waste was simply thrown out on to the river bank here. In the 1840s, the tireless Count Chotek had the city council clear things up. Prague's first riverside promenade was then laid out on a floodproof foundation of solid granite blocks. The embankment was originally named after Emperor Francis, whose statue used to stand in the little open space to the landward side.

In 1883 the waterworks personnel were rehoused in new premises at the tip of the row of buildings of varying dates which protrude into the river along Novotného lávka (Novotný Pier). The water-workers' offices were converted into the Bedřich Smetana Museum in 1936. The building's exterior is lavishly decorated with sgraffito (incised plaster) depicting Swedish soldiers being banished in 1648. The interior is filled with letters, musical scores, pictures, and other Smetana memorabilia. A modern statue of the composer is placed at the very tip of the promontory, from where there is an almost-too-perfect view across the water to Malá Strana and the castle.

▶ **Betlémské náměstí (Bethlehem Square)**   *118A1*

Metro: Národní třída

This pleasant little square, embedded in a maze of narrow streets in the southern part of the Staré Město (Old Town), is dominated by the twin gables of the **Betlémská kaple (Bethlehem Chapel)**▶. This stern structure is famous above all as the church whose rafters once resounded to the radical sermons of Jan Hus. The chapel was founded in 1391, well before the radical cleric's time, as a place where Prague's poor could hear sermons preached in their native Czech tongue rather than in Latin. Over the centuries it gradually fell into disrepair, and was finally demolished at the beginning of the 19th century. The growing importance of Jan Hus to burgeoning Czech nationalism was such that efforts to rebuild the chapel began as early as 1869, though completion had to await the advent of Communism. The plain interior emphasizes the importance of preaching, rather than elaborate religious ceremony. To one side are the quarters where Hus lived and worked. Also on the square is the **Náprstkovo muzeum (Náprstek Museum)**▶, devoted to ethnography.

▶▶ **Celetná (Celetná Street)**   *118C2*

Metro: Náměstí Republicky

Mostly pedestrianized, this ancient street follows the Royal Way from the Prašná brána (Powder Tower) on the

---

"Be kind to the chapel"
Among the last words to be uttered by Jan Hus before being burned at the stake in Constance were these. His exhortation was heeded by the Communists, who included the great preacher in their canon of "progressives," and who set the church restorers to work within months of coming to power in 1948.

edge of the Old Town to its very heart, the Staroměstské náměstí (Old Town Square). Behind charming Baroque and Rococo façades stand buildings of much greater antiquity, though at the corner with Ovocný trh there stands one of the outstanding structures of Czech Cubism, the **Dům U černé Matky Boží (House at the Black Madonna)►►**. Designed by Josef Gočár in 1911, it combines angular forms with respect for its venerable surroundings in a masterly way. The little figure of the Black Madonna in the gilded cage which once graced the building's Baroque predecessor is attached to its façade.

Opposite is the Pachta Palace, once the mint, built in 1759 and with a balcony held up by figures of miners, a tribute to those who actually dug out the precious metals processed here. Further down the street are any number of interesting details, such as the Madonna and Child adorning the portal of the undulating Baroque façade of No. 23, or the antique inscriptions in German and French at No. 22 advertising Gundle's, the royal jewelers. No. 11, now a souvenir shop, has a fine Baroque *pavlač* or courtyard, while No. 12, the Hrzánů palác (Hrzán Palace), has ornate sculptural decoration. As the street bends before entering Old Town Square, there is an entrance to the south portal of the Týn Church (see page 138). Adjoining it is No. 3, the home of the young Kafka, with a secret window looking down into the church interior.

Flood protection
Fed up with the erratic behavior of the Vltava, which in spring tended to take a shortcut across the Old Town, the citizenry decided on a drastic solution; in the mid-13th century the ground level of the whole area was raised by up to 10 ft. What had previously been the first floor of houses now became their cellars, and as you go down the flight of steps into a vaulted basement restaurant or nightclub, you may well be entering a Romanesque or early-Gothic shop or living room.

Outstanding Czech Cubism: the House at the Black Madonna on Celetná

■ **David Oistrakh described Bohemia as "the musical heart of Europe,"** and composers and performers from this small nation seem to have done more than their fair share to enrich the continent's musical traditions. Even the most casual visitor to Prague will be struck by the musicality of the scene; as well as orchestral concerts and operas, there are chamber music and organ recitals, solo performances, jazz, pop, folk, and the brassiest of military bands....■

Dechovky

This is the Czech name for the tuneful polkas, waltzes, and marches blasted out by the country's innumerable brass bands. Before World War I, Czech bandleaders monopolized the military bands of Austria-Hungary, and this kind of music, best played in the open air, is still popular, especially if the band's repertoire includes *Škoda lásky* (*Roll out the Barrel*) by Jaromír Vejvoda (see page 224). A good place to hear *dechovky* is the Národní dům Vinohrady (Vinohrady National House) on a Saturday afternoon.

Czech fiddler in Old Town Square

Concert halls The venues sometimes upstage the music. It would be difficult to imagine more splendid settings than the lavishly restored interiors of the 18th-century Stavovské divadlo (Estates Theater), the 19th-century Národní divadlo (National Theater) and Státní opera (State Opera), or the Art Nouveau Smetanova síň (Smetana Hall), while performances beneath the cathedral's Gothic vaults, in the sober walls of the Bazilika svatého Jiří (St. George's Basilica), or among the Baroque magnificence of the Kostel svatého Jakuba (St. James' Church) all have their own magic.

A chamber concert benefits from the gilt and chandeliers of a Baroque palace, and a "little night music" gains from being played in the intimate setting of a walled garden—and what street musician could hope for a better spot than Karlův most (Charles Bridge) or a traffic-free street in the Staré Město (Old Town)?

Music and Mozart Bohemian music-making goes back a long time. The Hussites used to fortify themselves before battle with a rousing chorale, but it may have been the later suppression of the Czech language that led the people's energy and talent into music and gained them the reputation they have enjoyed ever since. In the 18th century, every village schoolmaster was a musician, and many a pupil went into the world as a bandsman, member of a courtly orchestra or as a composer, some going abroad—such as Jiří Antonín Benda, to Prussia, or Josef Mysliveček, to Italy.

Bohemia's soil proved fertile ground for Mozart, appreciated in Prague as he had never been in Vienna. Beginning in 1787, he came here four times, staying with his friends the Dušeks in the Bertramka, their delightful country house in Smíchov. "My Praguers understand me," Mozart declared, after both *Figaro* and *Don Giovanni* had received rapturous receptions. It seems they not

Music in Prague

only understood, but loved him; after his pauper's death in Vienna, more than 4,000 Praguers mourned him at a great funeral mass in Chrám svatého Mikuláše (St. Nicholas' Church).

German and Czech In Mozart's time, and well into the 19th century, Prague music spoke in German; Weber was director of the Estates Theater from 1813 to 1816, conducting the 50th performance of his *Freischütz* there; it was here, too, in 1854, that Wagner presented his *Tannhäuser*. Later in the century, the note struck was a Czech one, characterized by Smetana's operas, *The Bartered Bride* and *Libuše*, and by his symphonic poem *Má vlast* (*My Country*). Many of Dvořák's genial outpourings were also based on Czech folklore and traditional music.

Both composers received their due from the nation; a gala performance of *Libuše* opened the National Theater, where Smetana was musical director and conductor. From humble beginnings as a butcher's son in the village of Nelahozeves, Dvořák became professor at the Prague Conservatory (the first in Central Europe) and then its director. A direct line of descent links Dvořák with several 20th-century composers: Josef Suk studied with him, then became his son-in-law, in his turn helping to mold the musical output of Bohuslav Martinů, who spent most of his working life in the U.S.

Mozart, Smetana and Dvořák all have museums devoted to them. Mozart's happy times in Prague are recalled at the Bertramka (see page 191), while Dvořák's memory is celebrated in the exquisite little Baroque summer palace known as the Vila Amerika (see page 183). Both places form a fascinating setting for concerts. Smetana's museum (see page 126) is splendidly sited on the Vltava embankment with lovely views of the castle.

Plastic people
The Communist regime was happy to promote traditional *dechovky*, but was less enamored of pop music. One of the great Czech singers of the 1960s, sometimes compared to Ella Fitzgerald, was Marta Kubišová. Her support for the Prague Spring ensured that her voice was silenced throughout the 1970s and 1980s, while the wonderfully named group, The Plastic People of the Universe, even had private performances in supporters' apartments suppressed by the police. After 1989, pop's prestige soared, not least when the Rolling Stones were honored by their foremost fan, the president himself.

Every night is Mozart night in Prague

129

ARSTOUR PRAHA

Amadeus

Mozart Interfest

STARÉ MĚSTO

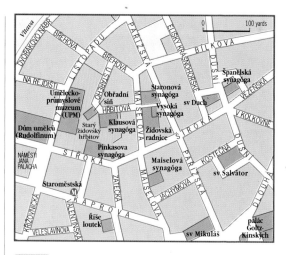

Third Reich theme park
By a cruel irony, the Nazis were kinder to the physical fabric of the Josefov than the turn-of-the-century town planners had been; their intention was to preserve what was left of the ghetto as a "Museum of a Vanished Race," and to this end, confiscated Jewish artifacts were gathered here from all over the country. Once the Final Solution had been achieved, the synagogues would have been turned into a showcase for the stolen treasures, and the ghetto streets would have been filled with actors impersonating the former inhabitants, all in a macabre anticipation of the theme parks of today.

▶▶▶ Josefov (Joseph's Town)   118A3

Metro: Staroměstská

Jews had lived in the area between Staroměstské náměstí (the Old Town Square) and the bend in the Vltava from the 12th century onwards, and the tightly packed district eventually became known as Židovské Město (Jewish Town). At the end of the 19th century, when much of Prague's ancient ghetto was demolished to make way for grand boulevards such as Pařížská, a small cluster of buildings was spared, grouped around the ancient cemetery; they include the town hall and several synagogues, among them the Staronová synagoga (Old-New Synagogue), begun in the mid-13th century and the oldest such structure north of the Alps.

Jews in Prague The Jewish presence in Prague goes back a thousand years, possibly even longer. In the early 10th century, Jews were already established in two areas, in Malá Strana and just outside the Staré Město (Old Town) near today's Národní metro station. In 1179 the Church demanded the segregation of Jews from Christians, and in the mid-13th century King Otakar II's plans for rebuilding Malá Strana made no provision there for its Hebrew community.

The city's Jews were accordingly relocated within the Old Town, in what became the ghetto, kept behind the walls which separated them from the Christians and, equally importantly, protected them from at least some of the regular outbursts of violent anti-Semitism. Here they governed themselves, in the 16th century producing such memorable figures as Mayor Maisel, one of the richest men in Europe, and the great Rabbi Loew, creator of the "Man of Mud," the Golem, and adviser in occult matters to Emperor Rudolf II.

The ghetto Hemmed in behind its walls, the ghetto suffered terribly from overcrowding. Some 7,000 people lived here in Rudolf's time, and more than 12,000 by the 18th century, when some much-needed improvements, including street paving, were finally carried out. In the 1780s, the enlightened Emperor Joseph II abolished most of the laws restricting Jewish participation in the life of the community, not in order to emancipate the Jews but to encourage them to assimilate.

By 1867, all forms of legal discrimination had been removed, and the ghetto, its walls torn down in 1848, had been renamed Josefov (Joseph's Town or Josefstadt), in honor of the liberalizing emperor. By this time, many of the more prosperous members of the community had already left for more salubrious quarters in the suburbs, where numerous new synagogues were constructed. Jewish intellectual life continued to flourish in the sharper air of the city center, producing world-class writers of the caliber of Kafka, Kisch, Brod, and Werfel (see page 137).

Persecution Not least because Emperor Joseph II had decreed it, Jewish life was conducted in German when not in Hebrew. At the turn of the century, Czech nationalism, not noted for its pro-Jewish stance, gave Prague's Jews some uneasy times. The establishment of the tolerant and progressive First Czechoslovak Republic in 1918 allowed Jews some justifiable optimism about the future but this was, alas, to be short-lived.

As the 1930s wore on, more and more Jewish refugees arrived, first from Germany, then Austria, then from the annexed Sudetenland. In 1939, when what was left of Czechoslovakia was dismembered by the Third Reich, there were 118,000 Jews in Bohemia-Moravia.

Buried treasure
The fate of the immeasurably important collection of Jewish objects assembled by the Nazis in Prague, and now administered by the State Jewish Museum, has never been free from controversy. The Jewish community has long disputed its ownership, and while much of it is on show, some of it has remained locked away in storage, such as at the Spanish Synagogue. The Communists proved themselves unworthy heirs of this heritage, twisting its meaning as the anti-Zionist tide flowed more or less strongly in the Soviet Empire, and opening and closing museums and displays at will.

The Second Czechoslovak Republic (September 1938 to March 1939), doing its desperate best to accommodate its Nazi neighbor, flirted with its own version of state anti-Semitism, reawakening a streak of prejudice that had never quite disappeared from national life. By the end of World War II, nearly 78,000 Jews had perished, most of them passing through the Terezín ghetto on their way to the death camps. Today, only 1,250 Jews live in Prague, more than half of them over the age of 70.

The Star of David shines out from a dark background redolent of the somber history of Bohemia's Jews

Man of mud
Rabbi Loew's Golem (see page 23), the prototype of all Frankenstein monsters and later robots, was molded from clay scraped from the river. When the Golem ran amok, it was only with some difficulty that the rabbi succeeded in turning him back into inert earth. The crumbling corpse of clay was laid to rest in the loft of the Old-New Synagogue; the door was then locked and the keys thrown away. The few brave spirits to have made their way into this secret space have either seen nothing at all or returned ashen-faced and trembling.

The Old-New Synagogue The fascinating Gothic building dominating Červená ulice is the **Staronová synagóga (Old-New Synagogue)▶▶▶**. With its high brick gable and atmospheric interior, this is one of the most evocative monuments of European Jewry. The name of the synagogue may be due to its replacing an earlier place of worship on the site and consequently being called the "New" synagogue, then earning its present ambiguous name when another "new" establishment was built near by in the 16th century. A more attractive explanation is that its name in German, Alt-Neu, is a corruption of the Hebrew *Al tnai*, meaning provisional or conditional; legend has it that the synagogue was built with stone flown here by angels from the Temple in Jerusalem, whither it will have to be returned with the coming of the Messiah. Whatever the origin of the stone, some of it seems to have been chiseled into shape by the Christian masons working on the nearby Anežský klášter (Convent of St. Agnes).

The atmospheric interior of the Old-New Synagogue; the bimah *(pulpit) and overhead chandeliers can be seen here, as well as the banner donated by Emperor Ferdinand II*

Royal permission for the construction of the synagogue was given in 1254, and its floor is well below street level—almost certainly on the original level of Staré Město (the Old Town) before the town was raised as a defense against flooding. In a city where nothing is straightforward, there is, of course, an alternative explanation; namely that the foundations had to be lowered in order to prevent the gable from overlooking (horror of horrors!) a nearby Christian church.

Decorations The interior is approached through a door with a tympanum beautifully decorated with a carving of a vine; this important Jewish symbol has 12 roots for the 12 tribes of Israel, and four branches for the four rivers of Creation. Beyond the barrel-vaulted vestibule is the main hall, tall for its width, and with five-part ribbed vaults instead of the usual four (four-part rib vaults were avoided because they could be seen as representing the Christian Cross). In the middle is the *bimah*, or pulpit, surrounded by a Gothic grille. Above hang splendid chandeliers dating from the 16th to the 19th centuries. There is also a banner that was given by Emperor Ferdinand II in recognition of Jewish participation in the fight against the Swedes in the Thirty Years' War. There is fine foliage carving around the corbels, one of which, on the south wall, has been left unfinished, a further reminder of the "provisional" status of the synagogue. Until the 15th century, women worshippers sat beyond the window slits in a separate space.

In the past, the synagogue was used as a meeting-place and, until the ghetto lost its separate jurisdiction, as a law court. Nowadays, its principal function is that of a tourist attraction, and the breath of its thousands of visitors is eroding the very fabric of its walls. Even so, it remains a place of worship, one of only two serving the much-reduced Jewish community of Prague.

The High Synagogue Opposite the entrance to the Old-New Synagogue is the **Vysoká synagóga (High Synagogue)►**. This dates from 1568, but its Renaissance appearance has been much altered over the years. Now given over to displays of ceremonial textiles, it used to adjoin the **Židovská radnice (Jewish Town Hall)►** alongside; this delightful building dates from slightly earlier but was rebuilt in Rococo style around 1760. It has a playful little belfry, with a clock whose hands move counterclockwise around the Hebrew letters of its face. The town hall is the center of Jewish life in Prague, complete with kosher restaurant.

133

Suburban synagogues
Memorials to once-thriving Jewish communities can be seen all over the Prague suburbs in the shape of abandoned synagogues. Some now serve as warehouses and others have become Christian churches. The big Vinohrady synagogue was hit by an allied air raid towards the end of World War II and left to burn by the Nazis. In Smíchov, the synagogue was used as a storage depot, but has now been returned to the Jewish community.

A fraction of the 12,000 tombstones in the Old Jewish Cemetery. The cemetery itself dates from the mid-15th century

The Old Jewish Cemetery The presence of the high-walled Starý židovský hřbitov (Old Jewish Cemetery)►►► on U stárého hřbitova is betrayed by the tall trees drawn up towards the light, which falls in dappled gloom on the 12,000 tombstones scattered over its undulating floor. The oldest of its kind in Europe to survive, the cemetery dates from the middle of the 15th century, when the Jews were forbidden to bury their dead beyond the ghetto walls. By the time the last burial took place in 1787, the available space had been used over and over again, with the dead being interred up to 12 deep in places: estimates of the total number laid to rest here vary between 20,000 and 80,000.

Some of the leaning tombstones seem about to topple as the earth heaves in frozen motion around them. In style they range from Gothic to Rococo, some of them decorated with the symbol of the deceased. On many are notes placed by visitors, held in place by a pebble; the tombstone most often singled out for this purpose is, inevitably, the grand one commemorating Rabbi Loew.

The days when the cemetery was an island of strangely disturbing tranquility can only be imagined now, such is its popularity. It is watched over by uniformed guards, and visitors are confined to a roped-off trail. Efforts to clean it up and indulge in some tasteful landscaping have not met with the Jewish community's wholehearted approval.

The Ceremonial Hall By the main cemetery gate is a neo-Romanesque building, the Obřadní síň (Ceremonial Hall)►, in which there are harrowing displays on the theme of the Holocaust, including children's art from the Terezín death camp. To the far side of the cemetery entrance is the Klausova synagóga (Klausen Synagogue)►, a Baroque structure of 1694, much altered subsequently; its displays include a fine cycle of burial paintings dating from 1780 to 1830. On the far side of the cemetery is the Pinkasova synagóga (Pinkas

Embedded in a later building is this glorious Gothic oriel window, a fragment of the Carolinum's original edifice

Synagogue)►►. This was built in 1479 by Rabbi Pinkas on the foundations of what was probably the ghetto's very first synagogue, a Romanesque building of the 11th century. It was rebuilt again in 1535, and extended or altered on several subsequent occasions. It is now a memorial to the 77,297 Czech Jews killed by the Nazis, whose neatly lettered names cover its walls.

Maiselova (Maisel) street recalls the name of the ghetto's 16th-century mayor, as does the **Maiselová synagóga** (Maisel Synagogue), endowed by him and fancifully remodeled in neo-Gothic style at the end of the 19th century. At present it houses an exhibition of silver. The **Španělská synagóga** (Spanish Synagogue), a little distance away on Dušní street, was built in Moorish style for the Jews expelled from their native Spain by Philip II; it now serves as storage space.

► **Karolinum (Carolinum)**   *118B2*
Corner of Ovocný trh and Železná street
Named after its founder, Emperor Charles IV, the Carolinum was the first university to be established in Central Europe. Set up rather inauspiciously in the year of the Black Death (1348), its interesting educational aim was "to increase the fame and glory of the Kingdom of Bohemia." Originally it had no premises of its own; professors' houses were used for lectures and degrees were awarded in the cathedral. From 1383 it acquired its present home, a rebuilt mansion with a graceful oriel (bay) window projecting from its façade. Jan Hus was the university's most famous rector and, until the Counter-Reformation, the university was a bastion of Protestantism. Apart from the oriel window and some arches not much is left of the medieval building; it was remodeled in the 18th century and thoroughly restored after partial destruction in the street fighting of May 1945.

Student split
The Carolinum was originally open to Germans, Czechs, and Poles. The Hussite emphasis on the use of the Czech language irritated the German-speaking students so much that in 1409 they upped and left to found their own university at Leipzig. In the late-19th century, animosity between the partisans of Czech and German was again so acute that the Carolinum was split once more, each faction claiming to be the rightful successor to the institution founded by the 14th-century emperor.

FOCUS ON — *Prague in words*

■ After several centuries of sleepy inactivity, Prague's literary life suddenly awoke in the 19th century. The long-suppressed Czech language had been revived by the likes of Jungmann and Palacký, and turned into an expressive medium quite the equal of any world language, while the intense and enclosed life led by the dwindling German-speaking population of Prague gave rise to an extraordinarily rich literature in that language as well....■

136

Survivors

Some Jewish writers took as their theme life in Prague under the Nazis. Jiří Weil (1900–1959) wrote *Life with a Star*, an account of underground life during the occupation, while Arnošt Lustig and Ivan Klíma worked their concentration-camp experiences into some of their writing. Klíma is perhaps the most adept chronicler of the absurdities of everyday life under Communism; until 1989 his short stories could only be published abroad or in *samizdat* (underground) versions.

The country's best-loved woman novelist was **Božena Němcová** (1820–1862). Born in Vienna, Němcová lived part of her life in Prague, though her enormously popular *Babička* (*Grandma*) deals with rural life. A Praguer through and through, **Jan Neruda** (1834–1891), was brought up in Malá Strana; his pithy stories about the life of the ordinary folk of his part of town, *Tales of the Little Quarter*, won him the title of "The Dickens of Prague." Neruda earned his living as a journalist, a trade common to many of the city's other literary figures.

Jaroslav Hašek (1883–1923) was editor of the maga-

"Arconaut". Franz Werfel

zine *Animal Life* until the proprietor dismissed him; it had become clear that the pages were being filled with accounts of unlikely creatures which were entirely the product of Hašek's imagination. Hašek's surveillance by the secret police seemed justified when his career in the Austro-Hungarian army ended with capture by the Russians and subsequent adherence to the Red Army, where he briefly became a commissar.

Kafka & Švejk

PRAGUE

© Fun Explosive

Hašek died of drink before his masterpiece *The Adventures of the Good Soldier Švejk in the Great War* was completed, but his blue-chinned, innocent-eyed malingerer in baggy pants lives on, his exposure of the absurdity of authority striking a sympathetic note among Czechs (though they won't thank you for calling them a "nation of Švejks").

While Hašek was churning out his absurdist satires in Czech, Prague's German

Prague in words

writers were equally productive, though not all of them were able to tolerate the city's claustrophobic ambience. **Rainer Maria Rilke** (1875–1926) soon left, but not before describing the city of his birth in poetry and in his *Two Tales of Prague*. **Franz Werfel** (1890–1945), literary lion of the famous Café Arco, eventually found his home in Hollywood.

The writer whose work seems most deeply infused with the atmosphere of Prague is, of course, **Franz Kafka** (1883–1924), even though the city's name hardly appears in his fiction. Kafka characterized Prague as a "little mother with claws," and he lived almost all his life unable or unwilling to escape the confines of Staré Město (the Old Town), Malá Strana and the castle.

Kafka's novels and short stories evoke a sinister, darkly-lit world where the individual is at the mercy of unaccountable and implacable authority; there can be little doubt that Kafka's imagination fed off the literal and political topography of bureaucrat-ridden Prague in the last days of Austrian rule, even though the full, horrific realization of his vision had to await the coming first of Nazism and then of Communism.

Kafka wanted his work burnt, but his literary executor, Max Brod (1884–1968), the doyen of Prague's German-Jewish literary set, refused to carry out his friend's wishes. Brod thereby contributed unknowingly to the growth of today's Kafka industry, one of whose principal products is the T-shirt, imprinted with the haggard features of the tubercular author, incongruously covering the ample tummies of numerous visitors to the city.

Outwitting the censors
Deft dealing with censorship enabled Bohumil Hrabal to publish works like *Closely Observed Trains* and *I Served the King of England*. Milan Kundera, together with Josef Škvorecký, found life under Communism intolerable after 1968, and much of their writing, including Kundera's *The Unbearable Lightness of Being* and Škvorecký's *Engineer of Human Souls*, was not published in their native country until after 1989.

137

Prague poet Rainer Maria Rilke

One of the giant globes in the Clementinum's Library Hall

Tin-nosed Tycho's Týn tomb

Among the several splendid tombstones to be found in the Týn Church is that of Tycho de Brahe, the Danish astronomer who briefly served as Emperor Rudolf II's imperial mathematician. He is remembered for the gloomy prophecies which put poor Rudolf in a panic more than once, for his metal nose (his real one had been sliced off in a duel), and for the manner of his passing: not wanting to leave the emperor's table to relieve himself, Tycho expired in agony from a burst bladder.

▶▶ **Klementinum (Clementinum)**   *118A2*

Access from Křížovnická street, Karlova street or Malé náměstí

Metro: Staroměstská

Occupying an area second only in extent to that of the castle, the Clementinum was a Counter-Reformationary megastructure founded in 1556 by the Jesuits as the base for their vigorous campaign to re-Catholicize Bohemia. The vast complex included schools and a college, a library, a theater, a publishing house, and an observatory tower; to make way for it, the Dominicans were evicted from their monastery near Karlův most (Charles Bridge), several dozen houses were demolished and roads were diverted. Today the Clementinum is the country's greatest repository of books, housing several libraries—including the National Library and the University Library. Built around a series of courtyards, it presents a rather blank face to the outside world. Its most assertive façade, adorned with effigies of emperors, runs a full 300 ft. northwards from the Kostel svatého Salvátora (Church of the Holy Savior) along Křížovnická street.

The entrance from Karlova street is near the Baroque church which lent its name to the whole undertaking. Kostel svatého Klimenta (St. Clement's Church) was built over a medieval church in 1715. It is now an Orthodox establishment, used by one of the city's smaller minorities, the Greeks, some of whom are descendants of the civil war partisans given refuge in Czechoslovakia by the Communists.

To visit the Clementinum's splendid interiors you are supposed to be a bona fide bibliophile with a reading ticket, but an air of studious confidence should get you past the porter's lodge and, so long as you do not disturb the readers, you are unlikely to be ejected. Among the spectacular spaces, with original murals and stucco work, are the Mozart Hall, the Mathematical Hall and the Library Hall, the latter with original bookcases, ceiling paintings, and an amazing row of ancient globes. Crowning the complex is the observatory tower, topped by a figure of Hercules carrying a celestial sphere.

▶▶ **Kostel Panny Marie před Týnem (Church of Our Lady before Týn)**   *118B2*

Staroměstské náměstí (Old Town Square)

Metro: Staroměstská or Můstek

The central church of the Staré Město (Old Town) is also its most distinctive landmark. Up close, its dark stonework is hidden behind the bright façades of the houses on the east side of Staroměstské náměstí (Old Town Square), but seen from a short distance away, its sinister-looking steeples and spiky belfries seem to rocket skywards, only stopped from puncturing the clouds by the golden spheres attached to their tips.

The Týn Church was built from 1365 onwards as the place of worship for foreign merchants working in the nearby Týn or Ungelt (the Customs House and money exchange). The church soon became a center of Hussitism, enjoying the patronage of King George of Poděbrady, the "Hussite king." His statue once graced the gable, together with a gold chalice symbolizing the Utraquist cause with which he was associated. Both disappeared after the Battle of the White Mountain, the chalice being melted down to help make the figure of the Madonna which replaced it.

The silvery-gray stonework of the lofty interior is set off by the dark wood of pews, altars, and furnishings, by the somber paintings, and by the glimmer of gilt and candles. The vaulting, with its emblems, is a Baroque replacement for the Gothic roof destroyed by fire in 1689. Among the many works of art is an expressive Gothic *Calvary*, a late-15th-century pulpit, an early Renaissance altar featuring John the Baptist, and a number of fascinating tombstones. High up in the south aisle wall, a blank window looks down into the nave from the house in which Kafka spent his childhood.

Profitable customs
Just to the east of the Týn Church is the charming Týn Court, also called the Ungelt, the German term for the customs tariffs levied on goods traded by foreign merchants. When these fees were abolished in the 1560s, the chief customs officer had done so well for himself that he was able to build the magnificent arcaded mansion that dominates the courtyard today.

Týn Church bathed in the evening light

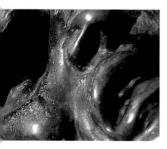

■ **The sense of Prague as a city deeply marked by history is accentuated by the presence almost everywhere of public sculpture. The Baroque saints gesticulating on Karlův most (Charles Bridge) are familiar from many a photograph, but there are figures and faces from every era, standing on parapets, occupying important positions in squares or, more modestly, attached to walls in the form of memorial plaques....■**

To arms!
Thousands died in the last days of World War II as the people of Prague rose against the Nazis several days before the Red Army arrived. All around town, bronze plaques bear the names of the victims of the last-ditch bullets and bombs of the Gestapo and the S.S. Well turned-out Young Pioneers stood guard over these sites under Communism, to commemorate the Prague Uprising. Even now flowers are placed in memory of those who fell.

Forgotten tyrants The most monumental of all memorials was also the most short-lived. A monstrous granite statue of Stalin dominated the city from the Letná plain for a mere seven years, from 1955 to 1962, before it was blown up and its fragments used as paving slabs.

But Stalin's is by no means the only name to have been erased from the record. Nowadays the attempt made by the Communists to set their seal on Prague in stone is suffering the same fate as that undergone by the Habsburgs in the early part of this century. After 1918, the Franz Josef station was renamed in honor of U.S. President Wilson, and after 1989 the wheel of fortune removed Communist leader Gottwald's name from a metro station, leaving it plain Vyšehrad. Emperor Franz I disappeared from the elaborate mid 19th-century fountain on what is now the Smetanovo nábřeží (Smetana Embankment), and today the figures of cloth-capped workers and red-cheeked maidens are no longer as prominent in the townscape as they once were. Many a red star or hammer and sickle has now gone the way of the Baroque Marian column pushed down by a nationalist crowd at the end of World War I, and the Soviet tank in Smíchov (see page 197) was first painted pink and then removed altogether.

Elegant statuary in the gardens of the Wallenstein Palace

Saints and scholars Most of the city's Baroque sculpture, thankfully, has failed to upset the crowd in quite this way; Nepomuk and the other saints favored by the Counter-Reformation continue to process gloriously across Karlův most (Charles Bridge). Burgeoning Czech nationalism added its own layer of meaning to an already animated townscape in the late-19th century; scholarly Josef Jungmann has sat thoughtfully in his square since 1878. The most inspired

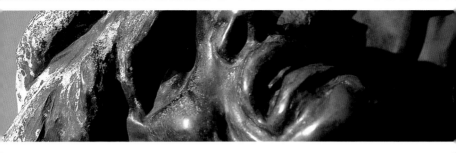

sculptures of this era came in a cluster at the beginning of the 20th century, including the striking monument to Jan Hus standing upright among his fellow-countrymen in the heart of the Old Town, and Wenceslas sitting on his sprightly steed at the top of his own square, Václavské náměstí.

In some ways the most striking of all is the memorial to the historian-turned-politician František Palacký. His massive seated figure in stone represents reality, while the spirited bronze figures soaring above depict the world of the imagination, a potent set of symbols for Czechs who so often have had to live in their minds in the face of an implacable reality. Palacký's monument stands in the square named after him on the Vltava embankment; it was the work of Stanislav Sucharda who, like Myslbek with Wenceslas and Šaloun with Hus, devoted more than a dozen years of his life to his inspirational task.

As well as a square, Palacký has a bridge named after him, though the statues which once adorned it have been removed to the lawns of Vyšehrad; representing figures such as Libuše and her consort Přemysl, they too belonged to the world of the imagination, to that mythical Czech past which so fired the zeal of 19th-century romantics.

The interwar First Czechoslovak Republic wasn't quite so given to the grand gesture, but many of its otherwise sober buildings have sculptural decoration that is worth far more than a passing glance. Look out for Rabbi Loew on the New Town Hall in Mariánské náměstí, or the legionnaires' adventures on the Rondo-Cubist façade of No. 24 Na Poříčí.

Parachutists' plaque
The sinister slit opening from Resslova street into the crypt of the Kostel svatého Cyrila a Metoděje (Church of Saints Cyril and Methodius) in the Nové Město (New Town) is still peppered with bullet holes. Above it is a somber wall plaque commemorating the sacrifice of the parachutists who died here at the hands of the Nazis, as well as the death of the Orthodox clergymen who had sheltered them (see also page 167).

The famous statue of Wenceslas in the square that bears his name

STARÉ MĚSTO

Tragic Jan
On January 16, 1969, Jan Palach, a 21-year-old student, poured petrol over himself and set himself on fire in Václavské náměstí (Wenceslas Square) in protest against the previous August's Warsaw Pact invasion. His death four days later touched the nation deeply, and hundreds of thousands attended his funeral. For a while, but not for long, Red Army Square was renamed Jan Palach Square by furious students. The official renaming had to wait 21 years until 1990 when, in a ceremony attended by President Havel, due honor was paid to the youth whose act of immolation had made him a national symbol.

Guardian of the source–fountainhead in Malé náměstí

▶▶ **Křížovnické náměstí (Knights of the Cross Square)** *118A2*

Metro: Staroměstská

The small square bounded by the Karlův most věž (Charles Bridge Tower) and by two Baroque churches in contrasting styles makes a magnificent entrance to the Old Town, marred only by its use as a main north–south traffic route.

The centerpiece of the square is a statue of Emperor Charles IV, placed here in 1848 on the 500th anniversary of the foundation of the Karolinum (Charles University), named after him (see page 135). The base of the railings makes an uncomfortable perch for some of the tourists congregating around the eastern end of Karlův most (Charles Bridge). The pressure of too many people has long since reduced the square's patches of lawn to dust. The Royal Way crosses the north–south riverside highway at this point; vehicles burst forth from the tunnel to the south, maiming amazingly few of the pedestrians sauntering blithely in their path.

The square's two churches preside calmly over this somewhat chaotic scene. The first built was the **Kostel svatého Salvátora (Church of the Holy Savior)**, begun in 1578 by the Jesuits not long after they had started work on the Clementinum (see page 138), to which the church was soon attached. It has a theatrical façade with plenty of outsized statuary. Joined to its eastern end, down Karlova street, is the Vlašská kaple (Italian Chapel).

The more sober façade, with statues strictly confined to their niches, belongs to the **Kostel svatého Františka Serafinského (Church of St. Francis Seraphicos)**. This was erected in the 1680s over the Romanesque foundations of the Knights of the Cross monastery, which had guarded the eastern end of the old Judith Bridge. Part of the bridge tower survived the Baroque rebuilding of the monastery and can still be seen. The church was given its splendid dome in a deliberate attempt to outdo the upstart Jesuits next door; it now echoes the even grander, but somewhat later, dome of St. Nicholas in Malá Strana.

▶ **Malé náměstí (Little Square)** *118B2*

Metro: Staroměstská

Not square, but triangular, this charming space along the Royal Way southwest of Staroměstské náměstí (Old Town Square) is focused on a fountain surrounded by a delightful Renaissance wrought-iron grille. Most of the buildings are Baroque, built on much earlier foundations. The most striking is No. 3, given elaborate and colorful sgraffito decoration by Mikoláš Aleš in 1896, while No. 13 has an interesting early shop front.

▶ **Mariánské náměstí (St. Mary's Square)** *118A2*

Metro: Staroměstská

The back entrance to the Clementinum (see page 138) stands on one side of this square, while opposite is the Art Nouveau Town Hall, built in 1912. The façade is appropriately grand and is decorated with reliefs and sculptures, including one by Ladislav Šaloun of Rabbi Loew, the learned creator of the monstrous Golem.

► **Náměstí Jana Palacha
(Jan Palach Square)** *118A3*

Metro: Staroměstská

With one side facing the Mánes bridge over the Vltava, this square and its splendidly pompous civic buildings formed part of a 19th-century attempt to give at least part of Prague's riverside a dignified, "Parisian" feeling. To the north are the neo-Renaissance School of Decorative Arts and the **Rudolfinum** (also known as the **Dům umělců**, or **House of Artists**), an even more lavish example of the same style, with extensive exhibition spaces and a 1,200-seat concert hall. Its name commemorates the Habsburg Crown Prince Rudolf, but people prefer to associate it with that other, stranger owner of the same name, Emperor Rudolf II. The monumental edifices were completed simultaneously in 1884.

The Church of the Holy Savior on Krížovnické náměstí, seen here against sunset, took more than a century to complete (1593–1714)

Provisional parliament
From 1918 to 1939 the Rudolfinum served as the home for the legislative assembly of the newly created Czechoslovak Republic.

House of history
History has been made in the Obecní dům. On October 28, 1918, the First Czechoslovak Republic was proclaimed here. More recently, in late 1989, intense discussions took place between Party bureaucrats and members of the Civic Forum, to work out the details of the transfer of power from the former to the latter.

▶▶▶ Obecní dům (Municipal House) 118C2

Náměstí Republiky (Republic Square)
Metro: Náměstí Republicky
This glorious confection of a building (under restoration until 1997) is an example of Czech Secession style at its most exuberant, and was built in the early years of this century to provide the city with a whole array of facilities, from grandiose halls and reception rooms to places in which to eat, drink, and be merry.

History The old Royal Court had stood on this site, becoming increasingly derelict and ending up being used as a barracks. In the course of the 19th century, the German population of Prague had more or less appropriated nearby Na Příkopě (On the Moat) as their own, calling it Der Graben (see page 172). Here were the German restaurants, the German club, and the drinking dens from which, on Sundays, scar-faced students would emerge to challenge any Czech who dared show his face. To counter this misappropriation, the Czech-dominated city council decided to develop the Royal Court site; here a prestige building was to arise which would proclaim the glory of the Czech nation and Prague's place in it. The architects joined forces with the leading sculptors, painters, and decorative artists of the time to create a major monument of European Art Nouveau which still has the power to stun today.

Inside The building occupies a triangular site with the two principal wings and a main entrance facing Náměstí Republiky (Republic Square). Above the ornate metal canopy, an enormous semicircular mosaic pays an elaborate *Homage to Prague*, flanked by writhing statuary and topped by a green dome glittering with gold. A hard act to follow, the ostentation of the entrance is nevertheless matched, if not outdone, by the interiors, not all of which are open to the public (though a guided tour may penetrate into normally closed rooms). There's no problem about getting into the restaurant (to the right) or the café (to the left), though you may have to wait for a table. This is the best place to imagine yourself back in the bourgeois atmosphere of pre-war days, when the comfortably-off would join the cultured for coffee.

The Prague Spring is heralded in the splendid **Smetanova síň** (Smetana Hall) every year with a bold blast of that composer's *Má vlast* (*My Country*) from the resident orchestra, the Czech Philharmonic. This hall is by far the biggest space in the whole complex and one of the most elaborately decorated. Beneath the dome are seats for 1,300 people, who can, if their attention wanders, enjoy portraits of composers, the ceiling fresco or various sculptures, including one of a pot-bellied cherub and another of a passionately dancing couple.

Other rooms with an ornamental overload include the **Sál Primátorský** (Lord Mayor's Salon), with paintings by Mucha and decorative lettering proclaiming such Orwellian slogans as "Freedom with Strength" and "Unity and Love." Every feature has received the same meticulous attention to detail, right down to the drapes

Art Nouveau encrustations adorn the interior of the Obecní dům

(with their extraordinary curtain cord) or the metalwork of the ventilation grilles. Equally worth inspection are the Rieger Hall, the Palacký Hall, and the Sladkovský Hall, plus the Empire-style pastry shop decorated in pastels and gilt.

► **Prašná Brána (Powder Tower)**   118C2
Náměstí Republiky (Republic Square)
One of the most photographed of the city's landmarks, the Gothic Powder Tower was built in the late-15th century in honor of King Vladislav II Jagiello as a ceremonial departure point for his coronation procession. It replaced an older tower, one of 13 that once stood guard over the Old Town but which fell into decay when the Habsburgs decided to confine their coronation ceremonies to Vienna. When the old Royal Palace next door was turned into a barracks, the tower became a gunpowder store, hence its name. It owes its present hypermedieval appearance to the avid 19th-century restorer, Josef Mocker, but it is well worth the climb for an intimate view over the Old Town rooftops.

The Gothic Prašná brána (Powder Tower) is joined by a bridge to the Obecní dům

■ **The skyline of Staré Město (the Old Town) is studded with the towers, spires, and domes of a dozen and more churches. Some proclaim their importance with a great show of self-confidence; St. Francis and St. Savior try to outdo each other across Křížovnické náměstí (Knights of the Cross Square–see page 142), while Staroměstské náměstí (Old Town Square) is dominated by the bristling spikes and steeples of the Týn Church (see page 138), its somber stonework contrasting with the smooth stucco of nearby St. Nicholas (see page 152)....**

In the Middle Ages and later, the Old Town had about 30 churches in all; some were attached to monasteries, some served exclusive communities composed of foreign merchants, while others were simple places of worship for the parish. Several new churches were added in the 17th and 18th centuries in the theatrical Baroque style so expressive of the values of the Counter-Reformation, though most apparently Baroque buildings are refacings of older, Gothic edifices.

Holy Cross The oldest of the Old Town's churches is the tiny Romanesque rotunda of the Kaple svatého Kříže (Holy Cross Chapel) on Karolíny Světlé street, an endearingly plain little structure dating from the early 1100s. Originally sited on the ancient highway linking Vyšehrad in the south to the ford across the Vltava to the north, it was nearly demolished in the 1860s to make way for an apartment building; members of the awakening conservation movement saved it, and provided the neo-Romanesque railings which still protect it. Inside are fragments of 14th-century wall paintings.

St. Giles' The Gothic grandeur which once dominated the town is still hinted at by the massive presence of the Kostel svatého Jiljí (St. Giles' Church) on Husova street. One of its sturdily buttressed towers is capped by a low tiled roof, the other by a copper-covered steeple. The Dominicans were given the church in 1626 after being made to cede the Clementinum to the Jesuits; they are back once again, after suffering similarly cavalier treatment at the hands of those 20th-century Jesuits, the Communists. The Dominicans were responsible for remodeling the Gothic interior, and it is fitting that one of Prague's most prolific participants in this city-wide process of "Baroquification," the painter Václav Vavřinec Reiner, is buried here.

St. Gall When the Old Town was extended southwards in the early 13th century, the new quarter was given its own church, the Kostel svatého Havla (St. Gall) in Havelská street, a Romanesque building reconstructed in Gothic style in the 14th century. Strongly Hussite, it—like

Monument to Vratislav
The monument to Count Jan Vratislav z in the Church of St. James is the most ostentatious in the city. As Lord High Chancellor of Bohemia, Vratislav spent much of his time in Vienna, where he commissioned the Austrian master of Baroque architecture, Fischer von Erlach, to build his Chancellery. Satisfied with the result, Vratislav gave von Erlach the job of designing a tomb which would remind posterity of his greatness. The architect certainly succeeded, though it is perhaps his name and that of the young sculptor Brokov (who actually carried out the work) which are better remembered today. The awesome figure of Chronos (Time), with hourglass and hollow eye-sockets, is especially striking.

so many of the other conquered strongholds of Protestantism—was given to a monastic order after the Battle of the White Mountain in 1620. The new owners, the Carmelites, dressed the church in fashionable Baroque clothes, tailored in this case by the great Santini, whose hand can be seen in the richly modeled façade.

St. James An even more magnificent Baroque rebuilding can be seen in the Kostel svatého Jakuba (Church of St. James) in Malá Štupartská street. Founded by the Minorites in 1232, it still has its Gothic cloister, built a century later, though the church itself was gutted in the great fire of 1689 which devasted this part of the Old Town. Anticipating the glories of the interior, the doorways are surmounted by orgiastic stucco reliefs by the Italian Ottavio Mosto. Inside, the great length of the church recalls its Gothic origins, though otherwise no trace of medieval austerity remains beneath the exuberant Baroque décor, culminating in the altar painting in its stunningly sculpted frame. With excellent acoustics, St. James makes a magnificent setting for concerts.

A warning hand
St. James was the church of the Old Town butchers' guild. One day in 1400, one of their number was summoned to end the misery of a thief who had tried to pilfer jewels from the Madonna on the high altar; Our Lady unceremoniously grabbed his hand and would not let go. The only solution was severance, performed with aplomb by the expert with his cleaver. The withered hand and forearm still hang in the church in horrid admonition.

The long, glittering nave of the Church of St. James

Stand by your stall

Among the more conventional stallholders on Old Town Square you will see others whose wares are suspended from a pole. At the approach of council inspectors, whose job is to check trading licenses, the pole is placed on the vendor's foot. Since, in principle, his pole is not occupying any pavement space, no license is necessary.

Patrician houses survey the busy scene in Old Town Square

▶▶▶ **Staroměstské náměstí**
(Old Town Square) *118B2*

Metro: Staroměstská or Můstek

This splendid square has been the theater for many of Prague's most dramatic historic events, though nowadays it seems permanently thronged by visitors. The square's cobblestoned, traffic-free surface spreads out from the foot of the tall tower of the Staroměstská radnice (the Old Town Hall) and pivots on the extraordinary Art Nouveau memorial to Jan Hus. Streets and passageways discreetly enter the square; only to the north is the dense townscape blown open by the Pařížská boulevard, leading the eye out towards the river and Letná plain. Some of the city's finest old townhouses line two sides of the square; the ones to the east conceal the lower parts of the Týn Church (see page 138) which rears up above their roofs in an angry outburst of bristling spikes and steeples, in complete contrast to the polished Baroque forms of St. Nicholas' Church opposite (see page 152).

History The hub of the Old Town ever since its foundation, Old Town Square started as a medieval marketplace, a

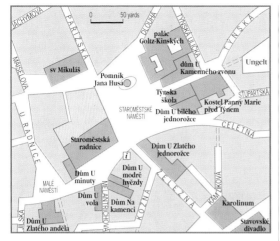

function gradually lost as its civic importance increased with the construction and gradual development of the Town Hall. The year of the Velvet Revolution, 1989, marked a return to this ancient market role, though today's traders concentrate on supplying tourists with souvenirs rather than the citizenry with life's necessities.

Over the centuries, the square served as the city's principal place of execution, and blood has flowed here as freely as today's cola and mineral water. In 1422, a gaggle of Hussites lost their heads and almost exactly 200 years later, in 1621, the lesson of the Battle of the White Mountain was rubbed in when 27 prominent Protestants were murdered. Their fate is commemorated by the 27 crosses in the stonework of the pavement just to the east of the Town Hall.

In 1945, in the fierce fighting between resistants and diehard Nazis, the north wing of the Town Hall was destroyed; the arrival of Red Army tanks marked the end of this episode, as it did of the Prague Spring in August 1968. In between, on February 21, 1948, the Communist seizure of power was celebrated by Klement Gottwald from the balcony of the palác Goltz-Kinských (Goltz-Kinský Palace), his triumphant speech greeted by a banner-waving crowd of supporters and militiamen who more than filled the square.

The Astronomical Clock Every visitor to Prague stands below the **Orloj (Astronomical Clock)►►►**, which—on the hour, every hour—reminds the world in its inimitable way of the passing of time: Death opens the show, saints and the Savior process, Vice and Virtue, Turk and Jew nod and dance, and a rooster crows an ending. The clock was made in 1410, and its mechanism perfected in the 1550s; its centerpiece not only tells the time, it also gives the position of the sun and the moon and much more. Below is a splendid painted calendar showing saints' days, the signs of the zodiac, and the labors of the months.

The medieval Astronomical Clock

The Old Town Hall The ancient buildings of the Staroměstská radnice (Old Town Hall)►► make up a charming, if incongruous, whole. To the right of the Astronomical Clock, at second-floor level, is the oriel (bay) window of the Gothic chapel, inserted in 1381 into the merchant's house which had been taken over by the city council as its meeting place in 1338. To the left is the main entrance, a fine Gothic doorway added around 1480, and further along is a superb Renaissance window whose inscription, *Praga caput regni*, is a proud reminder of Prague's prime position in the kingdom.

Inside the entrance are wall paintings by Mikoláš Aleš of legendary events in the city's history. The upper floors (whose accessibility depends on the progress of reconstruction work) provide access to the old council chamber and the George Hall. An intermittently functioning elevator spares visitors at least some of the climb to the top of the 210-ft. tower, from which there is a panoramic view of the Old Town and of the whole city.

Projecting from the collection of buildings which make up the town hall is the dům U Minuty (House at the Minute), a medieval house rebuilt in Renaissance times when it was given its sgraffito (incised plaster) figures of mythological and biblical figures—some of the most stylish in town.

The south side The curving south side of the square is lined with imposing townhouses, some with the grand arcades that are so characteristic of the city. The Dům U Zlatého jednorožce (Golden Unicorn House) used to be a music school directed by Smetana; beneath its Gothic portal and arcaded vestibule are 13th-century Romanesque cellars. No. 16 is an exuberant 19th-century attempt to be more medieval than the Middle Ages. Dům U bílého jednorožce is another Unicorn House (this time a white one) that stands on the corner with Celetná street; next to it is the Týnská škola (Týn School), its creamy Renaissance façade and cheerful gables a perfect foil to the great stony mass of the church behind.

The Gothic dům U Kamenného zvonu (House at the Stone Bell)►► spent much of its life convincingly disguised as a Baroque building, burdening the architects with a painful choice of options when the time came to restore it. Hiding its embarrassment behind scaffolding for many years, it has emerged with renewed confidence in its ancient origins, its fascinating rooms housing the temporary exhibitions of the Prague City Gallery. From its courtyard there is a surprise view of the looming towers of the Týn Church (see page 138).

With the adjoining palác Goltz-Kinských (Goltz-Kinsky Palace)►► a sudden step is made from the burghers' town of the Middle Ages to the pomp and pretension of the 18th-century Prague Rococo style, all pastel colors and stucco work. Above the books and CDs on the first floor are rooms showing selections from the rich Graphic Collection of the National Gallery.

The Hus Memorial The marvelous Pomník Jana Husa (Jan Hus Memorial)►►, rising from the middle of the square, is worth more than a quick glance. Around the turn of the century, the Czech-run city council turned its thoughts to marking the 500th anniversary of the martyr-

Chez Kafka
The Goltz-Kinský palace is one of many places associated with Kafka. For a while the building housed a German-language *gymnasium* (high school), most of whose pupils were, like young Franz, from Prague's Jewish population. Later, his father rented part of the ground floor for his haberdashery shop. The tormented writer's birthplace is just off the square, marked by a bust attached to the building behind the church of St. Nicholas.

dom of Hus in a fitting way. They found the right man in Ladislav Šaloun, a young sculptor eager to create a memorial in his own version of the Secession style. The work was unveiled in 1915 to cries of outrage from Habsburg supporters (who found its Czech nationalist overtones unacceptable), from traditionalists (who would have preferred something more traditional), and from progressives (who would have preferred something more progressive).

Since then, Šaloun's masterpiece has become one of the city's great symbols; the Nazis decorated it with swastikas, and, in late 1968, it was dressed in black drapes to mourn the passing of the Prague Spring. Nobler looking than in life (he was very short), the tall figure of Hus presides with immense dignity over an extensive landscape peopled with groups of figures representing the Czech nation crushed (to his right) and arisen (to his left). The idiosyncratic lettering on the base of the memorial includes the words *Pravda vítězí!* (Truth will prevail!).

Centerpiece of the Old Town Square is the Hus Memorial

A plague on your column!
A Baroque column once stood in the Old Town Square, erected in 1620 to honor the Virgin and to celebrate the defeat that year of Bohemian Protestantism. When the Habsburg Empire collapsed at the end of 1918, an enthusiastic crowd pulled down what had become a symbol of Austrian oppression.

STARÉ MĚSTO

Space for a competition
The north wing of the Old Town Hall, built in a romantic style in the early 19th century, was completely destroyed by enemy action in the course of the liberation in May 1945. The grassy space where it once stood has now become very popular in a city center somewhat short on such amenities. Although it is still the city council's intention to replace the bombed building, it has become more and more difficult to decide on how to set about this task with the passing of time. Architects have responded enthusiastically to the several competitions that have been held, producing designs ranging from the pseudo-historical to bizarre-futuristic, none of them considered suitable.

The church of St. Nicholas In startling contrast to the somber sculpture of the Hus Memorial is the brilliant white façade of **Kostel svatého Mikuláše (St. Nicholas' Church)►►**. This was originally built in the early 13th century as a place of worship for the German merchants when they moved from their quarters in Na Poříčí to the new focus of commercial life around Old Town Square. Like so many of Prague's central churches, it was one of those hotbeds of Hussitism which was handed over to a reliable Catholic order in the early 1600s. In this case it was the Benedictines who benefited, at least until 1787, when their monastery was one of many dissolved by Emperor Joseph II.

Before that they had had the church rebuilt by the great Baroque architect, Kilián Ignác Dientzenhofer, who gave it its present appearance, a striking combination of twin towers and a dome. The main, south-facing façade was not meant to dominate the townscape as it does today; it was built along one side of the narrow lane leading out of the square, and was intended to impress with its verticality when seen from this vantage point. It has been left oddly exposed by the construction of Pařížská avenue, around the turn of the century, and by the destruction of the north wing of the town hall by German bombardment in 1945. Squeezed onto a very constricted site, the church looks bigger than it really is, but the interior, not much more than the space covered by the dome, is nevertheless impressive. St. Nicholas is now the central place of worship of the Czechoslovak Church, successor to the Hussites of old.

View into the lofty dome of Staré Město's church of St. Nicholas, the work of Kilián Ignác Dientzenhofer

Walk Southern Old Town

The processional route of the Bohemian kings, on their way to being crowned in St. Vitus's Cathedral, followed a long and rambling path along what is now known as the Royal Way. You can follow part of this route on a short stroll, starting from the site of the royal court where the Obecní dům (Municipal House) now stands on Náměstí Republiky.

See map on page 118.

Pass through the **Prašná brána** (**Powder Tower**) and head westwards along **Celetná street** into Staré Město (the Old Town). The crowds now consist of tourists rather than applauding or mocking citizens, and the medieval houses have long since been given stylish Baroque and Rococo façades. The procession would cross Staroměstské náměstí (Old Town Square) and Malé náměstí

(Little Square), then head for the river along crooked Karlova (Charles Street). You should do the same, as far as the angle Karlova makes with Husova třída.

Just to the right, built to dominate a square which never materialized, is one of the city's grandest residences, the Clam-Gallasův palác (Clam-Gallas Palace), its portal held up by straining Titans. Here you can either continue with the crowds heading for Karlův most (Charles Bridge), or you can turn left down Husova, past No. 19 with its Venetian gables, and stop off at its neighbor, the enormously popular (and hence crowded) bar, the U Zlatého tigra (Golden Tiger).

■ **Former Czechoslovakia was very much a country of minorities. In the interwar First Republic, Czechs formed about half of the population, followed by roughly equal proportions of Slovaks and Germans and then by smaller groups of Hungarians, Ruthenes, Poles, Jews, and gypsies. Most Jews perished in the Holocaust, and nearly all the Germans were made to leave after 1945, while the Czech–Slovak split of 1993 left the Czech Lands and Prague with few Slovaks and no Hungarians, but with a growing number of gypsies....■**

German ghosts

Though the German presence in Prague has diminished substantially, the German language is still very widely understood. Signs in German are beginning to appear again after a long banishment; the street-name war was won by the Czech-dominated city council in 1894, when the previously bilingual signs were nearly all removed and replaced by Czech ones. Just one or two were overlooked: in the castle area the street sign for Jiřská ulice (George Lane) is accompanied by ghostly lettering spelling out Georgi Gasse.

Gypsies arrived in Central Europe around the beginning of the 14th century to an often chilly welcome, practicing their nomadic way of life on the margins of settled society. Many were killed by the Nazis and, after World War II, the Communists made a concerted effort to resettle the gypsy population, seeking to persuade them of the benefits of assimilation. Large numbers were encouraged to migrate to the west of the country to help repopulate the empty Sudetenland. Here their unwillingness to adopt the industrious ways of the expelled Germans helped confirm the already strong prejudice against them, though many industries could not have done without their labor.

Estimates of the number of gypsies in former Czechoslovakia vary between 500,000 and a million, with the highest concentration in eastern Slovakia. After 1989, prejudice was further fueled when the gypsy presence in Prague and other cities became more obvious. In a country where the liberal tradition was brutally broken in 1948, political correctness is a tender plant, and prejudice is freely expressed: one beauty contestant gained the plaudits of the

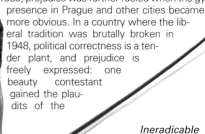

Ineradicable musicianship—a gypsy violinist

master of ceremonies, and of the studio audience, when she revealed on television that her ambition as a student lawyer was to clear out "black people" from North Bohemia.

Relegated to the very bottom of the social ladder, gypsies suffer the multiple social disadvantages of poor housing and health, illiteracy, and high infant mortality. In 1993 a further twist was added to their plight when a law was passed which refuses citizenship to anyone with a criminal record, no matter how trivial.

Vietnamese Another group who don't always find it easy to fit in are the Vietnamese, who originally came to work in Czechoslovakia and the other former Soviet bloc countries in return for aid given to their native land. Because of the difficulties at home, many do all they can to stay, working at whatever presents itself, often on the margins of legality, dealing in cigarettes and other contraband. There is a strong Vietnamese presence in the open-air markets of Prague and elsewhere in the Czech Republic.

Slovaks The break-up of Czechoslovakia has left many Slovaks stranded in Prague. In the past it had always been the policy to apportion government and other jobs equally; if a minister was Czech, his deputy would very likely be a Slovak (and vice versa). Many Slovaks with artistic and intellectual ambitions gravitated to the more cosmopolitan atmosphere of Prague, preferring it to that of "provincial" Bratislava. Forced to choose either Czech or Slovak citizenship, many opted for the former, giving great offence to their nationalistic-minded compatriots.

Greek ghosts
When the Communists were defeated in the Greek Civil War, many Greek partisans and their families fled to Yugoslavia. When this proved a less-than-congenial home because of Tito's defiance of Stalin, some moved on to a more sympathetic Czecho-slovakia. In the mid-1950s there were around 7,000 people of Greek origin in the country, some of them living in former German villages in northern Moravia which, for a while, had an entirely Greek character. The children of these refugees are now completely assimilated, two of them being famous as the pop-singing twins, Martha and Tena Elefteriadu.

The Estates Theater, a splendid setting for the première of Mozart's Don Giovanni

►► Stavovské divadlo (Estates Theater) 118C2

Ovocný trh

The only 18th-century theater in Central Europe to retain its original appearance, the Estates Theater first opened its doors in 1783 and will forever be associated with the name of Mozart, whose *Don Giovanni* had its first performance here four years later.

The neoclassical building, completely restored and reopened in 1991, dominates the newly pedestrianized spaces of the old Fruit Market (Ovocný trh). Its close neighbor is the Karolinum (see page 135), seat of the university, whose professors feared that the proposal of Count Nostitz to erect a theater here would infest the quarter with chorus girls (who doubled as prostitutes in the 18th century) who would distract the students from their studies. Nostitz went ahead nevertheless.

Carl Maria von Weber was the theater's director between 1813 and 1816; later it was associated with the Czech playwright, Josef Kajetán Tyl, whose comedy, *Fidlovačka*, was performed here often; this contains the song *Kde domov můj?* (*Where is my home?*), today's Czech national anthem. No visit to Prague is complete without attending a performance in these historic surroundings, invariably of a classical opera rather than contemporary theater.

► Uhelný trh (Coal Market) 118B1

In the early 13th century, the long strip of land between Staroměstské náměstí (Old Town Square) and the city walls was developed as an elongated marketplace, one end for fruit (Ovocný trh), the other for coal (Uhelný trh). For a while it formed a little municipality on its own known as Havelské město (Havel's Town). An immense medieval market hall, 600 ft. long, filled the space between the grand buildings lining Havelská and Rytířská streets where the little houses of V kotcích now stand. The hall has long since disappeared, but market traders still operate here daily. The triangular space of Uhelný trh itself is graced by a delightful classical fountain.

What's in a name?
The theater in the Fruit Market was originally named after its founder, Count Nostitz (Nostic in Czech), who intended it to be a thoroughly Germanic institution. It was in fact referred to as the "German Theater" for many years, before being renamed the Tyl Theater in honor of the composer of the Czech national anthem. After the theater was reopened in 1991 another (final?) change was made, this time to its 1799 name of the Estates Theater, referring to the fact that it was the theater of the aristocratic, estate-owning classes.

▶▶ **Uměleckoprůmyslové muzeum
(Decorative Arts Museum)** *118A3*

Ulice 17 listopadu 2

Set within a neo-Renaissance building, which does its best to look like the Louvre, the city's superb collection of Bohemian and European arts and crafts seems to attract few visitors, though this situation is likely to change as the extent and quality of its treasures become more widely known and, possibly, better housed.

The Czech contribution to the decorative arts seems to have climaxed in the early years of this century. Unfortunately, most of the museum's objects from this outstanding period are in storage, with only selections being displayed from time to time. Previously tolerated, this ridiculous situation is likely to change in the near future; in the mean time, the scope of the displays may well be widened by the use of temporary displays in the Rudolfinum and its neighbor, the School of Decorative Arts (see page 143).

Despite these shortcomings, the climb up to the second floor of this richly decorated, purpose-built palace of the crafts is well worth while for the excellent displays of furniture, glass, ceramics, porcelain, clocks, metalwork, and much else from Renaissance times to the 19th century. There is something here for everyone, from monumental pieces of Baroque furniture the size of small buildings, to the glassware for which Bohemia has always been famous. Prague was also one of the centers of the Biedermeier style, and there are fine examples here of its classically simple and elegant furniture.

157

The lavish interior of the Decorative Arts Museum almost overwhelms the exhibits

Havel's town
It would be nice to think that the name of Havelské město refers to some distant ancestor of the post-1989 Czech president, but the name is really just the Czech translation of St. Gall, a 7th-century Irish hermit, after whom the parish church of this part of town is named.

■ **Bohemia has always been known for the skill and ingenuity of its artisans, not least because of their longstanding tradition of metalworking and of glassmaking. The explosion of energy which accompanied the rediscovery of Czech nationhood in the late-19th and early 20th centuries also affected the whole range of decorative arts, helping to make the country one of the great centers of modern design and craft production....■**

158

Crafts and Communism
The achievements of the interwar period were not repeated under Communism, although there was no lack of support for official art. Work themes were, of course, popular, but often lacked the lightness of touch or simple humanity of the interwar artists, with too many studies of sturdy peasant girls and chisel-chinned tractor-drivers bringing in the harvest. Bombastic heroism, along Soviet lines, replaced careful observation or real sympathy in many monuments and memorials.

Karel Dvořák's jaunty Sailor, *a portrayal of the working man*

As with fine art and architecture, the outstanding contribution made by Czechs to the decorative arts is only just being rediscovered by a neglectful West, though it has to be admitted that keeping most of the national collection under lock and key for 40 years has not helped.

As the 19th century approached its end, Prague and the Czech Lands awoke from their provincial isolation and became aware both of international trends in design and of the rich heritage of local tradition and workmanship. Revival of historic styles—neo-Renaissance, neo-Baroque and Rococo—gave way to the nationalistically tinged realism of sculptors such as Myslbek, then to the swirling, organic forms of Art Nouveau, here termed Secese or Secession. Glassware in particular flourished, transmuting the forms and techniques of Emile Gallé into objects that are unmistakeably Czech in character, as in the products of the Loetz and Harrachov works.

An even more individual twist to artistic production was given by the foundation of the Association of Makers of Applied Art (Artěl) in 1908, an organization that aimed to give everyday objects—fabrics, furniture, books and clothes, toys and souvenirs—high aesthetic value. Artel's existence spanned four decades (it closed in 1934), overseeing several changes of style from Cubism to Functionalism; its objectives are best represented by the dynamic and optimistic period of the interwar era First Czechoslovak Republic.

Czech Cubism was not confined to painting and architecture, but resulted in strange and compelling objects of all kinds: the architect Pavel Janák designed furniture, wallpaper, coffee sets, and crystal-like pottery boxes as well as buildings, while some of the most extraordinarily angular furniture ever seen was made by another architect, J. Gočár.

The Paris Expo Czech achievements were recognized in the great Decorative Arts International Exposition held in Paris in 1925, when Czech designers and craftspeople came second only to France in the number of medals and prizes won. This little landlocked country may have lacked that icon of Art Deco, the transatlantic liner, but it excelled in the production of richly patterned glassware, ceramics, book-bindings, posters, metalwork, and jewelery.

Jaroslav Horejc's attractive figurines are paralleled by his dynamic, almost Celtic, brooches that feature

Sudeten specialties

The First Czechoslovak Republic inherited many of the industries of former Austria-Hungary, including most of its glass and ceramics factories. These were mainly located in Northern Bohemia, the old Sudetenland, an area almost exclusively inhabited by German-speakers, whose prosperity was based on a flourishing export trade. Households all across Europe once possessed porcelain from Carlsbad (Karlovy Vary), a tea-service or figurine from Dux (Duchcov) and glass from Gablonz (Jablonec) or Haida (Nový Bor). The Great Depression of the 1930s killed this trade; the region's impoverished and embittered German-speakers turned to the easy answers of Nazism, and thus contributed to the destruction of Czechoslovakia at the end of the decade.

Traditional glass-making techniques still survive today

subjects such as animals and athletic girls. The affluence implicit in Art Deco design did not exclude a sympathetic attention to the world of work and everyday life: the dignified and appealing sculptures of Otto Gutfreund and Karel Dvořák include the former's *Bobbin Woman* and the latter's wonderful whistling *Sailor*, as well as his *Foundryman* wiping the sweat from his brow. František Kysela worked with Marie Teinitzerová to create a stunning series of tapestries on the theme of work, in one of which (*Weaving*) a sheep is doing its best to help the weaver in his job at the loom.

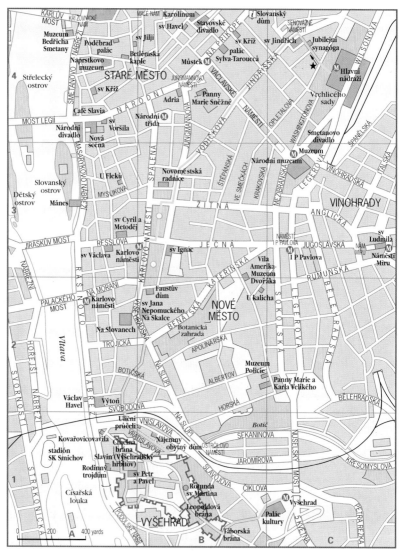

KARLŮV MOST · KŘIŽOVNICKÉ NÁM. · MALÉ NÁM. · Karolínum · Slovanský dům · i

Museum Bedřicha Smetany · Poděbrad palác · sv Havel · Stavovské divadlo · SENOVÁŽNÉ NÁMĚSTÍ

sv Jiljí · NA PŘÍKOPĚ · sv Kříž palác · sv Jindřich · Jubilejní synagóga

Náprstkovo muzeum · Betlémská kaple · Můstek · Sylva-Taroucca · WILSONOVA

STARÉ MĚSTO · JUNGMANNOVO NÁMĚSTÍ · VÁCLAVSKÉ · JINDŘIŠSKÁ · Hlavní nádraží

sv Kříž · Adria · Panny Marie Sněžné · NÁMĚSTÍ · Vrchlického sady

Café Slavia · Národní třída · sv Voršila · OPLETALOVA

MOST LEGIÍ · NÁRODNÍ · Smetanovo divadlo

Národní divadlo · Nová scéna · VODIČKOVA · Muzeum · ŠPANĚLSKÁ

Slovanský ostrov · U Fleků · Novoměstská radnice · ŠTĚPÁNSKÁ · KRAKOVSKÁ · MEZIBRANSKÁ · Národní muzeum · LEGEROVA · VINOHRADSKÁ · ITALSKÁ

Dětský ostrov · Mánes · MYSLÍKOVA · ŽITNÁ · VE SMEČKÁCH · VINOHRADY · ANGLICKÁ

JIRÁSKŮV MOST · sv Cyril a Metoděj · sv Ludmila · NÁM. MÍRU

RESSLOVA · JEČNÁ · NÁMĚSTÍ I P PAVLOVA · JUGOSLÁVSKÁ · Náměstí Míru

sv Václava · Karlovo náměstí · sv Ignác · KATEŘINSKÁ · Vila Amerika - Muzeum Dvořáka · I P Pavlova · RUMUNSKÁ

RAŠÍNOVO · NÁBŘEŽÍ · Faustův dům · U Kalicha · SOKOLSKÁ · BĚLEHRADSKÁ

PALACKÉHO MOST · Karlovo náměstí · sv Jana Nepomuckého Na Skalce · NOVÉ MĚSTO

Na Slovanech · BENÁTSKÁ · Botanická zahrada · BĚLEHRADSKÁ

TROJICKÁ · APOLINÁŘSKÁ

Vltava · BOTIČSKÁ · ALBERTOV · Muzeum Policie · Panny Marie a Karla Velíkého

HORSKÁ · BĚLEHRADSKÁ

Václav Havel · Výtoň · SVOBODOVA

Uliční průčelí · VNISLAVOVA · Botič · SEKANINOVA

Kovařovicova vila · VRATISLAVOVA · Chtěná brána · Nájemný obytný dům · OSTRČILOVO NÁMĚSTÍ

stadión SK Smíchov · Slavín (Vyšehradský hřbitov) · JAROMÍROVA

Rodinný trojdům · sv Petr a Pavel · SLAVOJOVA · ČIKLOVA · KŘESOMYSLOVA

Císařská louka · Rotunda sv Martina · Vyšehrad

Leopoldova brána · Palác kultury · PETRA REZKA

VYŠEHRAD · Táborská brána

0 — 200 — 400 yards · A · B · C

STRAKONICKÁ · HORŠEFÍ · SVORNOSTI · NA MORÁNI · SPÁLENÁ · NÁRODNÍ · NÁBŘEŽÍ · NA SLUPI · MA·STUPI · NUSELSKÝ MOST · 5 KVĚTNA

Opposite: St. Wenceslas stares down the square named after him

Right: the New Town Hall in Karlovo náměstí (Charles Square)

Nové Město Prague's modern, metropolitan lifeblood flows most strongly through the central streets of the New Town, especially in the area centered on Václavské náměstí (Wenceslas Square) and the "Golden Cross," the triangle it makes with the boulevards of Národní and Na Příkopě. Here are concentrated most of the stores and offices, cafés and hotels, bars, movie houses, and other places of entertainment frequented by the city's 1¼ million inhabitants, as well as their numerous visitors. Beyond this area the streets and squares planned 650 years ago by Emperor Charles IV still follow their original alignment, though most of the seemingly endless apartment houses lining them reflect the taste of the 19th century rather than that of the 14th century.

The New Town was the most ambitious of Charles IV's projects designed to turn Prague into a fitting capital for the Holy Roman Empire, whose crown he had inherited. It is the supreme example of medieval European town planning, flexible and farsighted enough to have accommodated all the changes of the succeeding 650 years. Part of the initial idea was to transfer some of the environmentally unfriendly activities of the Old Town (tanning, slaughterhouses, glue-making, metal-working, and so on) into more spacious surroundings, where they would not disturb students attending Charles's newly founded university, the Karolinum.

A pattern of streets was set out, centered on three marketplaces: a hay market, a horse market (today's Wenceslas Square), and a cattle market (now Karlovo náměstí—Charles Square). It was an instant success; within a few years, something like half the total area within the new walls was built up, and more than a hundred butchers were plying their messy trade in the stalls behind the Novoměstská radnice (New Town Hall), though the immigrant Jews the emperor attracted to the city preferred the intimacy of the old ghetto to the new quarters assigned them.

Orientation Both northern and western extremities of the New Town are bounded by the Vltava, at either end of its great bend; to the south is another natural barrier, the deep Nusle valley, crossed by the great bridge carrying metro trains and by the Magistral, the fume-laden expressway which seems to suck in the traffic of the whole metropolitan area. The highway runs along the line of walls the emperor had built to protect the eastern flank of his proud new city. Within these natural and man-made boundaries, the New Town extends over several square kilometres, and though it can be explored on foot, some of its attractions are far apart; this is one part of central Prague where judicious use of public transportation can benefit your sightseeing.

The Golden Cross The irresistible magnetism that the Golden Cross area exerts on strollers and sightseers has been recognized by the city authorities, who have kicked out the cars, ripped up the tramlines and laid down paving over much of the area. Wenceslas Square is no longer a through-traffic route, and although an eye needs to be kept open for the taxis roaring up and down, its central reservation now carries a floral display rather than trams.

   Crowds fill the wide tree-lined pavements, pouring in and out of the arcades and passageways to either side, or emerging from the subways which honeycomb the depths below. The swarming scene is surveyed from the top of the square by the huge Národní muzeum (National Museum) of 1890, just one of the city's great turn-of-the-century neo-Renaissance landmarks. The museum is complemented, on the riverbank, by the Národní divadlo (National Theater) of 1881, and, nearer at hand, by the Opera of 1888. The Hlavní nádraží (Central Station) of 1909 is a bold example of Prague Secessionist, or Art Nouveau, architecture.

Changing styles The New Town as a whole is something of a showcase for the architectural movements which followed one another in such rapid succession in the early

Leninist legacy
At the beginning of the 20th century, the early Baroque palace built by the architect Carlo Lurago for the Kinskys in the 1660s became the unlikely setting for the headquarters of the Czech Socialist Party. The comrades kindly made one of the back rooms available for the 1912 conference of the Russian Social Democrats, an occasion used by Lenin to engineer a Bolshevik takeover of the party. Inevitably, after 1948, the palace become Prague's Lenin Museum, with no fewer that 17,000 items relating to the life and work of the great man. Equally inevitably, the Vladimir Ilich memorabilia have now been removed from the public eye.

part of the 20th century. Most left their mark on Wenceslas Square, from the decorative extravagances of the Art Nouveau Evropa Hotel to the plate-glass and ferro-concrete functionalism of the Bata building.

The semi-suburban shopping street of Na Poříčí, in the north of the New Town, has the former Banka legií (Legionaries' Bank), perhaps the best example of that strange and uniquely Czech movement known as Rondo-Cubism (see page 209). Focused on Prague's second rail-road station, Masarykovo nádraží, this is a workaday part of town, though traces of more traditional architecture remain, such as the Baroque palaces named after the Kinský and Sweerts-Sporck families in Hybernská street.

Older buildings It is in the southern part of the New Town, around Karlovo náměstí (Charles Square) and beyond, that some hint can be sensed of the antiquity of Charles IV's new city. The Baroque buildings here include Dientzenhofer's masterpiece, svatého Jana Nepomuckého Na Skalce (St. John Nepomuk on the Rock), while in the square itself is the Novoměstská radnice (New Town Hall), begun in the 1360s. To the south is the Na Slovanech (Emmaus Monastery) still with its Gothic cloisters, as well as the Karlov monastery, its church modeled on Charlemagne's chapel at Aachen. The Muzeum Antonína Dvořáka (Dvořák Museum) is installed in the charming lit-tle 18th-century country house called the Vila Amerika, a reminder that parts of the New Town remained rural until the late 19th-century building boom.

A lifetime could be spent studying variations on the theme of the apartment building, but the most interesting specimens cluster by the riverside, particularly along Masarykovo nábřeží (Masaryk Embankment). Here, link-ing the embankment with the island known as Slovanský ostrov, is one of the monuments of the optimistic inter-war era, the Mánes Gallery, whose starkly functionalist white walls contrast with the dark stonework and onion dome of its neighbor, one of the old water towers which were used to feed the city's fountains.

At home with Havel
The post-1989 president used to reside in the top-floor flat at No. 77 Rašínovo nábřeží (Rasin Embankment). Just one of the cliff-like walls of apart-ment buildings that run all along the riverside from the National Theater to Vyšehrad, No. 77 was built by Havel's entrepreneurial grandfather. When released from one of his frequent spells in prison, Havel probably enjoyed more home comforts here than the policemen spying on his every move, who set up shop in a more or less permanent portacabin on the embankment.

163

The broad sidewalks of Václavské náměstí (Wenceslas Square) are always animated —with shoppers and strollers by day and night owls after dark

The Rondo-Cubist façade of the Adria Palace, dating from the early 1920s

► **Jungmannovo náměstí (Jungmann Square)** *160B4*

Metro: Můstek

This square owes its existence to there not being enough money to finish building the adjacent Chrám Panny Marie Sněžné (Church of Our Lady of the Snows—see page 184) whose nave would otherwise have occupied most of the space. It is a good place to draw breath between the excitements of Václavské náměstí (Wenceslas Square) and the more prosaic pleasures of Jungmannova třída (Jungmann Avenue) or Národní třída (National Avenue). The paved square features a statue of Josef Jungmann, but more remarkable is the Cubist street lamp. The authorship of this unique creation is disputed, but its crystalline surfaces still vibrate with the artistic excitements which suffused the early 20th-century city.

All around is evidence of the architectural innovation of that age. In the square itself is No. 17, a Constructivist building dating from 1938, but far more striking is the Adria Palace, built by Pavel Janák and Josef Zasche in the early 1920s; its first occupant was an insurance company, the Riunione Adriatica, a reminder of Prague's longstanding ties in Austro-Hungarian times with Trieste and the Mediterranean. The forbidding-looking and much blackened building is one of the key works of Rondo-Cubism, an experimental work prefiguring a planned transformation of the whole city which fortunately never happened. The palace is humanized to some extent by its sculpture, carried out by the likes of Jan Štursa, Otto Gutfreund, and Karel Dvořák. Its basement is laid out as a theater, which was for many years the home of the famous Laterna Magika (Magic Lantern—now in the Nová scéna building next to the National Theater).

Along Jungmannova třída is one of Prague's first truly modern buildings, the Mozarteum, built in 1913 by Jan Kotěra, while between 28 října and Perlová streets is the 1931 former Perla department store, one of those many Prague buildings that turn a corner with great aplomb.

Wordsmith Jungmann
An ardent patriot and indefatigable hunter through the archives, Josef Jungmann took 40 years to compile his amazing one-man dictionary of the Czech language, 4,500 pages long and published in five volumes between 1835 and 1839. The dictionary lifted Czech from its lowly status as a despised dialect to the level of a rich literary language, a point proved by Jungmann himself in his eloquent translations of Goethe, Schiller, Chateaubriand, and Milton.

■ **The mother of Prague museums, the Národní muzeum (National Museum—see page 178), presides over Wenceslas Square. This is one of those institutions where the architecture tends to overwhelm the exhibits, which here are meticulously arranged to celebrate the 19th century's genius for collecting and categorizing anything that moved (as well as much that didn't)**

Apart from the National Museum, Nové Město (the New Town) has a clutch of other collections. The little-known **Poštovní muzeum (Postal Museum)**▶ at Nové mlýny 1239/2, off Revoluční street in the central New Town, is an obvious must for philatelists, but not without interest for the way its exhibits illustrate the tortured course of recent Czech history.

Both the **Muzeum policie (Police Museum)**▶ at Ke Karlovu 1 and the **Vojenské muzeum (War Museum)**▶ at U Pamatniku 2 had to take a deep gulp after 1989 and decide how they were going to re-present themselves. The police have reorganized remarkably quickly and their slick displays present a clean-cut image of the force, worthy successors to the benign-looking blue-helmeted policemen of pre-war times; even so, their presence in the old Karlov convent overlooking the Nusle ravine still seems incongruous.

The military museum is housed in an interwar building at the foot of Žižkov hill, and the staff are still engaged in revising their version of Czech participation in this century's conflicts, whether through the Resistance or through service in other nations' armed forces, such as the Royal Air Force or the Red Army.

The most immediately appealing of all the New Town's museums, however, is the **Muzeum hlavního města Prahy (City Museum)**▶▶ at Na poříčí 52 (just beyond the overpass). Not only does it contain many mementoes of a past Prague, but it is also home to the incredible labor of love known as the Langweil Model, an amazingly accurate representation of the city as it was in the early decades of the 19th century (see panel).

Meticulous modeler
Antonin Langweil's 1:148 scale model of Prague is a fascinating record of the city of his time (the 1820s and 1830s). The cathedral (see page 59) is only half-completed and no one has yet thought of driving Pařížská through the ghetto. The riverside embankments and promenades are unbuilt, the watermills are all working, and the strange structures along the Vltava which look like modern offices or apartment buildings are great piles of timber, built up from the logs floated down the river by intrepid raftsmen.

165

Below: Post Office plaque from the early days of Czecho-slovakia

Left and top: items on display in the city's Police Museum

Memorial on Resslova, just off Karlovo náměstí, to Heydrich's assassins and the clergy who sheltered them (see panel opposite)

Defenestration No. 1
The old Prague habit of dealing with your opponents by hurling them from the nearest window got off to a good start at the New Town Hall in 1419. A Hussite crowd rampaging around the square had stones thrown at it from the town hall's windows. The infuriated mob, led by a cleric, Jan Želivský, stormed upstairs and threw the culprits, Catholic German councilors, out of the windows into the square, where they were crudely murdered. After due judicial process, firebrand Jan met his own fate, losing his head to the executioner's ax.

► **Karlovo náměstí (Charles Square)**   *160B3*
Metro: Karlovo náměstí

Until 1848 this vast expanse was known by the somewhat less dignified name of the Cattle Market, the biggest of the trio of marketplaces planned for his extensive New Town by Emperor Charles IV. Two of the main roads cutting through the square have names equally redolent of a countryside which for hundreds of years was only a short walk away; Žitná (Rye Street) and Ječná (Barley Street).

From the 1860s onwards Charles Square was beautified in a way which would no doubt have surprised the emperor; the efforts of Count Chotek and his landscape gardeners turned it into a tree-filled public park, populated these days by a considerable number of statues of famous Czechs, as well as by weary shoppers, hospital patients and commuters not yet able to face the metro ride home.

The New Town Hall Even though the square was chosen as the site for the **Novoměstská radnice (New Town Hall)►**, it never seems to have acquired the civic cachet or importance of either Staroměstské náměstí (Old Town Square) or Václavské náměstí (Wenceslas Square). A chapel in the center was used by Charles to display the crown jewels and the religious relics of which he was so fond. Later, the Hussites held their animated meetings around the chapel; it was here that their pact with Basle was proclaimed and the texts written on the walls in Czech and Latin. The chapel disappeared at the end of the 18th century, but well into the 1800s an odd assemblage of buildings occupied much of the center of the square, which was crossed by muddy trackways and used for exercising horses and storing timber.

The Town Hall was begun soon after the square had been laid out, probably in the 1370s. Unlike the Staroměstská radnice (Old Town Hall), which was formed from existing buildings, this was built from the start, though it had to be rebuilt more than once, particularly after a great fire in 1559. Its vaulted Gothic hall has survived, but the splendid trio of Renaissance gables was removed when the city was unified in 1784 and the mayor and all his men moved to the Old Town Hall. The building then suffered at the hands of various occupants—lawyers, scribes, and jailbirds—before its importance as an historic monument was recognized in the early 1900s and its traditional appearance was conscientiously restored.

St. Ignatius Most of the buildings lining the square are typical of the New Town; that is, undistinguished replacements, in various styles, of the structures that had stood there before being overwhelmed by the building boom of the late 1800s and early 1900s. Half of the east side is occupied by the Jesuits' New Town stronghold: their Kostel svatého Ignác (Church of St. Ignatius) and its adjoining college of 1667 correspond to the Old Town's Clementinum (see page 138). The college has been a hospital since the Jesuits were sent packing by Emperor Joseph II in 1773.

Faust House At the corner of the south side of the square stands a substantial town mansion with a promising name, the Faustův dům (Faust House). The house acquired its Faustian associations through the residence here, first of Prince Václav of Opava, who immersed himself in occult practices, then of the Englishman Edward Kelley, one of Rudolph II's band of alchemical adventurers. The man responsible for the "Baroquification" of what was originally a Renaissance building was a Count Mladota, whose own chemical experiments were probably innocent, but enough to confirm the mansion's sinister reputation.

Defeat by hosepipe
At 4 a.m. on the morning of June 18, 1942, the whole of the area west of Charles Square was cordoned off by the S.S. Their suspicion that the parachutists who had assassinated Reichsprotektor Heydrich were holed up in the crypt of the Kostel svatého Cyrila a Metoděje (the Church of Saints Cyril and Methodius) proved correct when the first troopers to enter the building were met with a hail of fire. All attempts to flush the defenders out failed until the fire department attempted to flood the cellars. Even then, the desperate men pushed the pipe out again using a ladder. Finally, though, they were overcome; as the water rose around them, they used their last bullets on themselves.

Statue of Jan Evangelist Purkyně, natural historian, in the Charles Square Gardens

The Vltava

■ **More than in many cities, Prague's river welds the different parts of the city together, joining just as much as it separates and defines. With its bridges, dams, old mills and waterworks, islands and embankments, it is an endlessly fascinating component of the townscape in its own right, as well as a potent source of myths and legends....■**

The Vltava in art

The Vltava is inextricably linked to the Vyšehrad rock and the legend of Libuše (see page 30) which was taken up so enthusiastically by the nationalistically inclined artists and poets of the Romantic period, though they tended to skim over the princess's propensity to use its waters as a waste-disposal unit for her discarded lovers. The most compelling poem to the Vltava, however, is a musical one, the second movement of Smetana's *Má Vlast* (*My Country*), in which the river's every mood is brilliantly evoked.

Ride in one of the pleasure steamers that ply the waters of the Vltava...

The young Vltava has two branches, one cold (the Studená Vltava) and one warm (the Teplá Vltava); both rise among the conifer forests of the Šumava uplands in Southern Bohemia. After winding around medieval Český Krumlov and leaving behind busy České Budějovice, the Vltava then runs for most of its course in a rocky wooded gorge, where a succession of dams has turned it from a wild watercourse into a series of calm lakes. Attractive tributaries, such as the Berounka and the Sázava, give an idea of what the untamed river must have looked like before hydroelectricity took its toll.

Below the bluff at Vyšehrad the river widens out, its calm surface a mirror for the city to admire itself in; it then narrows again as it is diverted eastward by the Hradčany–Letná heights. Another great bend swings it back on to its original course, creating a peninsula across which the Trojský zámek (Trója Château) on the far bank looks back towards Prague's castle. At Mělník, the Vltava's waters are absorbed by the Elbe (Labe in Czech), to flow eventually into the North Sea downstream from Hamburg.

Bridges The Vltava is one of the reasons for Prague's existence since its shallowness at this point made it relatively easy to ford. At the end of the 10th century the ford gave way to a timber bridge, succeeded by the Judith Bridge, the first bridge to be built of stone. This was itself

The Vltava

replaced in the 14th century by the incomparable Karlův most (Charles Bridge). Today, the city's bridges are among its glories; some of them, including the Art Nouveau structure named after Svatopluk Čech, are as ornamental in their own way as the Charles Bridge. Their sculptural decoration is best appreciated close up, but the finest general view is of several bridges in sequence seen from the lookout point at the western end of Letná plain.

Navigation The dams upstream have tranquilized the river's previous violent changes of mood. Spring floods used to sweep through the Staré Město (Old Town) until the town's whole level was raised at the end of the 13th century; the massive piers and sturdy cutwaters of the Charles Bridge remain as a testimony to former perils. The Vltava no longer carries much commercial traffic, though pleasure steamers and rowboats still animate its surface, along with the ducks and swans. Nevertheless, downstream from Prague the Vltava is still a navigable waterway of some importance for barges heading for Germany and other destinations along the far-flung European canal system. A huge port was built on the Vltava south of Prague some years ago, through which all the construction materials for the new Southwest Town passed.

Shaping the river The Vltava still supplies Prague with (not very palatable) water. In the old days, the stream was held back by dams (some of which are still very much in evidence) and its waters were distributed directly around the city from a series of water towers, such as those that survive on Novotného lávka and Slovanský island. The river also drove innumerable mills, of which there are a few picturesque traces on Kampa island.

Until the 19th century the riverbanks and islands changed shape and form constantly in response to the unpredictable river. Pioneer town planner Count Chotek began the process of stabilizing and beautifying the embankments in the early 1800s, and the islands were subsequently made to give up their tendency to wander all over the place. Members of Prague's 19th-century gun lobby used to hone their skills on Střelecký ostrov (Shooters' Island), today a pleasant park with unusual views of the city on either bank, while Štvanice island, where the gentry once hunted, is now the site of a sports complex.

River rafting
The construction of the dams in the middle reaches of the Vltava helped put an end to a centuries-old means of transportation. Right up to World War II loggers would lash rafts of timber together in convoys up to 600 ft. long and pole them downstream to the riverside yards in Prague which feature so prominently in Langweil's model of the city (see page 165), an adventurous journey which now seems to belong to another age altogether.

169

...or be more energetic and propel yourself in a rented row boat

Walk New Town to Vyšehrad

This long walk (allow three hours) takes you through the busy Nové Město (New Town) to its southern edge, where the old fortress of Vyšehrad offers one of the best (but least-known) panoramas of the city.

See map on page 160.

Start at the **Hlavní nádraží**, Prague's central station. This has had several names, originally being dedicated to the Habsburg Emperor Franz Josef. Then, in gratitude for the American President's help in ousting the Habsburgs and founding the First Czechoslovak Republic in 1918, it became Wilsonovo nádraží. Obviously unpalatable to the Communists, this title vanished in favor of plain Hlavní nádraží, which simply means Main Station, the name in general use today, though a plaque reminds us that the previous name of Wilsonovo nádraží was officially reinstated to mark the 1990 visit of President Bush.

The station buildings of 1901–1909 are one of the great monuments of the Prague Secession, lavishly ornamented inside and out by some of the leading decorative artists of the time. The temptation was resisted to sweep it all away when the expressway and metro were built in the 1970s, and on the whole the new reservations areas and concourses have been carefully integrated with the old structures. You should look into the grandiose departure hall with its half dome, and the high-ceilinged buffet is also worth a stop, whatever the state of the cooking or the clientele.

In Jeruzalemská street is one of the city's lesser-known synagogues, the Islamic-Revival **Jubilejní synagóga (Jubilee Synagogue)**, built in 1906 to replace others demolished during the redevelopment of the ghetto. **Senovážné náměstí (the Haymarket)** is one of the three great squares laid out in the New Town by Charles IV. It is guarded at its western end by Kostel svatého Jindřich (St. Henry's Church) and by a detached belfry, one of those archetypal Prague towers which owes more to the 19th century than to the Middle Ages.

The tramlines of busy Jindřišská street lead to Václavské náměstí (Wenceslas Square—see page 178), then along **Vodičkova street**. At No. 30 is the colorful Secessionist façade of what used to be Novák's department store, now a casino.

Park-like **Karlovo náměstí (Charles Square**—see page 166) offers a chance to recharge your batteries for the second part of the walk. Alternatively, you could walk down Resslova street to the **Kostel svatého Cyrila a Metoděje (the Church of St. Cyril and St. Methodius)**, where the parachutists responsible for assassinating Heydrich were cornered and killed (see pages 40 and 167).

On opposite sides of Vyšehradská street are the **Na Slovanech (Emmaus Monastery)** with its modern twin towers and the **Kostel svatého Jana Nepomuckého na Skalce (Church of St. John Nepomuk on the Rock)**, the latter making artful use of the steeply sloping terrain (for both see page 185).

The legend-encrusted height of **Vyšehrad** can be approached by means of Vratislavova street, or up the steep steps from the riverside. Some of Prague's unusual Cubist buildings cluster here; there are two (Nos. 2 and 30) in Neklanova street, which runs parallel to Vratislavova, and two more on the embankment, just before the riverside highway disappears through a romantic portal into the rock jutting out into the Vltava.

After exploring Vyšehrad and enjoying the views over the city and up and down the river, leave via the Táborská brána (Tábor Gate) and make for the giant Palác kultury (Palace of Culture) which overlooks the expressway spanning the deep Nusle ravine. This great monument to the pretensions of Communism is conveniently linked to Vyšehrad metro station.

Opposite: Prague's Secessionist main railroad terminal

Below: the Smetana Theater, now renamed the State Opera

Banks of Bohemia
In the last decades of the 19th century, the grim struggle between the competing Czechs and Germans was, in part, fought out on the unlikely battlefield of banking. To counter German and Jewish domination of industry and commerce, banks such as the Zemská built up huge capital reserves from the savings of Czech investors, which were then invested in specifically Czech enterprises. The architectural and decorative splendor of the Zemská was just as vigorous an expression of confident Czech nationalism as that of the National Museum.

► **Na Příkopě (On the Moat)**   160B4

Metro: Můstek or Náměstí Republicky

Running from the "Golden Cross," along the line of the Old Town fortifications, to the Obecní dům (Municipal House) in Náměstí Republiky (Republic Square), this is one of the capital's main streets, now partly pedestrianized and always full of shoppers, tourists relaxing, and customers coming in and out of the numerous banks.

The moat referred to in the name of Na Příkopě (On the Moat) formed part of the Old Town's defenses until it was filled in in 1760 and laid out as a carriageway with trees planted along it in boulevard style. Newly fashionable, it was lined with aristocratic palaces, most of which gave way, in the late-19th and early 20th centuries, to the palaces of commerce which determine its present-day character.

As the German population of Prague declined, they made Na Příkopě ("Der Graben" in German, on the model of Vienna's famous thoroughfare) the focus of their social life, particularly for the *corso*, or Sunday promenade. It was here that the students from the nearby German University would ostentatiously parade their colors, and woe betide any incautious Czech who challenged them—although many did! There was a German House and a German Casino as well as a number of cafés and restaurants, some of whose descendants are still very much in business.

Palatial premises The street begins with a bang at No. 1, a glass 1980s building from whose rooftop disco music blasts out over the whole of the Golden Cross area. The clock comes from the old department store which stood on the site. More mundane concerns are dealt with behind the granite façade of the State Bank (No. 3), a sober structure of 1908. No. 4, built in 1870 in Empire style, was originally the city's first department store, the Dům elegance, the "House of Elegance;" it is held in place by a slender sliver of the big Koruna palace which turns the corner with Vaclavské náměstí (Wenceslas Square).

An idea of what the townscape looked like before the building boom of the late-19th century is given by the finest remaining palace, No. 10, the Sylva-Tarouccâ palace, designed by Kilián Ignác Dientzenhofer in the 1740s for the Piccolomini family of Siena. Opposite, at No. 7, above the Restaurant Pelikán, is what remains of the Secession façade of the 1905 U Dorflera building. On the corner with Panská street is the Kostel svatého Kříže (Church of the Holy Rood), an unusual (for Prague) Neoclassical

Stalwart figures stand atop the parapet of No. 3 Na Příkopě, the address of the 1908 State Bank

No ornamentation was too elaborate for the early 20th-century Zemská Bank

Literary cafés
Much of Prague's literary life in the early part of the 20th century was led in the cafés frequented by authors and journalists, as well as their admirers and hangers-on. The German-speakers' favorite café was the Arco, and they prided themselves on their nickname of "Arconauts." The Czechs preferred the Union, affectionately known as the "Unionka," but common ground was found in the Slavia. The Arco still exists (at Hibernská 16), the Union gave way to an office building in the 1950s and the fate of the Slavia, in the hands of private owners, is currently uncertain.

structure of 1824. It faces one of the city's more famous holes, a "prime site awaiting redevelopment," which for many years was used as a yard by the builders involved in the construction of the metro system.

Nekazánka street is crossed by a bridge linking the two halves of what was once Bohemia's best-known bank, the Zemská (Provincial—now called the Živnostenská banka). To the right is the later section, in Neo-Renaissance-cum-Secession style, built 1911–1912 and adorned with a decorative mosaic. The principal part of the bank is grander altogether. Its architecture is full-blooded Neo-Renaissance, its interior ornamented with a lavishness comparable to that of the Národní muzeum (National Museum). Grand stairs lead from the vestibule, with its paintings by Max Švabinský, up to the main banking hall. Business proceeds apparently undistracted by the glamor of the surroundings—mosaic floor, statuary, stained glass, coats of arms, and paintings of *Thrift* and *Industry*. The entrance is guarded by statues of Slav warriors of fiercer and more convincing mien than the harmless-looking security men beside them.

Next door to the bank, at No. 22, is the old Vernier palace, once the cultural redoubt of the Germans but since 1945 renamed the Slovanský dům (Slavonic House), with restaurant, café and exhibition halls. Na Příkopě comes to an end with a cluster of somewhat faceless banks and administrative buildings, poor compensation for the cafés full of turn-of-the-century chatter that they replaced.

■ Towards the end of the 19th century, tired of the endless recycling of historical styles—Neo-Gothic, Neo-Renaissance, Neo-Baroque—designers and architects turned to new sources for inspiration, particularly to nature. The rigid rules of the architectural pattern book gave way to sensuous and colorful ornamentation based on flowing, sinuous lines. Like its Viennese counterpart, the Czech contribution to this movement became known as Secession (*secese* in Czech), and it marked the Prague townscape with some of its most distinctive buildings....■

Universal art
Art Nouveau conceived of itself as an all-embracing movement in the arts, and its traces can be seen in engineering structures such as the Čechův most (Svatopluk Čech Bridge). This bridge is guarded at both ends by figures perched on pylons, with other sculptures facing up- and downstream; it also has specially designed lampposts and railings which do far more than merely fulfill a functional purpose.

The flowing female form was a favorite Secession subject

The first building to appear in the new style was No. 12 Václavské náměstí (Wenceslas Square), the Peterkův dům (Peterka House), designed in 1898 by Jan Kotěra, who had worked with the great Viennese architect, Otto Wagner. Here the decorative scheme is still relatively sober, but further up the square, on the opposite side, is the far more prominent presence of the Evropa (Europa) Hotel of 1903, as sumptuous inside as it is out. Its high-ceilinged café is always crowded with locals as well as sightseers sampling its authentic turn-of-the-century ambience.

The 1903 department store known as U Nováků, in nearby Vodičkova street, is the equal of the Evropa in ornamental extravagance, with a huge mosaic by Jan Preisler flowing over its façade. The building is now a casino and nightclub. Its architect was Osvald Polívka, who was also responsible for the far-from-identical twin office buildings in Národní třída (National Avenue); the more decorative No. 9, built for the publisher Topič, is close to the German Jugendstil in spirit, while No. 7, the old Prague Assurance building, was influenced more by the Viennese Secession.

The Municipal House The structure which set the seal on the Prague Secession was not a hotel, shopping complex or an office building, but a local government office. The Obecní dům (Municipal House—see page 144) was commissioned by the city council in 1903 as a multi-purpose building with halls, galleries, meeting-rooms, restaurants and many other communal facilities. Given that the Czech Lands had not yet gained their independence, the Municipal House was also intended to be one of the representative buildings of the Czech nation. It fulfilled this role with a display of the utmost lavishness. Polívka, together with Antonín Balšánek, was the architect, working with a team

of artists, designers, and sculptors whose names—Mucha, Preisler, Šaloun, Špillar—were a roll-call of the progressive artistic establishment of the day.

The central station Of less symbolic importance perhaps than the Obecní dům, but hardly less lavish, was the main railroad station, completed in 1909. Named at first after Emperor Franz Josef and later after the American President Wilson, it has twin towers, a great domed entrance hall, and restaurants and buffets now largely abandoned in favor of the fast food-stuffs available in the vast underground concourse added in the 1970s.

Ingenuity and ornament
Buildings such as the Obecní dům are among the monuments left by what was a fairly short-lived movement (it did not survive World War I), but they are far from alone in a city which was experiencing a building boom at the time. All over the center, and more particularly in the closely packed tenements of the Nové Město (New Town) and the inner suburbs, can be found examples of Art Nouveau ingenuity and ornamental exuberance, often difficult to distinguish beneath a coating of grime. Look out for such wonders as the pair of gloriously rounded female figures distracting visitors to No. 96 Široká street, or their skinnier sister in Kaprova street (both in the Old Town).

Top: detail from the Art Nouveau concourse of the Hlavní nádraží (Main Station), designed by Josef Fanta in 1909

Detail from the Čechův most bridge

František Bílek
This highly individual artist exercised a considerable influence on his contemporaries, including the sculptor of the Jan Hus Monument, Ladislav Šaloun. Frustrated by color-blindness, Bílek gave up painting and turned to sculpture and architecture, designing his own villa in Hradčany (Mickiewiczova 1). The house, its setting and its contents are permeated with Bílek's intense religious feeling, and are intended to symbolize summer, the Egyptian-style columns representing ripening ears of corn. Bílek's work can also be seen in the cathedral (see page 63), and his sculpture of *Moses* stands near the Staronová synagoga (Old-New Synagogue—see page 132).

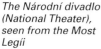
Fiery drama

Not long after its opening performance the National Theater was burnt down, probably because of a fire started accidentally by workmen putting the finishing touches to the roof. The nation rallied around and within months the money needed for rebuilding had been collected again. Reconstruction was supervised by Josef Schultz, who subsequently built the Národní muzeum (National Museum), and the project was completed very quickly, enabling the theater to be reopened within two years.

The Národní divadlo (National Theater), seen from the Most Legíí

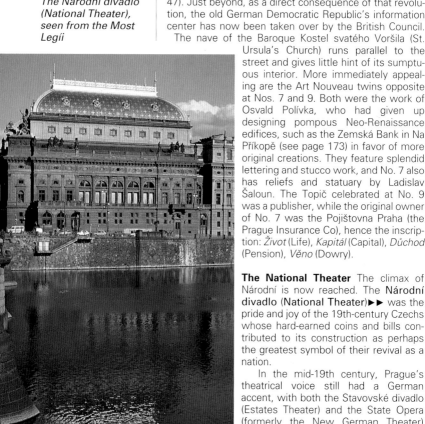

► **Národní třída (National Avenue)** 160A4

Metro: Můstek or Národní třída

Like Na Příkopě (see page 172), this important city-center street, with its stores, offices, and institutions, was laid out along the line of the Staré Město (Old Town) walls in the late-18th century. It runs from Jungmannovo náměstí, in the east, to the huge pile of the Národní divadlo (National Theater), brooding over the Vltava to the west.

Marking the eastern end of the street in almost as emphatic a way as the National Theater is the chunky mass of the Adria palace (see page 164). Few of the buildings along Národní can compete with this Rondo-Cubist fortress for sheer presence. The Empire-style structure on the north side, No. 37, built 1813–1825, is the great-grandfather of the countless apartment buildings built in Prague subsequently, while the 1970s K-Mart/Máj department store is a triumph of rational planning rather than a distinctive contribution to the townscape.

The sidewalk on the south side is arcaded in places, and beneath one of the arcades is a small bronze memorial. This marks the site of the so-called "Massacre" of November 17, 1989, when a student demonstration was viciously put down by the riot police, the incident which became the overture to the Velvet Revolution (see page 47). Just beyond, as a direct consequence of that revolution, the old German Democratic Republic's information center has now been taken over by the British Council.

The nave of the Baroque Kostel svatého Voršila (St. Ursula's Church) runs parallel to the street and gives little hint of its sumptuous interior. More immediately appealing are the Art Nouveau twins opposite at Nos. 7 and 9. Both were the work of Osvald Polívka, who had given up designing pompous Neo-Renaissance edifices, such as the Zemská Bank in Na Příkopě (see page 173) in favor of more original creations. They feature splendid lettering and stucco work, and No. 7 also has reliefs and statuary by Ladislav Šaloun. The Topič celebrated at No. 9 was a publisher, while the original owner of No. 7 was the Pojišťovna Praha (the Prague Insurance Co), hence the inscription: *Život* (Life), *Kapitál* (Capital), *Důchod* (Pension), *Věno* (Dowry).

The National Theater The climax of Národní is now reached. The **Národní divadlo (National Theater)**►► was the pride and joy of the 19th-century Czechs whose hard-earned coins and bills contributed to its construction as perhaps the greatest symbol of their revival as a nation.

In the mid-19th century, Prague's theatrical voice still had a German accent, with both the Stavovské divadlo (Estates Theater) and the State Opera (formerly the New German Theater) producing their performances in that

The glittering interior of the National Theater is decorated with allegorical and historical themes by leading artists of the late-19th century

language. In 1868 František Palacký laid the foundation stone of the building that was to put an end to what, for patriotic Czechs, was an intolerable situation. The structure was designed by Josef Zítek, architect of the great classical colonnade at Carlsbad (Karlovy Vary). Working with him were the cream of the country's artistic talent, painters and sculptors, such as Aleš and Myslbek, who came to be known as the "National Theater Generation."

The riverside site helped the building become an instant landmark, but Zítek angled its enormous bulk so that from the street it forms a pleasing but not overwhelming composition with the bridge and Petřín hill beyond. The sculptures crowning the cornice proclaim the theater's high importance, while the interior is sumptuous in the extreme, covered in wall and ceiling paintings, crowded with statuary, and with a stunningly painted stage curtain by Vojtěch Hynais.

The theater was opened with a triumphal performance of Smetana's *Libuše* in 1881. By the 1960s it was showing signs of wear and its technical facilities had become outmoded. Finally, it was closed down for six years, while restoration took place. Reopened in 1983, the refurbished theater gives as much pleasure as before, though controversy still rages about its new annexe, the Nová scéna; built using glass blocks, this extension certainly makes an odd contrast to its senior partner.

Save the Slavia!
Opposite the National Theater stands the Café Slavia, long famous as a meeting place for intellectuals and their hangers-on, and celebrated in the poetry of Nobel-Prize-winner, Jaroslav Seifert. Its post-1989 closing (by new foreign owners) was a terrible culture shock for its old habitués, who included the president. The owners' indifference to their promise to restore the place to its former character at first provoked outrage and then, in autumn 1993, resulted in action. The keys were found and the Slavia was "occupied." Accumulated trash was cleared away and coffee served to anyone who cared to join in. This "occupation" was only temporary and the Slavia remains closed, although an eventual reopening seems probable.

(Map labels:)

NA MŮSTKU
PROVAZNICKÁ
ČKD dům
28 ŘÍJNA
NA PŘÍKOPĚ
Můstek
palác Koruna
Lindt
Ambassador
Bata
Zlatá husa
Peterkův dům
Juliš
Adria
Assicurazione - Generali
Alfa palác
Můstek
JINDŘIŠSKÁ
VODIČKOVA
Družba
Melantrich
VÁCLAVSKÉ NÁMĚSTÍ
Lucerna palác
Evropa
ŠTĚPÁNSKÁ
Jalta
VE SMEČKÁCH
OPLETALOVA
KRAKOVSKÁ
sv Václav
Muzeum
WILSONOVA
MEZIBRANSKÁ
Národní muzeum
LEGEROVA
0   100 yards

►►► Václavské náměstí
(Wenceslas Square)   160B4

Metro: Můstek or Muzeum

Almost half a mile long, this world-famous focus of city and national life is really more of a tree-lined boulevard than a square. Its pavements and carriageways rise gently towards the statue of St. Wenceslas, poised on his horse in front of the long façade of the Národní muzeum (National Museum). No traces remain of the original buildings lining what Emperor Charles IV's town planners called "the Horse Market," a name that stuck until 1848. By then lined with Baroque and Rococo houses, the square had acquired such airs and graces that the old name seemed completely inappropriate; it was therefore rechristened in honor of the nation's patron saint. The building boom of the late-19th and early-20th century left its mark on the square, and for architecture enthusiasts it is now an unparallelled open-air museum of that vibrant time in the city's history.

Wenceslas Square vibrates with life today, though not always of the most salubrious kind. Filled with shoppers and strollers during the day, it becomes the haunt of every category of night owl when darkness falls. Czechs tend to dwell with relish on its nocturnal perils, but there is probably more risk to your person from the sausages on sale from the sidewalk booths than from any other quarter, though it is prudent to take precautions.

Historical events The most popular place to gather is the lower (northern) end of the square, but the best overall view is from the terrace in front of the National Museum. The Staroměstské náměstí (Old Town Square) may have been the theater for many of Prague's older historical dramas, but Wencelas Square has attracted some of the bigger audiences of modern times. The riots and near-revolution of 1848 started here, after thousands had assembled in the lower part of the square to attend a "Slavonic Mass." On October 28, 1918 the First Czechoslovak Republic was proclaimed from the base of Wenceslas' statue.

In March 1938 the Wehrmacht's panzer tanks intimidated the shocked onlookers while the planes of the Luftwaffe roared overhead. The Communists set up their May Day stand here and, in August 1968, the initially bewildered Soviet tank crews came to a halt here among the tens of thousands of milling protesters. A year later, Jan Palach chose a spot near the Wenceslas statue to commit his act of self-immolation. There were protests again in November 1989, broken up by riot police at first but gradually increasing in confidence; finally a crowd of perhaps half a million roared in triumph at the balcony appearance of Václav Havel and Alexander Dubček that marked the demise of the Communist regime.

The National Museum In August 1968, frightened by a car backfiring, a Soviet gunner raked the façade of the National Museum with heavy machine-gun fire, traces of which can still just about be made out. This lack of respect for one of the country's great institutions has stuck in Czech craws ever since, for the **Národní muzeum (National Museum)**►► is second only to the

Magisterial highway
The Magistral, which slices north–south through the city, is laid out along the line of the city walls. Never nice to be near, it has helped siphon traffic away from the city center, but on the down side is the resulting isolation of the National Museum and its neighbors, the strange 1970s Federal Parliament building and the State Opera.

179

Národní divadlo (National Theater) as a symbol of the 19th-century Czech revival. The museum was founded in 1818 by Count Kašpar Šternberk, though the building dates only from 1891, erected on the site left vacant by the demolition of the old Horse Gate that once stood here. It stands four-square on its elevated site, topped by a splendid gilded dome, but unhappily isolated from its immediate surroundings by the never-ceasing tide of traffic rushing north and south on the Magistral expressway.

Pedicab drivers await the tourists

Wenceslas Square rises gently towards the National Museum

NOVÉ MĚSTO

Another Wenceslas
The goatee-bearded bust of Václav (= Wenceslas) Havel surveys the interior of his Lucerna palace complex with a wry smile of satisfaction, as well he might. Havel was a developer, as well as a contractor, and the family fortune was founded on this key piece of city-center real estate, along with the equally futuristic leisure complex (restaurant, dance-floor, swimming pool) built on a cliff overlooking the Vltava at Barrandov, upstream from Prague.

Fulsome figures adorn the approach to the National Museum

Exploring the National Museum The National is one of those museums whose architecture is at least as important, if not more so, than its collections. The allegorical sculptures above the fountain outside (*Bohemia*, *Vltava*, *Elbe*, and so on) are relatively modest compared to the almost overwhelming pomp of the interior, which is approached by successive flights of extremely grand stairs. Beneath the dome is the vast Pantheon, with its large-scale historical paintings, innumerable busts and statues of Bohemian worthies, not to mention a tiled floor of great beauty.

The collections (Numismatics, Theater, Mineralogy, Paleontology, Zoology) are often written off as old-fashioned and boring (although the Prehistory Department is, oddly enough, very modern!); it is true that their spirit belongs to another age but this could be regarded as a source of fascination in its own right—the endless arrays of mineral specimens, for example, are displayed in showcases as old as the building itself.

The exhibits are, in any case, so extensive that everyone should find something of interest, and if enthusiasm flags there are unusual views down the square to the north (and somewhat less appealing ones into the unkempt tenements of Vinohrady to the south). The museum has a changing program of exhibitions using objects not normally on display, and these are often more stimulating than the main galleries. A final positive factor is that the museum opens its doors on Mondays when everything else is closed.

The statue of Wenceslas A statue of the country's patron saint stood in the square for many years before being replaced by the present version, the masterpiece of Josef Václav Myslbek (1848–1922), the greatest Czech sculptor of his age. His work on the **Wenceslas Statue▶▶** lasted many years, from its conception in 1887 up to its unveiling in 1912 and beyond, since the four statues of the other patron saints of Bohemia were only completed in the 1920s.

Wenceslas was originally to be portrayed as a rough-and-ready hero from the early days of Slavdom, but as the project advanced, and as the idea of a Czech nation

The Secessionist splendor of the 1903 Evropa Hotel

became more sophisticated, the horseman became the vigilant figure we see today, his lance erect and his sprightly steed poised to carry him, not into a sentimentalized past, but towards a hopeful future. The polished granite plinth is decorated with a simple frieze and is guarded by a wonderfully chunky chain. Just down the hill is the impromptu shrine (now institutionalized) to Jan Palach and other victims of Communism.

The Evropa The architecture of the upper end of the square is bland in comparison to the flamboyance of the museum. The 1950s Jalta Hotel on the right brings a breath of the Soviet seashore into this landlocked Central European metropolis, but the star of the scene is undoubtedly the Grand Hotel Evropa of 1903. One of the landmarks of the Prague Secession, it has a façade of great delicacy and intricacy which rises above the glazed arches of its famous first-floor café to culminate in a mosaic-encrusted gable and a roof ridge crowned with clusters of gilded eggs. The interior of the café retains all the atmosphere of the pre-World War I era, though locals are likely to be far outnumbered by tourists willing to pay the entrance fee now demanded.

Opposite the Evropa, between Štěpánská and Vodičkova streets, is one of those building complexes so typical of downtown Prague, deeply penetrated by the arcades which create an exciting, enclosed world of cafés, movie houses, boutiques and bars, dance-halls and nightclubs, a preview of the city of the future as conceived by the visionaries of the early 20th century. The visionary in this case was a practical one, Václav (or Vacslav) Havel, the enterprising engineer grandfather of the post-1989 president. The Wenceslas Square façade of his Palac Lucerna (Lucerna Palace) is very varied, and ranged with it is the Neo-Renaissace Wiehl House of 1896, with sgraffito decoration by Mikoláš Aleš, and the splendidly self-confident former Bank of Moravia of 1916, which turns the corner into Štěpánská street.

The Night of Wenceslas
This is the title of a thriller by Lionel Davidson, set in the sinister Prague of the 1960s. Innocent but ingenious hero Nick evades entrapment by the secret police by disguising himself as a waiter amid the seedy splendor of a hotel clearly modeled on the Evropa.

Můstek metro

The whole of the lower part of Wenceslas Square is hollow, consisting of an underground concourse which is the 1970s contribution to Prague's peculiarly labyrinthine character. The square's metro station, a busy interchange between lines A and B, is called Můstek (Little Bridge). This is a reference to the medieval bridge that crossed the moat in front of the Old Town walls, remains of which were unearthed during the construction of the metro and which are now displayed in the wall on the landing at the top of the main escalator, far beneath present ground level.

The tower of the 1914 Koruna palace at the corner of Na Příkopě and Wenceslas Square presents a more sober side of the Secession

Revolution balcony At No. 36 is the Melantrich publishing house; it was from the balcony of this building that Dubček and Havel spoke to the crowd in November 1989, marking the end of Communist rule in Czechoslovakia. The building housed the offices of the Socialist paper, *Svobodné Slovo* (*Free Word*), an appropriate enough location from which to celebrate, among other things, the rebirth of free speech.

Across Vodičkova from the arcade of the Lucerna palace, you can dive directly into another network of passageways. These lead to the Alfa palace, the secret heart of the severe-looking U Stýlbů building (1929) fronting on to the square, with the Alfa movie theater and Semafor theater in the basement deep below. At the back of the building is one of the city's most delightful surprises, the newly and expertly relandscaped Františkánská zahrada (Franciscan Garden—see page 125), providing welcome relief after too much sidewalk-pounding. Next door to U Stýlbů is one of the square's few surviving 18th-century buildings, the Adria Hotel, sparklingly renovated after a long period of decline.

Further north along this side of the square is a trio of early modernist buildings which have helped inspire so many nondescript imitations that it is easy for the lay person to overlook them. First comes the Hotel Juliš at No. 22, designed by Pavel Janák in 1931, then two stores; No. 6, the Bata store (for long the Dům obuvi, or House of Shoes) has now reverted to its original owners, the shoemaking company founded by Tomáš Bata and based in Zlín, the town dreamed up by Bata in the interwar period as an industrial Utopia. Like No. 4, the Lindt department store, it is a reinforced-concrete structure, and was one of the first in the city to proclaim its wares with ultramodern neon advertising slogans.

In contrast to these bastions of functionalism are two fine examples of that Art Nouveau delight in decoration which so offended the austere modernists among Prague architects: No. 12, the Peterkův dům (Peterka House) of 1898, is an early work by Jan Kotěra, while No. 8, The Golden Leg, with splendid sculptures holding up its bow window, is a pharmacy.

On the far side of the square, Secession style gives way to the Art Deco of the interwar years, though both the Ambassador and the Zlatá husa (Golden Goose) hotels date from before World War I. The corner with Na Příkopě is

presided over with considerable dignity by the tower of the Koruna palace of 1914.

This northern end of Wenceslas Square, the junction with 28 října and Na Příkopě, known as the Golden Cross, is one of the favorite places for Praguers of all kinds and their visitors to gather. Trams heading to all parts of the city used to stop here, but their rails have long since been torn up and replaced by tasteful paving, while most of their former passengers now travel by the metro far below.

► **Vila Amerika (Villa America—**
   Dvořák Museum)   *160B3*
Ke Karlovu 20
Metro: IP Pavlova
The southern part of Nové Město (the New Town) remained undeveloped well into the 19th century, a place of gardens, orchards, and even farmland. In 1720, Count Michna built a little summer palace here, an elegant two-story edifice set in a formal garden and flanked by a pair of pavilions. His architect was Kilián Ignác Dientzenhofer, newly returned from a long apprenticeship abroad, and his design has something of the light-heartedness, as well as the discipline, of the French château about it. The arcadian surroundings which persuaded Michna to build here have long since disappeared, but his pleasure palace was restored in the 1950s and turned into a delightful setting for the Dvořák Museum, which displays manuscripts, letters and photographs of the composer and his friends.

Batagonia
The Moravian shoemaker Tomás Bata made millions by supplying the Austro-Hungarian army with boots during World War I. He invested his wealth in the futuristic city of Zlín, using the most advanced architects of the time to create an extraordinary industrial Utopia which still looks modern today. Zlín, and Bata himself, were among the symbols of the First Czechoslovak Republic, being progressive, liberal, and dynamic in character. The Communists renamed the place Gottwaldov, after the first Communist Prime Minister, but it is now known as Zlín again.

183

Count Michna's country retreat, now the Dvořák Museum

■ When Emperor Charles IV laid out Nové Město (the New Town) in 1348, some Romanesque churches already stood among the fields now enclosed by the new city walls, or fringing the old road running south along the banks of the Vltava. Charles's comprehensive planning made provision for additional parish churches for the greatly expanded population, and convents for all the monastic orders not yet represented in the city, such as the Benedictines, the Carmelites, the Lateran canons, and the Servites....■

Charles's pet project
Charles IV intended to make Prague a fitting capital for the Holy Roman Empire of which he was ruler. The Karlov monastery church was no exception. Its octagonal nave is a copy of the 9th-century Imperial Chapel at Aachen, built by Charlemagne, the first head of the Holy Roman Empire.

Top and below: medieval art from Emmaus Monastery

The Emperor's vision left the New Town with an array of churches scattered all over its wide area, their number augmented by new building in the Baroque era. Some existing churches were "Baroqued" too, but others remain in their original Romanesque or Gothic state, reminders of the great age of this "new" town and of the even older settlements that predated it.

Ancient foundations The most striking of all the New Town's places of worship is the prettily named **Panny Marie Sněžné (Our Lady of the Snows)**, which used to dominate the lower part of Václavské náměstí (Wenceslas Square) until shut out of the scene by the ostentatious buildings of the turn of the century. The church still surprises, both inside and out, with its sheer height, even though it now only consists of the Gothic choir of what would have been a huge edifice taking up virtually all of today's Jungmannovo náměstí (Jungmann Square).

The church was founded by Charles IV in 1347, one year before the building of the New Town was officially begun. Three years later came a parish church for the northern part of the New Town, **svatého Jindřich (St. Henry's)** in Jindřišská street, not far from the older **svatého Petr (St. Peter's)** in Biskupská street, originally the church used by the colony of German merchants established in this part of town. Both buildings have detached bell-towers, and were subject to the attentions of the over-enthusiastic restorer, Josef Mocker, in the late-19th century.

Baroque theatricals No. age built or rebuilt churches more enthusiastically than the Baroque. The Jesuits built their collegiate New Town base complete with its sumptuous

church of **svatého Ignác (St. Ignatius)** on Karlovo náměstí (Charles Square) in the 1660s, while the Ursulines planted their convent on Národní Avenue in the 1670s, followed by their church—**svatého Voršila (St. Ursula)** at the beginning of the 18th century.

Prague's most prominent Baroque architect, Kilián Ignác Dientzenhofer, designed what is perhaps his masterpiece, **svatého Jana Nepomuckého Na Skalce (St. John Nepomuk on the Rock)** on Vyšehradská street; set on a restricted, steeply sloping site, this is a dynamic composition of almost sculptural sophistication, with twin towers canted inwards rising over a double staircase. Dientzenhofer also seems to have been responsible for **svatého Cyrila a Metoděj (Saints Cyril and Methodius)**, a massive presence in Resslova street, the place where the assassins of Heydrich met their doom (see pages 40 and 167).

Monasteries Among the monastic foundations brought to the New Town by the emperor were the **Na Slovanech (Emmaus Monastery)**, opposite St. John Nepomuk on the Rock, and the **Karlov**, on Ke Karlovu street, whose deep-red domes overlook the Nusle bridge. Na Slovanech was badly damaged in one of the city's few World War II air raids, but retains a medieval cloister with fine wall paintings. In the 1960s it was given an extraordinary twin spire of twisting concrete.

Baroque altar in the Church of Our Lady of the Snows

PRAGUE SUBURBS

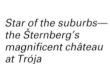

Star of the suburbs—
the Šternberg's
magnificent château
at Trója

ČERNÝ VŮL

STATENICE

KAMÝCKA

SUCHDOL

HOROMĚŘICE

SEDLEC

BOHNICE

LYSOLAJE

TROJ

Zoologická
zahrada

Trojský-
zámek

PŘEDNÍ
KOPANINA

3

NEBUŠICE

BABA

Hotel
International

6

Šárecký potok

DEJVICE

Stromovka

VOKOVICE

EVROPSKA

BUBENEČ

7

Vodní nádrž
Džbán

OŘECHOVKA

MILADY HORÁKOVÉ

Letenské
sady

1

STŘEŠOVICE

HRADČANY

DOL
LIBOC

VELESLAVÍN

Vila
Müller

MALÁ
STRANA

JOSE
STARÉ
MĚST

BŘEVNOV

RUZYNĚ

Letohrádek
Hvězda

Benediktinský
Klášter

6

380m

VÝPICH

Bílá hora

BĚLOHORSKÁ

NOVÉ
MĚSTO

2

MOTOL

ŘEPY

PLZEŇSKÁ

PLZEŇSKA

5

Bertramka

Pivovar
Staropramen

KOŠÍŘE

SMÍCHOV

Kostel svatého Petr a Pavel
& Rotunda svatého Martina

368m

STODŮLKY

Na Vidouli

RADLICE

VYŠEHRAD

JINONICE

5

5

BRANÍ

ŘEPORYJE

Dalejský potok

HLUBOČEPY

1

BARRANDOVU

BARRANDOV

Pivovar
Braník

E50

MALÁ
CHUCHLE

HODKOVIČ

OŘECH

1

SLIVENEC

VELKÁ
CHUCHLE

MODŘANY

ZAD
KOPANINA

A

LOCHKOV

B

Prague suburbs Until the 19th century, urban growth was contained within Prague's 14th-century walls. Vineyards came right up to the edge of town and these later gave their name to a built-up suburb, laid out in the late-19th century, known as Královské Vinohrady, meaning "Royal Vineyards," or **Vinohrady** for short (see page 201).

Much earlier, the Bohemian kings and aristocracy had enjoyed country pleasures in areas set aside for that purpose; the Královská obora (Royal Enclosure), now the Stromovka—see panel on page 204—to the northeast of Hradčany dates from Charles IV's time, while to the west, in 1555, another royal park was provided with a most unusual hunting lodge in the shape of a star, called **Letohrádek Hvězda (Star Castle**—see page 195).

At the end of the 17th century, Count Sternberg constructed one of the great palaces of Prague, not in town but beyond the Vltava to the north. His superb Baroque **Trojský zámek (Trója Château**—see page 200) is to Prague almost what Versailles is to Paris. By this time, others were venturing into the countryside, building villas and converting farmsteads into summer residences.

PRAGUE SUBURBS

Suburban charms The charming old vintner's house called the **Bertramka** (see page 191) dates from this era; in 1784 it was bought as their summer place by Mozart's Prague friends, the Dušeks, and this is where the composer stayed whenever he came to the city. The Bertramka is in Smíchov, a name synonomous with factories and breweries today, although the area was once rural. The name Smíchov originates from *smiech* (mixed), a result of the mixed population who settled on plots of land belonging to the medieval monastery that once existed here.

Late 19th-century Prague grew rapidly, and even more so in the 20th century. The city's first industrial suburb was Karlín, bordering the Vltava to the east of the New Town. It was originally centered on the medieval village of Zabransko, but was renamed after Empress Karolína Augusta in 1817, soon after a hospital had been built in the district along the lines of Les Invalides in Paris. A riverside port was laid out and in 1845 the first railroad nudged its way into town, carried on a long, low viaduct into what is now Masarykovo nádraží (Masaryk Station). Today a vast district of heavy industries stretches out eastwards far beyond Karlín to Vysočany and Hloubětín.

To the south, Karlín is overlooked by the rocky spur of **Na Vrchu Žižkově** (Žižkov hill—see page 210), named after the great Hussite commander Jan Žižka, who defeated the armies sent against him by pope and emperor on this spot. The hill is crowned by his statue, set in front of the Národní památník (National Memorial), built as a memorial to World War I Czechoslovak legions and then taken over as the mausoleum of the Czechoslovakia's Communist nomenklatura. At the foot of the hill is the modern Vojenské muzeum (Military Museum).

Žižkov's name was also given to the proud working-class suburb which merges with Vinohrady. Here, among the endless middle-class apartment houses, stands the Kostel Nejsvětějšího Srdce Páně (Church of the Most Sacred Heart of Our Lord) of 1933, the greatest single work erected in Prague by the Yugoslav architect, Josip Plečnik.

Suburban struggles
Armies have never much liked street fighting, and most of Bohemia's invaders have preferred to do battle well outside the city walls. In 1620, 200 years after Žižka's stalwart defense of Vítkov hill, in what might be termed a replay, his countrymen were soundly trounced by imperial forces of Ferdinand II; the Battle of the White Mountain was fought on open land to the west of Hradčany, and the emperor's men only entered the city once it had been vacated by their opponents.

The statue of Jan Žižka, who gave his name to Žižkov hill

Cemeteries Beyond Vinohrady, to the east, are the city's biggest cemeteries, the **Olšanské hřbitov** (Olšany Cemetery) and the **Židovsky hřbitov** (New Jewish Cemetery—see page 202); among the innumerable graves are those of Jan Palach (in the former) and Franz Kafka (in the latter). Another cemetery was laid out in the last years of the 19th century on **Vyšehrad** (see page 206), the legendary rock that overlooks the Vltava river to the south of the New Town; the Slavín was intended to be the Pantheon of the Czech nation, and here are buried many authors and artists of all kinds who have enriched the country's cultural life.

Vyšehrad is also the name of the district running along the southern rim of the Nusle valley, which remained unbridged until the great Magistral expressway and metro viaduct was built in 1973. The valley is dominated by the great cement-faced mass of the **Palác kultury** (Palace of Culture—see panel on page 194), the Communist citadel completed in 1981.

Modern architecture Many of Prague's most fascinating modern buildings are located in the suburbs. Vyšehrad has its cluster of Cubist structures, while in **Barrandov** (see page 190), on the western bank of the river, are the famous film studios and the futuristic leisure complex known as the Barrandove terasy (Barrandov Terraces). The western suburbs have the city's most attractive (and expensive) houses. Barrandov has its streets of progressive villas, and there are other villa communities to the northwest of Hradčany in the **Dejvice** area (see page 191), notably at Baba and, in an earlier, less rigorous garden city style, at Ořechovka.

Below Baba is Prague's only thoroughgoing example of Soviet-style Social Realist architecture, the International Hotel, trapped in a 1950s time-warp. The other great landmark of that troubled time, the Stalin statue, was demolished in 1962. The huge figure of the dictator used to dominate the city from its plinth on Letenské sady (Letná plain— see page 194), some of which is laid out as parkland, while part formed the bleak location for the May Day parades of Communist times.

To the east of the plain is the **Národní technické muzeum** (National Technical Museum—see page 195), and east again the Holešovice district, its gloomy tenements looking like a chunk of the inner city that has jumped the river. Here are located Prague's Exhibition Grounds, the **Výstaviště** (see page 202), site of the great 1891 Expo.

189

Middle-class villas in the garden suburb of Ořechovka

Joachim Barrande
Barrandov perpetuates the name of the 19th-century French refugee who combined the role of railroad promoter, geologist and tutor to the Comte de Chambord, Pretender to the throne of France. Barrande is best remembered here for his meticulous geological studies of the limestones that create the rugged scenery of the Vltava gorge and the surrounding area. Barrande also left his huge collection of fossils to the Národní muzeum (National Museum—see page 180).

▶   **Barrandov**   *186B1*

Metro: Smíchovské nádraží, then Bus 105, 246, 247 or 248 to Terasy

What was once Czechoslovakia's Hollywood lies high up above the Vltava just south of Smíchov, among a tangle of main roads and railroad lines. Unlike its Californian counterpart, the center of the local film industry didn't just grow, but was laid out in 1927–1933 according to a sophisticated scheme prepared by the appropriately named town planner Max Urban. As well as the famous studios, his plan incorporated a Functionalist villa quarter and a futuristic leisure center, the Barrandovské terasy (Barrandov Terraces).

The villas are some of the most fascinating examples of interwar architecture to be seen in and around Prague, lining streets with names like Lumièrů and Filmašská. The Barrandov Terraces perch on a limestone cliff overlooking the river; incorporating clubrooms, a café, an open-air restaurant with dance floor and a swimming pool, they are an extraordinary fusion of architecture and landscape, topped by a landmark lookout tower, though sadly the complex has been neglected and only superficially restored.

▶▶▶   **Benediktinský Klášter**
(Břevnov Monastery)   *186A2*

Off Bělohorská ulice, 3km west of Hradčany
Metro: Malostranská, then Tram 22 to Břevnovský klášter
Břevnov is the site of one of most ancient of Bohemia's religious foundations, the Klášter svatého Markéty (Monastery of St. Margaret). In 1993 this monastery celebrated its 1,000th anniversary; its Benedictine monks had returned from their Communist-imposed exile only three years previously. According to legend, the monastery was built close to a clear spring by Prince Boleslav II and Bishop Vojtěch (or Adalbert) after they had shared the same dream. Břevnov became an important nucleus from which Christianity was spread throughout early Bohemia.

The pre-Romanesque crypt of the very first abbey church can be seen beneath the floor of its early 18th-century Baroque successor. The latter was built by Christoph and Kilián Ignác Dientzenhofer, and is a building of great calm and spaciousness, now fully restored. Other sumptuous buildings are gradually being reopened to the public; they include a superb ceremonial hall with ceiling paintings by the great Kosmas Damian Asam of Bavaria. Decades of neglect have left the Dientzenhofers' Baroque gardens a shadow of their former selves, but the delightful pavilion by the legendary spring is being restored.

The Baroque interior of the 1,000-year-old Břevnov Monastery

▶▶   **Bertramka (Mozart Museum)**   *186B2*
Mozartova ulice 2, Smíchov
Metro: Anděl, then Tram 4, 7, 9 or 58 to Bertramka
Prague was once surrounded by a ring of pleasant farmsteads to which the leisured classes would repair to enjoy

their summer weekends. A few have survived more or less intact, though there is little about their present surroundings to evoke the picturesque past.

Among these retreats is the restored Villa Bertramka, which belonged to Mozart's dearest Prague friends, the Dušeks. Mozart stayed here in 1786, in 1787, and again in 1791, the year of his death; it was here that he rushed the *Don Giovanni* overture to completion the night before the opera's première. The villa has been faithfully restored to its 18th-century appearance (it almost burned down in the 19th century) and is fitted out with Mozart memorabilia, including a piano on which it is quite possible he may have played.

▶ **Dejvice** 186B3

Metro: Dejvická

Emerging from the metro station you will find yourself by the city's biggest rotary, Vítězné náměstí (Victory Square). From here Jugoslávských partyzánů runs north to náměstí Družby (Friendship Square). Here stands Prague's salute to Social Realism, the wedding-cake Hotel International, a faithful copy of Stalinist structures such as the main university building in Moscow. Conscientiously decorated inside and out by some of the most able (and Party-approved) artists of the time, the hotel exhales the authentically oppressive atmosphere of 1950s Communism.

The turnaround in architectural thinking that the hotel represented can best be appreciated by visiting some of the "progressive" housing areas that were developed in the optimistic days of the interwar First Czechoslovak Republic; on the hill northwest of the International, for example, is the Baba Colony with its array of individually designed Functionalist houses and a fine view over the city (see also page 208).

Mozart memorabilia in the Villa Bertramka, where the composer completed his opera, Don Giovanni

Day of doom
Beyond Brevnov, to the west of Prague, stands the White Mountain, a desolate plain rising over 1,000 ft., where a decisive battle took place in 1621 between the Protestant Czechs and the Catholic forces of the Holy Roman Emperor. Defeat for the Protestants came swiftly. Within an hour their ranks were broken and the soldiers fled back to Prague in disorder. Their Winter King, Frederick, took a day to pack his bags (they filled a mile-long wagon train) before he, too, fled.

Living in a panelák

■ Something like half of Prague's population live in the high-rise complexes which seem to hem the capital in on all sides and which contrast so starkly with the historic buildings of the city center and with the more human scale of the older suburbs. Most of the apartment buildings were built from prefabricated concrete panels—hence their nickname, *"panelák."* In architectural and town planning terms, *paneláks* are completely unimaginative, but nevertheless they do offer many desirable amenities, particularly to those who do not possess them....■

Prague seems always to have had an acute housing problem, and in the period after World War II the authorities cast around for cheap and quick ways of solving it. The first developments to go up consisted of conventionally built low-rise apartment buildings, arranged in groups of around 1,000 units. Some of these can be seen on the airport road at Ruzyně, looking no better or worse than their counterparts elsewhere.

High life in Prague

The housing drive really got under way in the late 1950s, when prefabrication, on the Soviet model, became *de rigueur*. Factories would be set up on site to produce the panels, which were assembled by crane into towers, or slab blocks, usually five to seven stories in height, but sometimes reaching 12 stories. The method is only economical with long production runs, and the resulting housing areas are huge, with populations of up to 140,000. Their names reflect the anonymity of the environment they created—Severní město (North Town), Jižní město (South Town) and, biggest of all, Jihozápadní (Southwest Town).

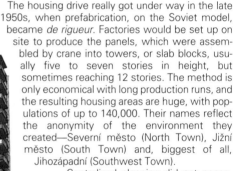

Centralized planning did not necessarily mean that amenities were smoothly scheduled to appear at the same time as the housing; new inhabitants often had to wait years for basic facilities, such as stores and schools, let alone landscaping and recreation areas. Many residents had to commute long distances in overcrowded buses or trams because no provision had been made for local employment.

There were some benefits, however, especially in comparison with old-style tenements which lacked bathrooms and had only communal kitchens; *panelák* dwellers at least had light, air (marginally less polluted than in

the city center), space, warmth, and hot water, the latter pumped from the district heating plants whose pipelines snake so strangely across the landscape in places. Rents were low and the hot water was unlimited.

Unsolved problems Over a period of 40 years nearly 250,000 apartments were built by the state or by cooperatives, although the building of *paneláks* was stopped in 1990/1991. In spite of this impressive achievement, shortages continue; young people are forced to live with their parents far longer than either generation would wish, and the luckless partners in a divorce frequently find themselves sharing the same accommodation indefinitely. For tens of thousands of people, it is only the possession of a second home that makes their housing situation bearable. On the edge of town, or deep in the countryside, the chalet or cottage provides an escape from ever-present neighbors, an opportunity to practice some do-it-yourself construction and create an individualized habitat, however temporary, without reference to the Housing Department.

Your own panelák Visitors to Prague may well find themselves accommodated in a *panelák* (see page 236 for details). If so, look upon it as an interesting way of experiencing at first hand how the ordinary citizens of the country live. The bleakness of the external environment often contrasts with the carefully created comforts and general hominess of the interior of the apartment, conceived though it may have been by planners and engineers as no more than a "machine for living in." Vandalism is far less of a problem than in equivalent projects abroad, and the inhabitants of a particular building will almost certainly conform to the *domácí pořádek* (*Hausordnung* in German, house rules in English) setting out a routine for the cleaning of communal spaces and so on.

Rent rises
Since 1992, rents in the publicly owned housing sector have begun to rise, and it seems unlikely that housing subsidies will continue indefinitely. The lavish heating arrangements, whereby the inside winter temperature has to be kept down by opening the windows, will probably be an early casualty.

193

Room with a view

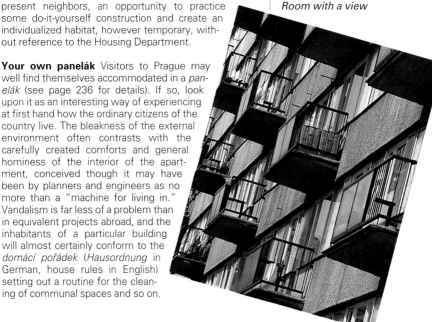

Palace of Culture
Another gross monument to Communist aspirations is the huge Palác kultury (Palace of Culture), looking across the Nusle valley towards the Nové Město (New Town). Begun in 1969, it was intended to mark the townscape in a monumental way, a Hradčany for the Party. No longer guaranteed well-drilled capacity audiences, the Palace of Culture is today struggling to fill its vast spaces, such as the 3,000-seat Congress Hall. The view north from its terraces is worth the walk up from Vyšehrad metro station.

This gilded goddess welcomes visitors to the Hanava Pavilion on Letná plain

► **Letenské Sady (Letná Plain)**   186B3
Metro: Malostranská, then Tram 18 or 22 to Chotkovy sady
The Letná plain presents an almost cliff-like face to the Vltava and the Svatopluk Čech Bridge below. A choice of paths leads up the landscaped slopes from the riverside embankment to the lip of the plateau. Here, a king-sized metronome ticks away where once a huge statue of Stalin stood, glaring balefully down to Pařížská on the far bank. The troupe of workers, peasants and soldiers lined up in solidarity behind the 31,000-lb. granite giant was nicknamed "The Meat Line" by irreverent Praguers.

Stalin and his supporters stood for seven long years, from 1955 to 1962. After the dictator had been denounced by Krushchev, his presence here became too embarrassing even for hard-line Czech Communists, and the monstrous figure was demolished—not without some difficulty, as it had been built to last.

Pavilions and parades More cheerful memories cling to the other structures overlooking the river and the city. To the west is the Hanavský (Hanava Pavilion), a lighthearted contribution to the 1891 Expo, now a discothèque. To the east is its circular steel-and-glass successor, the award-winning Czechoslovak pavilion from the Brussels Expo of 1958, now a panoramic restaurant.

The bleak spaces of the Letná hinterland are backed by the big Sparta stadium, scene of popular weekend markets as well as soccer and other sports. When Václavské náměstí (Wenceslas Square) became too cramped for the mass parades of May Day, the Communists set up their stand on the Letná, and it was here, too, that the biggest anti-Communist demonstration took place during the tense days of the Velvet Revolution.

►► **Letohrádek Hvězda
(Star Castle)**   186A2
Bílá hora (White Mountain), 6km west of Hradčany
Metro: Malostranská, Trams 22 to Bílá Hora, then Bus 179 to Libočka
This star-shaped hunting lodge, a fanciful essay in Renaissance geometry, was built in 1556 for Ferdinand, Archduke of Tyrol and Governor of Bohemia. Severe outside, its interior was lavishly fitted out to provide a luxurious setting for the revelry that invariably followed a good day's hunting. The vaults have some of the most sumptuous stucco work to be seen anywhere, but the days of revelry have long since gone, and the building is now a conscientious, but rather dull, museum to the 19th-century novelist Alois Jirásek, the "Bohemian Walter Scott," and to the painter, Mikoláš Aleš.

▶▶ **Národní technické muzeum**
(National Technical Museum)   *187C3*

Kostelní ulice 42
Metro: Vltavská, then Tram 1 to Letenské náměstí
This faceless building belies its fascinating contents, much of whose appeal is cultural as well as technical. The focal point of the museum is the great glass-roofed central hall. Here fragile flying machines, suspended from the ceiling, contrast with an array of railroad engines and vintage and veteran automobiles arranged on the floor. All around this focal point run several tiers of galleries, crammed with models and transportation memorabilia of all kinds.

A giant metronome now ticks away on Letná plain where Stalin's statue once stood

Explosive charge

One aspect of Czech technology little dwelt on in the Technical Museum is the armament industry. Czech weaponry has long been famous; the British Army's standard light machine gun for many years was the Bren, designed in **Br**no and manufactured under license in **En**gland. The virtually undetectable and locally-produced dynamite substitute known as Semtex has also achieved worldwide fame, or rather infamy.

The technological triumphs of interwar Czechoslovakia on display in the great hall of the National Technical Museum

Car crazy The Czech Lands were the industrial power-house of the Austro-Hungarian monarchy, and the inter-war Republic built on this heritage, producing heavy machinery of all kinds and becoming the fifth largest manufacturer of motor vehicles in Europe. Here is the special V12 6-litre Tatra 80 built in 1935 for President Masaryk, as well as the streamlined pre-war prototypes of the sinister black and bulbous Tatra limousines in which high Party functionaries were chauffered around in the 1950s and 1960s. Foreign names are represented too, such as Bugatti and Mercedes, and there is a wonderful Soviet 1952 Zis 110B, built like a Stalinist skyscraper.

Railroad development got off to a good start in Bohemia, though at first motive power was supplied by horses rather than steam. The nags were up and trotting along the 80 miles of the Linz–Budějovice line by 1828, though the Prague–Plzeň line only got as far as Lany before being abandoned. The first steam train puffed into Prague in 1845, but it was only at the start of the 20th century, at the zenith of steam, that handsome locomotives were built like the big express engine 375 007, fit to haul the Neo-Renaissance dining car constructed in the Smíchov workshops for the imperial family.

The Czechoslovak aero-industry was built up from scratch after World War I; by the late 1930s it was

producing business-like, but never-to-be-used bombers and fighters. The museum also covers navigation, including the barges that brought timber down the Vltava from the Bohemian Forest, and that curiosity, the Czechoslovak sea-going fleet, whose biggest vessel is the 33,000-ton ore carrier, *Košice*.

Other galleries in the museum deal in a surprisingly comprehensive way with such matters as time, sound, photography, geodesy, and astronomy; there is also a metallurgy section and a scale model of a coal mine.

▶   **Smíchov**   *186B2*

Metro: Smíchovské nádraží

One of Prague's oldest suburbs, Smíchov was industrialized with such enthusiasm in the 19th century that little trace remains of the rural arcadia which induced Mozart's friends, the Dušeks, to settle here at the Villa Betramka (see page 191). The Dušeks are buried in the local cemetery, the Malostranský hřbitov, a neglected spot that will appeal to all lovers of decay. Otherwise the place is known for its railroad station (the terminal for suburban trains), for the Staropramen brewery (founded in 1869), and for the Red Army tank, set on a plinth as a monument to Soviet tank soldiers, that used to grace náměstí Kinských (Kinský Square—see panel).

The Smíchov tank in its embarrassing coat of paint—see below

The pink Panzer
A T34 tank once stood, with its gun barrel cheerfully erect, in what used to be called náměstí Sovětských tankistů (Soviet Tank Crewmen's Square). This, according to official propaganda, was the first tank to roar into Prague on May 9, 1945, when Red Army tanks were a much more welcome sight than those that arrived in August 1968. No one quite knew what to do with the memorial after 1989 until the artist, Dávid Černý, came along and painted it pink (he was also the perpetrator of the German Embassy's four-legged Trabant—see page 108). The embarrassed government cleaned it up, but some members of parliament were outraged at this timidity and used their immunity from prosecution to color the unfortunate armored vehicle pink again. The tank has since been removed, to blush in private.

Bohemian beer culture

■ "The best beer in the world" is not a claim to be taken lightly, but even the most partisan drinker of his local brew may be inclined to change his mind when confronted with the superb beers brewed in the Czech Republic. These are by no means limited to the famous products of the breweries at Plzeň (Pilsen) and České Budějovice (Budweis); beers of equivalent quality are brewed all over the country in a hundred or so breweries. Some of these national institutions are, however, being threatened with foreign take-overs, so drinkers beware!....■

Dark monopoly

Prague's fourth brewery is the smallest in the country. Founded in 1499, U Fleků is named after Jakub Flekovský, who took over the ancient pub and beer garden in 1762. A compulsory stop on every tour-operator's circuit, U Fleků can seat 900 drinkers inside and out. Waiters continually resupply the happy guests with half-liters (pints) of the pub's own brew, a dark 13° beer only available here (it is supposed not to travel well).

Beer has been brewed in Bohemia since time immemorial. The first written records mention the names of brewers resident in Malá Strana in 1088, a trio named Sobik, Sesur, and Caston, and a maltsters' guild was formed in the Old Town in 1357. By this time Bohemian beer was already famous, not least because of the quality of the Žatec hops from which it was—and still is—made; the town of Žatec, in the north of the country, had long been shipping its products down the Elbe to Hamburg, where they were the stars of the annual Hop Fair. In Emperor Charles IV's time it was forbidden to export cuttings taken from these superlative plants.

Beer from Prague was in demand in Vienna, while the brew from Domažlice found favor as far away as Augsburg. Scientific treatises of the time reflect the seriousness attached to beer drinking; in 1585 Rudolf II's personal physician wrote a weighty tome entitled *De Cerevisia* (*On Beer*), while modern principles of production were established both by František Poupě (in his 1794 work *The Art of Beer Brewing*) and by the splendidly named Prague Polytechnic professor, Karel Josef Napoleon Balling. It was natural that the world's first brewing college and a research institute should find their home in Prague.

Monastic heritage It was those nodes of early medieval civilization, the monasteries, that first brewed beers commercially. The beer cellar called U Tomáše, attached to the old monastic foundation of St. Thomas's in Malá Strana, is a reminder of those days, though it no longer brews its own beers. Later, the citizens of free towns often had the exclusive right to brew and sell beer in their own boroughs, a monopoly challenged by enterprising aristocrats, such as the Schwarzenbergs, who set up their own breweries.

The great days of Plzeň began in 1842, when a group of such citizens amalgamated their rights and founded the "Burghers' Brewery" (*Bürgerbräu* in German, *Měšťanský pivovar* in Czech) whose Urquell/Prazdroj has slaked thirsts worldwide ever since. By the 20th century the Czechs' capacity for consuming and producing beer could only be challenged by the Germans and the Belgians. On

average, each inhabitant of Bohemia and Moravia is still responsible for putting away some 40 gallons a year, though in the case of some of the types encountered in Prague pubs, this figure can be exceeded in the course of a month without obvious strain.

Czech breweries have dropped in number from a total of 800 at the beginning of the century, to today's still-impressive 100. Prague, which used to have 35, now has four. The biggest (in Prague and in the country) is the Staropramen brewery in Smíchov. Founded in 1869, it produces what for many is a typical Czech beer, magically combining lightness and clarity with a full body and distinct flavor, a world away from the "Eurofizz" of some beers. Two other breweries in Prague whose products are worth sampling are the První pražský měšťanský pivovar in Holešovice, and the big Braník brewery in the suburb of the same name.

See you in the Chalice
The Chalice, U kalicha, was one of the Good Soldier Švejk's favorite watering holes. It was here that the Austrian secret police picked him up, allegedly for denigrating Emperor Franz Josef whose fly-encrusted portrait stood over the bar.

Card-playing imbibers in Wenceslas Square

Zámek and **hrad**
Zámek is usually translated in English by that non-English term, château. *Hrad* invariably refers to a fortified castle or stronghold, but *zámek* normally implies something less austere, a place for enjoying life rather than just sheltering from your enemies. A big *zámek* might be called a palace, a smaller one a country house or mansion. Infused as it is with the spirit of the French Baroque, Trója wears the name of "château" well.

The south, or garden front of the Trója Château

▶▶ **Trojský zámek (Trója Château)** *186B3*

U trojského zámku

Metro: Holešovice, then Bus 112 to Zoologická zahrada
Completed in 1685, and still sparkling from a recent thorough restoration, Trója and its gardens epitomize the Baroque taste for expansive living. They are Prague's closest equivalent to Versailles, but Trója is aristocratic, not royal; it was built as the summer palace of Count Wenceslas Adalbert Šternberg, the richest man in Prague after Count Černín. As his architect, Šternberg employed Jean-Baptiste Mathey, a man of many talents from Burgundy, who was responsible for starting the Baroque transformation of Prague's townscape. Here, among the former vineyards beyond the royal hunting park of Stromovka, Mathey not only erected a grand country house on the model of the Baroque châteaux being built in his native France, he also integrated it within a transformed landscape of geometrically laid-out gardens oriented on the spires of distant Hradčany.

The visitors' entrance is now on the north side of the château, facing the outbuildings which, with their painted ceilings, are almost palace-like themselves. The original entrance, however, was to the south, where the main axis of the garden leads past the symmetrically planned gardener's house and orangery to the superb staircase. This is a *tour de force* of Baroque sculpture, where battling Titans fight it out watched by various deities among a grandiose array of ornamental urns.

Inside, the succession of splendidly decorated rooms culminates in the Grand Hall, whose *trompe l'oeil* murals almost defy description in their lavish celebration of the Habsburg dynasty (everyone loves the turbaned Turk falling from the cornice). The château also houses the Prague City Gallery's 19th-century Czech Art Collection,

few of whose paintings compete successfully with the Baroque extravaganzas all around.

Charmingly located among the vine-clad slopes behind Trója Château is the little Chapel of St. Clair and a branch of the Prague Botanical Gardens, though more popular are the animals in the Zoologická zahrada (zoo); this was last taken charge of in the 1930s by the Functionalist architect, Josef Fuchs, and is now rather rundown.

Endless rows of run-down apartment buildings line the streets of Vinohrady

▶ Vinohrady   187C2

Metro: Náměstí míru, Náměstí Jiřího z Poděbrad (for the Church of the Most Sacred Heart of Our Lord), Flora (for Olšany Cemetery) or Želivského (for the Jewish Cemetery)

The name of this densely built up inner-city district (meaning "Vineyards") is a reminder that it remained almost completely countrified until well into the 19th century, the vines interspersed with gardens and cemeteries and cut through by the main road to Vienna. By the turn of the century an almost complete trans-formation had taken place; the area had become a borough with the rather grand official name of Královské Vinohrady (Royal Vineyards), developed along planned lines as a middle-class apartment district, with the occasional square and park.

The formerly grand tenements are now very shabby indeed, but Vinohrady remains a good address. The focus of the whole area is náměstí Míru (Peace Square), where the civic pride of the new suburbanites is expressed in important-looking civic buildings, such as Josef Mocker's neo-Gothic Kostel svatého Ludmily (Church of St. Ludmila).

To the north are the Riegrovy sady (Rieger Gardens), laid out in 1904 on north-facing slopes that offer good views over Nové Město (the New Town) towards Hradčany. Here is the headquarters of the famous football team, the T.J. Bohemians.

TV tower (Televizní vysílač)
Great controversy attended the erection of this monster of a building, which involved the demoli-tion of much of the old Jewish cemetery. Nearby residents claim that they can pick up broadcasts on virtually any domestic appliance and that their bodies are slowly being microwaved. There is, however, an amazing panorama of the city from the viewing gallery.

George of Poděbrady Square Vinohrady is too large an area to be explored easily on foot, but if you take the metro to Jiřího z Poděbrad (George of Poděbrady Square) you can visit one of Prague's most remarkable 20th-century buildings, the **Kostel Nejsvětějšího Srdce Páně (Church of the Most Sacred Heart of Our Lord)▶▶**. This wonderful church is the expression of the great originality and the deep piety of Josip Plečnik, President Masaryk's official architect in the 1920s. Designed in 1919 and completed in 1933, the church is monumental without being overwhelming, full of Plečnik's personal symbolism and love of fine materials. The great slab of a tower is flanked by obelisks; inside, the nave is a vast, unified space, with decoration and statuary all the more effective for its restraint. Underneath is a mysterious crypt.

Vinohrady cemeteries The metro runs further out to a vast tract of land occupied by Prague's biggest cemeteries, served by two stations, Flora and Želivského. Between the two stops is the entrance to the **Olšanské hřbitov (Olšany Cemetery)▶**, founded in the late-17th century to cater for the thousands carried off by the plague of 1680.

The most visited grave in the Olšany cemetery is probably that of Jan Palach; the ashes of the student who burnt himself to death in protest at the 1968 invasion are covered by a slab into which a prone figure of a man seems to be melting. Palach's body was removed in 1973 by the regime, which had gotten tired of sympathizers placing flowers on the grave. His body was cremated and reburied in his home village of Všetaty, but was returned here after 1989.

Želivského metro station serves a big suburban bus station and the **Židovský hřbitov (New Jewish Cemetery)**. This was laid out along generous lines in the 1890s, at a time when the city's Jewish population was growing—and dying—in greater numbers than ever before. Given today's much reduced community, it will take a long time to fill. Here is Franz Kafka's grave, and that of his sisters, marked by a dignified stone column, or stele. To the north is an Orthodox chapel and beyond it the War Cemetery. The latter contains the graves of Czechs who fell in World War I—immaculately maintained British war graves, mostly of Royal Air Force personnel—and a memorial to the Red Army men who were killed in the last days of World War II during the liberation of Prague.

▶   **Výstaviště (Exhibition Grounds)**   *187C3*

Holešovice

Metro: Holešovice, then Tram 12

The grounds where a great Jubilee Expo was held in 1891 are still dominated by the steel and glass Průmyslový pálac (Palace of Industry), a splendid giant of a building, with a candy-cane staircase twisting up inside its 150-ft. clock tower. The 146 pavilions of the Expo celebrated the industrial and other achievements of the Czech Lands; some of the 2 million visitors had an exciting journey from the city center, first by funicular up to Letná plain, then on to the Expo itself aboard a newfangled electric tram.

The Exhibition Grounds have proved remarkably robust, surviving all kinds of changes, and are as popular today as ever, catering for virtually everyone from health nuts to fans of brass-band music. Among the older attractions is a wonderful diorama of the Battle of Lipany, a circular painting that conveys something of the bewilderment of battle as well as its bloody side. Sounding potentially tedious, the **Lapidárium►** of the National Museum is housed in one of the original entrance pavilions. In fact, it consists of a fascinating collection of sculptural stonework from all over Bohemia, including many of the original works which once graced Prague's townscape and which have had to be replaced by copies. They include some of the statues from the Karlův most (Charles Bridge) and works by Petr Parléř, as well as the Marian Column from the Staroméstské náměstí (Old Town Square—see page 151).

Down the slope beyond the main buildings are all the old Expo facilities, plus new ones, such as the enigmatic Pyramid and the big black drum of the Laterna Animata, where performances draw on the famous Laterna Magika (Magic Lantern) for inspiration. For the 1991 centenary, a computer-controlled illuminated water feature of great complexity was installed, named after Křížik, the man who had been the driving spirit behind the original Expo. Nearby is an excellent example of Functionalist architecture, the Veletržní palác (Trade Fair Palace—see panel on page 208).

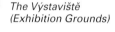

The Výstaviště (Exhibition Grounds)

Garden of trees
The Stromovka, or Tree Garden, started life as the Royal Deer Park, founded in the reign of John of Luxembourg in the early 14th century. Under Emperor Rudolf II, its lake was replenished with water from the Vltava, led through a long tunnel bored beneath Letná plain, quite a technical feat for the time. The greenery of the Stromovka remains a popular place of escape. Its centerpiece is the old Summer Palace, Gothicized in 1805, and now the somewhat incongruous home of the national periodicals library.

■ **The streets and highways in and around Prague sometimes seem as congested as those of any Western capital. The level of car ownership is high—much higher than in the rest of the country—with something like one car for every three inhabitants. Under Communism, possession of a car was seen as one way of taking control of your own life—not just a practical means of transportation but a symbol of escape from the restrictions of the everyday world....■**

Bridging the Botic brook
For many years the deep Nusle ravine—carved out by the modest little watercourse called the Botic—formed a formidable barrier between the New Town and the growing suburbs to the southeast. Many proposals were made for overcoming this natural obstacle, among them a futuristic 1927 project consisting of a bridge held up by a row of skyscrapers. Work on a viaduct carrying the approach road to the D1 highway was begun in 1939, interrupted by war in 1942, restarted in 1945, interrupted again by the advent of Communism in 1948, then finally completed between 1965 and 1973. It is ⅓ of a mile long and carries six lanes of traffic plus two footpaths, not to mention line C of the metro, slung beneath the traffic lanes. Originally named after Gottwald, Czechoslovakia's first Communist premier, it is now modestly entitled the Nuselský most (Nusle Bridge).

The prestige Tatra comes in any color you like—so long as it's black

Cars were never easy to come by. The waiting time for a new vehicle might be a decade or more, and its purchase price would eat up several years' salary. Even so, the money was found somehow and cars were bought, to be lovingly maintained, despite the fact that spare parts were as difficult to obtain as the original vehicle. Few car owners had a garage, so vehicles were parked in long lines outside *paneláks* (panel-built apartments) and protected by a strange contraption, something like a raincoat on a metal frame. Owners devoted a good proportion of their time to coaxing wheezing engines into life or restoring decayed bodywork, prolonging the life of the vehicle by whatever means available.

The Škoda The car itself would almost certainly be one of the makes turned out by the factories of the former Warsaw Pact countries: a Russian Lada, a Polski (Polish) Fiat, a Wartburg or spluttering Trabant from East Germany. But the people's car of the former Czechoslovakia was the Škoda, produced in quantity by the famous factory at Mladá Boleslav northeast of Prague, and the butt of many a patronizing joke in the West.
Škodas had a distinguished ancestry, reaching well back to the interwar period when Czechoslovakia was the fifth-biggest producer of motor vehicles in Europe. The Mladá Boleslav factory was a natural partner for Volkswagen when the huge German firm expanded into Eastern Europe after 1989, and the current Škoda, the zippy Favorit (described by BBC Television as "the bee's knees") seems set to restore the firm's former reputation.

Traffic jams Nevertheless, an increasing number of Western and Japanese cars can now be seen among the stalwarts of the former Eastern bloc during the rush-hour

or the great weekend exodus from the city to the country house. The latter journey is almost inconceivable without a car to transport the family, their pets and all the impedimenta needed to maintain the precious second home. Thus Friday afternoons and Sunday evenings see traffic jams on the main roads leading in and out of the city.

Blocked and slow-moving traffic generates more than its fair share of smog, and cars trying to enter Prague have sometimes been turned back by police because of a pollution alert. The pace of road-building to ease the pains of congestion has progressed on a more modest scale than that for most Western cities.

The historic city center is, of course, sacrosanct. Here, extensive areas have been given over exclusively to pedestrian use and motor vehicles are made to take the long way around. Much of this traffic is carried by the Magistral urban expressway, which channels the flood of traffic to the east of Nové Město (the New Town); there is an ambitious project to tunnel an equivalent highway on the west side of town, beneath Hradčany and Malá Strana on the far bank of the Vltava.

Not the people's car
These days, the Czech Republic's official car seems to be the BMW from neighboring Bavaria. Under Communism, and even before, it was the big black Tatra, a species now rapidly disappearing from the streets. Descendants of the T77, which had been a star of the 1934 Berlin Motor Show, these sinister-looking streamlined limousines seemed ideal for chauffeuring the Party nomenklatura and high-ranking secret policemen.

205

Keeping the precious possession clean

High castles
Literally translated, Vyšehrad means "high castle." There is another high castle, spelled Visegrad, above the Danube where the river has cut a gorge through the northern Hungarian mountains not far from the Slovak border. Visegrad was a Renaissance palace rather than a fortress, built by King Matthias, the Hungarian monarch who also ruled the Czech Lands for a while. It was chosen as the highly symbolic site for the first summit meeting of the post-Communist heads of state of Hungary, Poland and what was then still Czechoslovakia.

Romanesque remnant in Vyšehrad—the 11th-century St. Martin's

▶   **Vyšehrad**   *186B2*

Metro: Vyšehradská

The rocky bluff of Vyšehrad has carried the potent charge of legend and history since Princess Libuše fell into a swoon here and foresaw the founding of Prague (see page 30). For a while, in both the 10th and 11th centuries, it formed an alternative royal seat to Hradčany. Boleslav II (967–969) built a palace and a citadel here as well as a church whose remains lie beneath today's neo-Gothic Kostel svatého Petr a Pavel (Church of St. Peter and St. Paul). The oldest building to survive intact is the Rotunda svatého Martina (St. Martin's Rotunda), built in the reign of Vratislav II (1061–1092) and one of the small number of these circular structures scattered around the city. When royalty moved back to Hradčany, Vyšehrad lost its importance, though the Habsburgs refortified it in the 17th century to keep a watchful eye on the potentially troublesome Praguers.

In the 1860s Prague was declared an open (in other words indefensible) city and the fortress was abandoned by the Austrian military, just in time to be taken over as a potent symbol of Czech nationalism, a considerably more militant force than the imperial army which had just been thrashed by the Prussians at the Battle of Königgrätz. Vyšehrad was celebrated in drama (Grillparzer's *Libussa*), in poetry (Zeyer's *Vyšehrad*), in painting (by Mikoláš Aleš and many others), but above all in Smetana's opera *Libuše*, given a triumphal performance at the opening ceremony of the Národní divadlo (National Theater).

From the 1870s, what had been a simple old parish graveyard became the Národní hřbitov (National Cemetery), the final destination of the Czech nation's great and good. The ardent medievalist Josef Mocker did his best to make the Church of St. Peter and St. Paul even more Gothic than it had been before. In the 1920s the whole area was landscaped, and today it makes a pleasant place to spend an idle hour or two, not least because of the magnificent views of the Vltava, both upstream, towards the crags of Braník and Barrandov, and downstream, towards Hradčany.

Principal sights Vyšehrad can be approached from below, via the Cihelná brána (Brick Gate), or more or less directly from Vyšehradská metro station through the Leopoldová brána (Leopold Gate). Inside the Brick Gate is a small and well-presented exhibition telling the story of the city fortifications, while mysterious passageways lead to the Vyšehrad casemates, the underground works of the Baroque fortress.

Most visitors come here to inspect the National Cemetery, also known as the **Vyšehradský hřbitov (Vyšehrad Cemetery)▶▶**, sparing perhaps a

207

The spires of St. Peter and St. Paul rise over the peaceful National Cemetery, Vyšehrad

passing glance at the Neo-Gothic splendors of St. Peter and St. Paul.

The cemetery is indeed a fascinating place, less grand and more intimate than one might expect from a national pantheon. Here are the names with which every Czech (and many a foreigner too) is familiar: Alfons Mucha and Mikoláš Aleš, Jan Neruda, Božena Němcová and Karel Čapek, Antonin Dvořák and Bedřich Smetana. Many of the individual tombs have outstanding sculpture, but the focus of the cemetery is the Slavín, the pantheon itself, where 50 of the nation's foremost sons and daughters are interred, watched over by statues representing the *Grieving Homeland* and the *Rejoicing Homeland*.

On the lawns to the south of the church are big sculptures by Myslbek, removed from the Palacký Bridge in Nové Město (the New Town) and not looking entirely at home here, even though they do include the figures of *Libuše* and *Přemysl*. Beyond is a little bastion with a small exhibition (other exhibits are shown in the deanery) and then the ramparts, offering an almost complete and well worthwhile circuit walk.

At the foot of the rock, with seemingly no connection whatsoever with Vyšehrad's world of myth and legend, is a little cluster of buildings representing that uniquely Czech Cubist architectural movement (see page 209) that briefly flourished before World War I.

■ Some of the foundations for what later came to be known as the International Style in architecture were laid in the interwar years in Czechoslovakia, in the progressive and optimistic atmosphere of the First Republic. Unornamented, strictly functional buildings in glass, steel and concrete appeared not only in Prague, but in provincial centers such as Brno, giving the country a heritage of modern architecture largely unappreciated during the long decades of the Cold War, but now being enthusiastically rediscovered ....■

Wartime exploits commemorated at the Legionaries Bank

Slow conversion
One of the biggest and, some would say, one of the ugliest early modern buildings in Prague is the Trades Fair Palace on Dukelských hrdinů třida in Holešovice, designed by Oldřich Tyl and the Brno architect Josef Fuchs in 1924. The palace has been undergoing an exceptionally lengthy (even by Prague standards) conversion into the capital's gallery of modern art.

Whole districts were developed with estates of boxlike, white-painted concrete houses, often designed by an individual architect for a particular patron. The **Baba colony** (see page 191), perched on the brow of a hill and laid out in 1928–1934, is the most spectacularly sited of these developments, though there are others, notably the villas clustering around the famous film studios at **Barrandov** (see page 190). The most outstanding individual house, however, is the **Vila Müller** in Střešovice by the Moravian architect Adolf Loos, its severe exterior concealing a highly original and flexibly planned interior (see panel opposite).

Václavské náměstí (Wenceslas Square), that great outdoor museum of modern architecture, naturally has good examples of the genre, particularly the **Bata** building at No. 6, with its walls made entirely of plate glass, and its neighbor, the former **Lindt** store at No. 4 (see page 182). Modern architects loved light and air to circulate freely around their buildings, and this was achieved by the cross-shaped plan of the **Všeobecný penzijní ústav (Pensions Institute)** of 1932 in Žižkov (see panel on page

210), one of the first truly modern office buildings. The **Trades Fair Palace** of four years earlier is a pioneering megastructure of a building (see panel opposite).

Cubist architecture The triumph of Modernist architecture, after World War II, was so complete, its output of buildings so vast, and the design of many of them so banal that it may now be difficult to recapture the "thrill of the new" that structures such as the former Pensions Building must have provoked when they were first built. More immediately appealing to many will be their predecessors, built in the Cubist and uniquely Czech Rondo-Cubist styles.

Architectural Cubism flashed and sparkled into brief life just before World War I, breaking down the façades of buildings into an angular pattern of prisms making bold play with light and deep shade. Obvious inspiration came from the paintings of the French Cubists (which had been exhibited in Prague), but the style also harks back to the stellar vaulting of Bohemian Late Gothic and the revivalist games played by the Baroque architect Santini.

No visitor to Prague can fail to notice Josef Gočár's **Dům U černé Matky Boží (Black Madonna House)** guarding the corner of Celetná street with Ovocný trh in Staré Město (the Old Town), a stark statement of a building which nevertheless harmonizes well with its Baroque neighbors. The biggest concentration of Cubist buildings is, however, to be found in the suburbs, beneath the Vyšehrad rock, where a cluster of villas and an apartment building were designed by Josef Chochol.

Cubism's last fling came after World War I, when a block of flats was erected by Otakar Novotný in 1919–1921. Now somewhat upstaged by the Hotel InterContinental, its colored façade is a link with Rondo-Cubism, which tried to develop a specifically national style, based on Slav folklore, with its love of color and rounded forms. Even shorter lived than Cubism, Rondo-Cubism left some extraordinary structures dotted round the town, such as the massive **Adria Palace** in Národní třída (National Avenue) and, most flamboyant of all, the richly ornamented former **Legiobank (Legionaries Bank)** at No. 24 Na Poříčí.

"Ornament is crime"
Such was the rallying cry for modern design uttered by Adolf Loos, who wanted to reduce—or rather elevate—architecture to its essential components of form and function. The potentially stark result can be studied at the villa he built for the Müller family at No. 14 on the street called Nad hradním vodojemem high up in the pleasant suburb of Střešovice. Although one of the Czech Republic's nouveau riche citizens recently tried to purchase the house, it has been saved for the nation and it may be that this key work of Modernism will become accessible to the public as a museum itself.

Modernist shoebox—the Bata building

The White Cathedral of Prague
This is the name given by architectural historians to the Všeobecný penzijní ústav (the Pensions Institute), a building that looks like an extremely ordinary high-rise office building in náměstí Winstona Churchilla (Winston Churchill Square) in Žižkov. It is in fact one of the key buildings in the story of modern architecture, begun as early as 1928, at a time when most new offices were being dressed up in historical clothes of one cut or another. Steel, glass and concrete were combined with rational planning to produce this monument to Functionalist architecture (see page 208).

Out-doing Žižkov hill is Prague's television tower

Les Invalides de Prague
To the north of Žižkov hill is Karlín, another industrial suburb which stretches down to the Vltava. In the middle of the view is an enormous 18th-century structure resembling a barracks. This is a mere fragment of what was intended to be a vast complex, built to house the invalids of Prague and its surroundings; it was designed by the great Austrian architect, Fischer von Erlach, who was inspired by Les Invalides, built in Paris in 1706.

 Žižkov 187C2

Metro: Florenc

The closely packed tenements of "Red Žižkov" were built towards the end of the 19th century, at the same time as the middle classes were settling in Vinohrady to the south. Left-wing politics and trade unionism flourished among the factories, gasworks and railroad yards of the district, inspired perhaps by memories of an earlier fight for justice that took place here when a small Hussite force routed the numerically far superior imperial army sent to crush them. The hill was renamed Žižkov in honor of one-eyed Jan Žižka, the Hussite commander; the Národní památník (National Memorial) with his statue is a landmark visible from all over Prague.

Battles and crusades Na Vrchu Žižkové (Žižkov hill) is a long, narrow ridge running east–west, aimed like the bolt from a crossbow at the heart of Prague. Invading armies—the Swedes in 1638, the Prussians in 1756—used it as a gun-emplacement from which to bombard the city into submission. At other times it served as a site where the corpses of executed criminals were exposed to view.

Its greatest moment of glory came before all this unpleasantness, in July 1420. The pope had proclaimed a crusade against the heretical Hussites, and an imperial army had been gathered from all over Europe to exterminate the heretics. Both Vyšehrad and Hradčany were occupied by the crusaders, but the Hussites, under Žižka, stood their ground on the Vítkov Hill, using the pews from a nearby church to make a palisade across the narrowest part of the ridge. From here they held off the assault made by the imperial cavalry, the emperor grinding his teeth as the corpses of his finest horsemen piled up on the rocky ground. The day was decided by a flanking attack made by Žižka's own cavalry; these were farmers mounted on their rustic steeds, less polished perhaps than their knightly opponents, but more than their equal when it came to the battle.

Statues for heroes When the Czechoslovak Republic was founded, this place of glory seemed an appropriate location for the **Národní památník (National Memorial)**▶. This consists of a monumental granite slab of a building intended to mark the independence the country had gained in 1918; although it was not completed until 1932, it lent itself perfectly to adaptation by the Communists as the Party shrine *par excellence*.

The huge Žižka statue alongside (the biggest equestrian sculpture in the world) was completed in 1950. In 1953, President Gottwald died of a chill caught while attending Stalin's funeral, and, like the Soviet dictator and Lenin before him, he was embalmed. His preserved corpse was then put on show here in a glass coffin, to be saluted reverently by troupes of kerchiefed Young Pioneers on their outings to the capital. Other Party grandees were laid to rest here too, as were the remains of the Unknown Soldier, a member of the Czechoslovak Army Corps killed in the fierce fighting for the Dukla Pass in 1944.

Supplementing the earlier, nationalistically tinged decoration by artists such as Max Švabinský, this weird place of worship was then fitted out with an appropriate iconography, including the bronze doors, with their reliefs celebrating centuries of working-class struggle.

Not surprisingly, the monument is now an embarrassment to its custodians, and suggestions are welcome for an appropriate new use. In 1989, what was left of Gottwald and his cronies was spirited away, in a preemptive move against possible vandalism. Decay has begun to affect the desolate tracts of steps and paving outside, and only the occasional dog-walker seems to frequent the rundown parkland that covers the steep slopes. But the view westward over the city center still makes the climb worth while, best seen in the morning when the sun is behind you.

At the foot of the slope is the **Vojenské muzeum (Military Museum)**▶, built at the same time as the memorial. The museum houses extensive collections related to Czech and Slovak participation in the conflicts that have taken place in the 20th century—the Legionaries' exploits in World War I, exiles serving with the RAF or the Red Army in World War II, partisan and Resistance work at home, and even the anti-gas unit sent out to the Gulf War of 1991.

Mummy to dummy
Klement Gottwald's corpse resisted the embalmers' efforts to preserve it for all eternity. Despite being lowered every evening into a refrigerated underworld, with faithful technicians in attendance around the clock, his complexion turned a ghastly yellow-green and his extremities began to crumble. In the end master puppeteers were brought in from the Barrandov film studios to replace what could not be saved, though it remains unclear to this day just which parts of the wily leader were mummy and which dummy.

EXCURSIONS

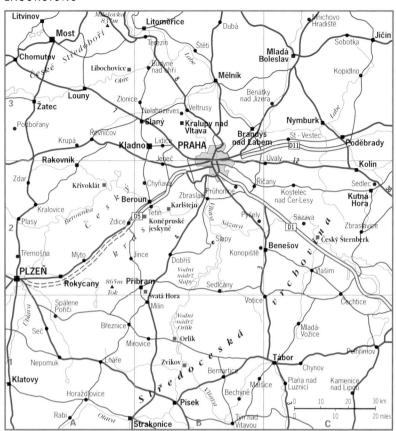

Choosing a map

Under Communism, many maps were regarded as state secrets and were not available to the public. Plans are underway to remedy this, and good maps or plans exist for most of the places you are likely to visit. For driving, the best map is at 1:200,000 scale, published in individual sheets or in atlas form as the *Velky Autoatlas* (Kartografia Praha). For walking, use the 1:50,000 *Turistika Mapa* (VKU/Klub Ceskych Turistu).

The rustic rooftops of medieval Krumlov

Excursions The Czech Republic is a small country divided into the two provinces of Bohemia and Moravia. Since Prague sits squarely at the center of Bohemia, it is theoretically possible to reach almost any destination in that province from the capital in the course of a day. Tour operators offer day excursions to the "triangle" of spa towns in western Bohemia—Karlovy Vary (Carlsbad), Mariánské Lázně (Marienbad), and Františkovy Lázně. Tours also go to the exquisite medieval cities of the south—České Budějovice and Český Krumlov. If you are venturing this far afield, however, it would be worth considering spending at least a night or two away from Prague in order to savor the pleasures of such towns more fully (and possibly save a lot of money by using public transportation to get there and back).

The options There are plenty of destinations nearer to Prague that will give you an idea of the richness of the Czech landscape, with its castles, country houses and parks, its ancient towns, large and small, and its grim reminders of more recent history, such as **Lidice** (see page 214), the village destroyed in revenge by the Nazis, or **Terezín** (also page 214), the fortress town they turned into a ghetto.

A destination so popular that it is virtually compulsory is the dramatically sited castle at **Karlštejn** (see page 226), built in the 14th century by Emperor Charles IV to house the crown jewels. Karlštejn, together with Archduke Franz Ferdinand's lavishly furnished residence at **Konopiště** (see page 220), was heavily restored in the 19th century, but there are plenty of other strongholds in a more authentic state, such as medieval **Křivoklát** (see page 227) or Renaissance **Nelahozeves** (see page 216), the latter dominating the village in which the composer Dvořák was born.

The Vltava leads upstream from Prague to the great Baroque abbey at **Zbraslav** (see page 224), the home of the country's finest sculpture collection, then to the Schwarzenbergs' fortress at **Orlík** and romantic **Zvíkov** (see page 230). **Konopiště** (also page 220) has lush grounds, as does **Průhonice Park** (see page 220) just beyond the city limit. On the way to the old royal town and vineyards of **Mělník** (see page 217) you should visit the château at **Veltrusy** (see page 216), dreaming away among the water-meadows of the Vltava. **Plzeň** (Pilsen—see page 228), the metropolis of western Bohemia, has far more to offer than its world-famous beer, while medieval **Tábor** (see page 232) preserves something of the atmosphere of Hussite times.

The Counter-Reformation of the 17th and 18th centuries turned Bohemia into a sacred landscape, putting an onion dome on every village church, lining roadsides with chapels and calvaries, and promoting pilgrimages, above all to **Svatá Hora** (**the Holy Mountain**—see page 230), the great Baroque complex high above the old silver mining town of **Příbram** (also page 230). Mining made **Kutná Hora** prosperous too, and here some of the huge quantities of gold and silver extracted were turned to stone, in the shape of the greatest Gothic edifice outside Prague, the glorious Chram svaté Barbory (Cathedral of St. Barbara—see page 218).

Drive **Lidice and Terezín**

At the start of this 84-mile roundtrip to the north of Prague you should take highway No. 7 past Ruzyně Airport, then highway No. 551 towards Kladno until you reach the village of Lidice.

After visiting Lidice, return to highway No. 7 and drive as far as Slaný, where you turn northwards, following highways No. 30 and No. 8 to Terezín. Return to Prague via highway No. 8.

Escape from Terezín
Just downstream from gloomy Terezín, where the Ohře river joins the broad Elbe (Labe), is Litoměřice, a more normal place altogether, and the center for the surrounding orchard country and the České Středohoří (Central Bohemian Uplands). In the Middle Ages the town's market, held in the big main square, was one of the most important in Europe, and there are echoes of past splendors in buildings such as the arcaded town hall, the sgraffitoed Černý orel (Black Eagle House) and the landmark Mrázovský dům (Chalice House), its roof crowned by a huge communion chalice. The cathedral was rebuilt by an Italian architect, Giulio Broggio, between 1663 and 1681; his son, Ottavio, born in Litoměřice, followed in his father's footsteps, building or remodeling many of the town's churches in Baroque style, including All Saints Church and the delightful little chapel of svatého Václava (St. Wenceslas).

▶▶ **Lidice** *212B3*

Few acts typified the brutality of the Nazi domination of Bohemia-Moravia more completely than the razing of this small mining village in reprisal for the assassination of Reichsprotektor Heydrich on May 27, 1942. On June 10, on the flimsiest of pretexts, the population of Lidice was rounded up by the S.S. and the Gestapo. The men were herded into a farmyard and shot, and the women sent to concentration camps together with their children, all except for a few thought capable of being "Germanized." The village was then destroyed with characteristic thoroughness and its name erased from the records "forever." But this Nazi terror had the opposite of its intended effect; Lidice's name resonated around the world, soon becoming a synonym of German ruthlessness and Czech suffering.

After the war the village was rebuilt. The trim new houses and community buildings of New Lidice stand a short distance away from the site of the old village, which has become a memorial park. A colonnade and bastion overlook the valley where the foundations of the medieval church and other buildings can be discerned, while a rose garden and recently planted trees testify to the continuing validity of Lidice as one of the great symbolic sites of World War II. The small museum is all the more moving because its exhibits and short film evoke the sheer ordinariness and innocence of village life before it was so arbitrarily snuffed out.

▶▶ **Terezín** *212B3*

The foundation stone of this grim fortress town was laid by Emperor Joseph II of Austria in 1780, who built it to block a possible Prussian move on Prague. The town, named Theresienstadt after the emperor's mother, Marie Theresa, was laid out on a checkerboard pattern, its massive brick walls and bastions the very latest in Baroque defense technology. The Ohře river was diverted to form a moat, beyond which stood another seemingly impregnable fortification, the Malá pevnost (Small Fortress).

When the Prussians did decide to invade, in 1866, they ignored Terezín, thrashing the Austrian army at Hradec Králové (Königgrätz) well to the east. Terezín was abandoned as a fortress, but kept its garrison, as it does today. The Little Fortress became a political prison, one of whose most celebrated inmates was Gavrilo Princip, the Bosnian Serb who triggered World War I by his assassination of Archduke Franz Ferdinand in Sarajevo in 1914. Princip died here of tuberculosis before completing his sentence.

LIDICE AND TEREZÍN

Memorial at the ghetto cemetery in Terezín

Gaiety in the ghetto
Terezín's population included a disproportionately large number of the country's intellectual and artistic élite. With no work and few responsibilities, people were free to create, to "dance in the shadow of the gallows" as one of them put it. Cultural life was intense; in particular, all kinds of music were composed and performed, from the childrens' opera *Brundibár* to the syncopated rhythms of the Ghetto Swingers. Viktor Ullman, now considered one of the great composers of the 20th century, wrote the opera *The Emperor of Atlantis* here. The Nazis suppressed the opera, rightly seeing its lead role as a Hitler figure, and its première had to wait until after the war.

The murky past of the Little Fortress appealed to the Gestapo, who took it over as a prison in 1940. A year later, the inhabitants of Terezín were given notice to quit and were replaced by the first contingents of Czech Jews. A semblance of normal life was maintained, notably during visits by inspectors from the International Red Cross or when the cameras turned to make a propaganda film with the deceitful title *The Führer Gives the Jews a Town*. In all, some 150,000 individuals passed through Terezín, many of them dying here, many more perishing in death camps such as Auschwitz-Birkenau. Even after liberation by the Red Army in May 1945, hundreds were to fall victim to typhus.

The past hangs heavily on Terezín, with its dour barrack buildings and parade ground park. Most visitors head for the Little Fortress, which has become a museum. In the town is the Muzeum ghetta (Ghetto Museum), which tells the true and terrible story of the place. No one should miss the film shown at frequent intervals in the movie theater, and even more moving are the works of art and ingenious artifacts made by those who suffered here during their inhumane imprisonment.

Some of the massacred menfolk of Lidice

EXCURSIONS

𝒟rive Veltrusy, Nelahozeves and Mělník

This 56-mile roundtrip to the north of Prague starts on highway No. 8 (the Dresden road) which leads first to Veltrusy. After stopping there, continue along the highway, crossing the Vltava and then turning left for Nelahozeves. From this castle, return to highway No. 8, then turn right on to highway No. 16 for Mělník.

For the return to Prague, follow highway No. 9 past the town of Neratovice.

The Chotek's country house at Veltrusy

Old Bohemians
The Choteks were one of the most notable families of old Bohemia. Václav Anton was the kingdom's governor, his son Rudolf the instigator of Europe's first industrial exhibition, held in Veltrusy in 1754. In the early 19th century, Count Karel Chotek laid out the Prague's riverside embankments. When Archduke Ferdinand was assassinated in Sarajevo in July 1914, his beloved wife Sophie Chotek died by his side.

▶ **Veltrusy**   *212B3*

The riverside woodlands just to the north of the village of Veltrusy make a popular campsite for weekenders and vacationers. Beyond the tents and chalets is the "Island," a vast area enclosed by an arm of the Vltava which was chosen in the early 18th century by Václav Anton Chotek as the site for an altogether more aristocratic form of country life. Here he built a highly original star-shaped mansion with a great dome at its center, approached by a sculpture-laden external stairway and pierced by a passageway at ground level. This device allows views through formal gardens laid out in the French manner to the immense park laid out by Chotek's heirs in the "English" style, complete with an extensive array of garden buildings and fanciful structures, among them the "Doric Temple," the "Cave with a Ruin," the "Egyptian Cabinet," and the "Temple of Friends of the Countryside and Gardens."

▶ **Nelahozeves**   *212B3*

This otherwise unremarkable village on the banks of the Vltava is dominated by its massive Renaissance castle, and is famous as the humble birthplace of Antonín

Dvořák, the Czech nation's most beloved composer. This butcher's son was born in 1841 in the house which is now a (fairly modest) museum. In 1990, amid much celebration, a new statue of Dvořák was erected on the adjacent common in the center of town.

The castle was begun in the 1550s by Florián Griespek and its rather plain walls are much enlivened by splendid sgraffito (incised plaster) work. It has now been returned to its erstwhile owners, the Lobkovic family, who hope to display progressively more of their huge collection of old masters here including such stars as Bruegel's *Haymaking*, previously on show in Prague's National Gallery.

►► Mělník   212B3

Crowning the terraced vineyards high above the Labe (Elbe) river are the castle and church of this old royal town, visible from far away across the flat farmlands that are typical of this part of Bohemia.

Mělník's castle goes back to a Slavic fortress of the 9th century. Later, Queen Ludmila brought up her grandson, the "Good King" Wenceslas, here. In the 18th century, like Nelahozeves, the castle passed into the ownership of the aristocratic Lobkovic family. They left the central courtyard with its Gothic and Renaissance ranges much as they found it, preferring instead to live in their palace in Prague.

Now back under Lobkovic ownership, ambitious plans are underway to revive the place. A number of rooms have already been restored and filled with Lobkovic furniture recovered from various ministry buildings in Prague. A gallery of modern art is proposed, and the ancient cellars are being brought back into use as the rightful center of Mělník's wine production.

With its attractive arcaded square and the remains of its walls, the old town clusters comfortably around the castle. The kostel svatého Petr a Pavel (Church of St. Peter and Paul) began as the castle chapel in the 11th century, and a Romanesque tower recalls its early origin; the main body of the church is Gothic, its tall tower topped by cheerful Baroque decorations.

Regal vines
Not content with remodeling the townscape of Prague, progressive Emperor Charles IV left his mark on Mělník, too. As well as being king of Bohemia, he was ruler of Burgundy, and in the 1360s it was from this noblest of wine regions that he ordered vines to be packed in honey for safe transit and brought to Mělník to form the basis for what is still Bohemia's biggest vineyard (albeit only about 1.5 sq. m. in extent). Mělník wines enjoy a variable reputation, sometimes dismissed as sour, sometimes praised as being the equal of "real" Burgundy. Before World War II, Prague nightclubs were filled with the sound of champagne corks popping from bottles labeled "Château Mělník."

Mělník remains little changed from this early engraving

Drive Kutná Hora

Kutná Hora lies 44 miles east of Prague. To get there you can take the D11 expressway, highway No. 12, or highway No. 133, the latter being the most scenic route.

Return to Prague on either road.

Misfortunes of a monument
The bronze statue of Masaryk outside Kutná Hora's Italian Court encapsulates the ups and downs of modern Czech history. Erected in 1938 by "The Society for the Erection of a Monument to T. G. Masaryk," it was destroyed by the Nazis in 1942, replaced in 1948, pulled down by the Communists in 1959 and, finally (?), restored in 1991.

▶▶ **Kutná Hora**   212C2

Bigger than London in its medieval silver-mining heyday, Kutná Hora is now only a shadow of its former self, though there are plenty of reminders of its days of glory, foremost among them the great Gothic cathedral.

Serious mining began in the 13th century when a chaotic settlement of sheds, shacks, and mineshafts grew up, its lack of planning reflected in the town's labyrinthine layout today. At the beginning of the 14th century the kingdom's coin-making activity was centralized in the city's Vlašský dvůr (Italian Court), named after its resident Italian bankers and technicians. In the 15th century new shafts were sunk to the then-stupendous depth of 1,800 ft. Kutná Hora's *coup de grâce* came in 1770 when much of the town was destroyed in a great fire.

The cathedral Most visits to Kutná Hora begin at its incomparable **Chrám svaté Barbory**▶▶▶, a cathedral dedicated to St. Barbara, patron saint of sappers (military minefield experts) and miners. Its unique triple-tented silhouette, marked by flying buttresses, pinnacles, and spikes, rises above the southwestern heights of the town like "an encampment of angels" (Brian Knox).

Begun in 1388, at the height of the city's prosperity, Chrám svaté Barbory was intended to be the equal of the great cathedrals of northern France. When the money ran out, the ingenious architect of the Vladislav Hall in Prague, Benedict Ried, was brought in to engineer a solution to the less-than-half-completed structure. His vault, finished in 1547, is one of the triumphs of late Gothic architecture, its endlessly fascinating pattern of intersecting segments of circles floating weightlessly high above the floor of the nave. The cathedral's other treasures include an array of late 15th-century wall-paintings, some of which depict the activities of the miners and minters, which paid for Ried's virtuosity.

The town One of the best views of the town, straggling along its hilltop, is from the cathedral esplanade, from which the immensely long façade of the Baroque Jezuitska Kolej (Jesuit College) stretches northwards. Beyond is the 13th-century building (known as the Hrádek) which

Gothic glory—St. Barbara's cathedral, Kutná Hora

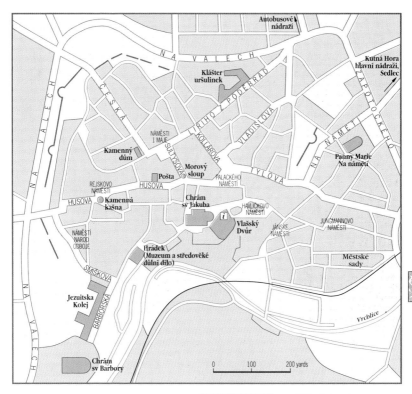

houses the Muzeum a středověké důlní dílo (Mining Museum), whose underground shafts can be visited; next comes the tall tower of the church of svatého Jakuba (St. James) and finally the Italian Court.

Much remodeled in the 19th century, the Italian Court is home to the remains of the 17 minters' cells where coins, such as the "Prague groat," were struck; the cells are overlooked by the chapel's oriel (bay) window, convenient for the morning prayers which began the day's work. Municipal business is still conducted inside; there is also a small museum with enough Prague groats and other coins to satisfy the most enthusiastic numismatist.

A stroll around the uncannily quiet streets reveals further sights, such as the 12-sided Gothic fountain in Rejskovo náměstí and a number of venerable burghers' townhouses, of which the most splendid is the high-gabled Kammený dům (Stone House) of 1490.

Stained-glass saint in St. Barbara's

The skeletons of Sedlec
This suburb of Kutná Hora has a huge medieval abbey church, rebuilt early in the 18th century by the inventive architect, Santini, in a strange weaving together of Gothic and Baroque elements. The nearby cemetery chapel contains even stranger compositions. Soil sprinkled here in the 13th century from the Holy Land made Sedlec a fashionable place to be buried. In the 19th century the remains of some 40,000 people were arranged into fantastic patterns. These include a chandelier with strings of jawbones and the complicated coat of arms of the Schwarzenbergs, who paid for the work.

EXCURSIONS

Drive Průhonice, Konopiště and Český Šternberk

Heading southeast on the D1 expressway out of Prague, this 67-mile roundtrip begins just on the city outskirts at Průhonice. From here, continue along the expressway until you reach highway No. 3, the Tábor road, which takes you to Konopiště.

After visiting Konopiště Castle, follow the signs to nearby Benešov; drive through the town following highway No. 112, then turn left onto highway No. 111 for Český Šternberk. This highway will then take you back to Prague.

Bohemian bears
The country's emblem may be a lion, but bear pits were a favorite feature of Bohemian castles. The one at Konopiště still contains a live bear, while one of its former denizens stands stuffed in the castle's smoking room. The skins of others, shot by the S.S. who resided here during World War II, adorn the floor.

220

Český Šternberk Castle, amid Bohemia's meadows and forests

► **Průhonice** *212B2*

Průhonice basks in the reflected glory of its park, and hopes that tourism will make its fortune. There is a golf course, and the country's first motel, ultra-chic in its day, adjoins the expressway. The park itself is one of the biggest in a land not short of country seats set in extensively landscaped grounds. It was laid out at the end of the 19th century by Count Silva-Taroucčã who, as Austrian Minister of Agriculture, knew a thing or two about trees. His dendrological passion was expressed on this nearly 500-acre estate through the lavish planting of native and exotic trees; over 1,000 different species are represented, making Průhonice an ideal place for botanical studies. The natural-seeming successors to the Count are the administrators and researchers of the Academy of Sciences, who occupy the Neo-Renaissance castle he built overlooking one of the lakes.

►►► **Konopiště** *212B2*

The origins of Konopiště Castle go back to a stronghold of the late-13th century, but it is best known as the palatial residence of Archduke Franz Ferdinand d'Este, ill-fated heir to the Habsburg throne.

Like a number of Bohemia's castles, Konopiště's striking outline, rising from the surrounding woodland, is

partly a product of the late 19th-century taste for romantic medievalism. Franz Ferdinand acquired the place in 1887, and employed the eminent expert, Josef Mocker, to engineer an atmosphere more medieval than the Middle Ages themselves, though modern conveniences, such as elevators and central heating, were not neglected.

The intensity of the archduke's obsessions are evident throughout. Head huntsman of the Habsburg Empire, he is estimated to have killed one animal for every hour of his life. The horns of his victims line the castle corridors leading to the rooms he furnished, museum-like, with fine furniture from his d'Este inheritance. He was a passionate collector, competing with England's Edward VII for memorabilia of St. George and the Dragon, while his stunning collection of arms and armor will enthrall the most pacifistic of visitors.

A tour of the interior finally becomes a claustrophobic experience, however, and it is a relief to escape on to the high terrace outside. Here, too, the restless mind of the archduke was at work. Not content with transforming the castle interior, he re-landscaped the grounds, laying out a superb rose garden, planting up the wider parkland with exotic trees and, needless to say, creating several hunting preserves.

An intriguing Habsburg
Frustrated at Emperor Franz Josef's unwillingness to consider the changes that might have saved the Habsburgs' ramshackle realm, his nephew and chosen successor, Franz Ferdinand, set up an "alternative Cabinet" to plan reforms. But he too was rigid in his own way (as you might guess from his portraits), and it seems unlikely that his rule would have given the peoples of Austria-Hungary sufficient say in its affairs to reconcile them to Habsburg rule. In any case, he never had the chance; in Sarajevo in June 1914, the archduke's Czech chauffeur made a wrong turn; his inability to reverse quickly gave the Bosnian Serb assassin, Gavrilo Princip, plenty of time to empty his revolver into the chests of the archduke and his wife. This act precipitated the war Franz Ferdinand had hoped to avoid, and led directly to the dissolution of the Austro-Hungarian Empire.

An old Bohemian battler buried among Franz Ferdinand's military memorabilia in Konopiště Castle

▶ **Český Šternberk**   *212C2*

The wooded valley of the River Sázava is a popular recreation area for Prague weekenders, enthusiastic patrons of any available guided tours. One such tour takes visitors around the famous monastery in the town of Sázava, while another goes around the castle at Český Šternberk, a classic example of a crag-top stronghold dominating a river crossing. In the 18th century, what had been a medieval stronghold was converted into a Baroque residence, with a succession of richly furnished, heavily stuccoed and sometimes oddly shaped rooms somehow crammed into the confined spaces of this old fortress lining the narrow rocky ridge. Sharp-eyed visitors will notice the occasional appearance in the décor of the Šternberg emblem—a star (*stern* in German).

FOCUS ON
Prague's countryside

■ **Within easy reach of the capital are many of Bohemia's most attractive landscapes, and even the more dramatic scenery of the country's frontier highlands can be reached in the course of a long day excursion. Like most big-city dwellers, Praguers rush to the countryside at weekends and at vacation time, making good use of its varied recreational facilities. The weekend cottage, or *chata*, has become a cult and these buildings can be seen dotting the landscape in all parts of the country....■**

The *chata*

Variously translated as "country cottage," "chalet," "second home," "summerhouse," or "lodge," *chata* (pronounced "khata") is the generic term for the buildings in which most Czech city folk seem to spend their weekends. The privileged have a real house of some kind, perhaps an old farm or an isolated woodman's cottage. The less privileged have to erect their own. Various off-the-rack designs are available, the oddest being the A-shaped timber chalets which would look incongruous in any landscape. Some people took decades to build their second home, scorning the ready-made and using whatever materials came to hand.

Characteristic Czech countryman

Prague lies roughly at the center of the province of Bohemia, at the point where the Vltava has carved a valley through the plateau extending east and west of the city. To the north, the river enters the country's most extensive area of flat land, the fertile Polabí plain along the Labe (Elbe) river, much of it characterized by endless fields of sugar beets. The monotony is relieved only by the occasional hill, such as the rounded summit called Říp from which chieftain Čech, the great-great-grandfather of the nation, is supposed to have surveyed the prospect and found it good.

Generally speaking, this part of northern Bohemia is not tourist country and most Praguers turn their attention southward. Here the terrain is more varied, cut by the Vltava and its tributaries, such as the Sázava and the Berounka. These rivers flow through narrow wooded valleys that sometimes take on the character of gorges, with their dramatic cliffs and rock outcrops.

Where limestone occurs, as in the Český kras (Bohemian Karst) around Karlštejn on the Berounka, many of the typical features of karst country are to be found, including caves and sinkholes, as well as unusual flora and fauna. This is also good hiking country, covered, like much of rural Bohemia, with a dense network of well-signposted footpaths, best explored with the aid of one of the excellent large-scale maps now being published with a key and notes in various languages (see panel on page 212).

The Vltava itself is one of the favorite destinations of city-dwellers. Since the construction of a whole series of dams the river has lost its former wildness and settled down to life as a series of calm lakes, not so good for white-water enthusiasts, but wonderful for sailing and generally high jinks by

the water. The most popular lake is Slapy, which has large colonies of weekend cottages, beaches of imported sand, hundreds of houseboats, and innumerable tents and cabins.

Village life While the vacationers crowd around the water's edge, village life goes on in the wider country-side. Within an hour or so's drive from Prague many of the traditional features of the southern Bohemian land-scape begin to appear. Czechs regard this area, stretching southward towards the Šumava uplands, as the arche-typal Czech countryside, dotted with villages whose fea-tures were sentimentalized by Josef Lada (the illustrator of the *Good Soldier Švejk*): the village pond with its pol-larded willows, the gabled farmhouses in peasant Baroque style, the dominant church with its spire or onion dome, the road lined with fruit trees winding out into the patchwork quilt of tiny fields, the wayside shrine or calvary, the huntsman's blind perched on its spindly legs on the edge of the forest.

Some of this character was swept away by the forced collec-tivization imposed under Communism. The colorful pattern of different crops growing on the long strips of land farmed by indi-vidual peasants has given way to huge open fields growing a single crop. The church may not have survived because anything that smacked of religion was subject-ed to systematic neglect, if not outright demolition. The huge farm buildings of industrialized agriculture stand in intimidating proximity to more tradi-tional structures; the villagers themselves "modernized" their old dwellings with great thoroughness. Enough, though, remains to make touring around the countryside in a car more than just worth while, and as individual responsibility and pride return, Bohemia's countryside may well regain its former cheerfulness.

Summertime sculler on the Vltava south of Prague

Zbraslav

Zbraslav is 8 miles south of central Prague and can easily be reached by car along highway No. 4. Alternatively, you can take the metro line B to Smíchovské nádraží, then buses 129, 241, 243, or 255 to Zbraslav. You can even take a boat trip down the Vltava to Zbraslav from the quay beside Prague's Palackého most (Palacký Bridge).

Roll out the polkas
Zbraslav was the birthplace (in 1902) of the bricklayer's son, Jaromír Vejvoda. Brass bands were in the young boy's blood; there were a couple of dozen Vejvoda bandsmen making music in the Zbraslav area at the time, including his father and grandfather. Jaromír surpassed them all. Though his name is hardly known outside the country, he wrote one of the world hits of the century, the rip-roaring polka whose Czech name translates as *The Pity of Love*. If you are American, you will almost certainly know this better as *Roll Out the Barrel*; if you are German then you will recognize it as *Rosamunde*.

▶▶▶ **Zbraslav**   212B2

This small and rather dusty place on the Vltava used to be a favorite destination for a steamboat trip from Prague, and although there is still a landing stage here, the town is cut off from the river by the busy road running south to Slapy, so few come here now. Despite this, Zbraslav is still well worth a visit, since its abbey is the rather unlikely home of one of the country's greatest art collections, the National Gallery's Collection of 19th- and 20th-century Czech Sculpture. The reason why the collection is housed in this rather inaccessible spot remains unexplained, though the grandeur of the abbey's Baroque architecture makes an intriguing contrast to the inventiveness and originality of the works on display, some of them the most immediately appealing sculptures you are ever likely to see.

The abbey buildings The abbey's origins go back to the 13th century, when Cistercian monks settled on the spot once occupied by a royal hunting lodge. Their Gothic buildings were destroyed in the Thirty Years' War and replaced in the early 1700s by the present palatial Baroque structure. Not long afterwards, the monks were thrown out and a sugar factory was installed in some of the abbey buildings. A panel in the pediment of the entrance pavilion recalls the munificence of Cyril Dobenín, an industrialist who, in 1911–1927, "restored what industry had destroyed."

The palatial abbey stands in a sculpture-strewn park with an ornamental canal to the north. Approached through the entrance pavilion, the main building and its flanking wings are arranged around a courtyard. Inside, high cloisters give unexpected and tantalizing glimpses into the rooms beyond, the most sumptuous of which is the Great Hall with its painted ceiling.

The exhibits The first floor spaces are grand enough to house monumental works by many of the artists who contributed to the embellishment of Prague's street scene in the late-19th century. Inevitably, Myslbek dominates, not only with the four figures of saints and the head of Wenceslas from the statue in Václavské náměstí (Wenceslas Square—see page 180), but with a big Crucifixion and an equally imposing seated Schwarzenberg, here in the role of cardinal.

The move away from this imposing but finally rather pompous semi-official art is charted on the second floor. Art Nouveau intensity of feeling pervades Rodin-like figures by Ladislav Jan Šaloun, passionate couples by Josef Mařatka, and a rather affected Orpheus by Jaroslav

Horejc. There are lyrical figures of boys and maidens by Jan Štursa, including a double of the skinny figure of Victory who graces the garden of the Belvedere in Prague (see page 68).

By contrast, much of the work of Otto Guttfreund explores the interplay of realism and abstraction, though his most endearing figures are those of people going about their daily business. Glorification of work and workers, and labored treatment of social themes later became a tediously repeated theme of official Communist art, but in the 1920s and 1930s there was a freshness, humor, and affection in the studies of everyday life by observers such as Guttfreund, Karel Dvořák, and Jan Lauda. Karel Pokorný's *Bread Line*, presided over by a stout policeman, strikes a more somber note.

The last rooms are filled with the dreams and nightmares of the postwar period, a characteristically Czech mixture of wit, fantasy, and horror, by no means to be missed. Michal Gabriel's *Pták* (*Bird*) may make you jump as it fixes you with its beady eye, but your surprise could not be greater than that of the *Rudé Právo* reader scanning the headlines of this Communist Party newspaper on November 17, 1989 (the day the Velvet Revolution began).

Outside, in the well-wooded park, Guttfreund's family group take it easy, undisturbed by Otakar Švec's motorcyclist speeding along. By the canal, a strange bride made of bits and pieces from the junkyard seems to be draining the vital bodily fluids from an array of recumbent suitors.

Victim of Stalin
The sculptor of the Zbraslav motorcyclist, Otakar Švec, moved on from fascination with the elegance and power of machines to the more monumental preoccupations of the Communist era: in 1950, he accepted the commission for the gigantic statue of Stalin overlooking Prague. Five years later, increasingly aware of the banality of what he had been doing, and in daily receipt of letters denouncing him as a traitor, he gassed himself, only days before the unveiling ceremony.

225

The National Gallery's collection at Zbraslav Abbey includes a stunning collection of modern sculpture

EXCURSIONS

Drive Karlštejn and Křivoklát

These two castles both lie along highway No. 116, to the southwest of Prague. Karlštejn is a mere 18.5 miles from the city center, and is reached via highway No. 4, then highway No. 116. Suburban trains also run to Karlštejn from Smíchovské nádraží (Smíchov Station) or, if you would prefer a guided tour, there are many bus trips available in Prague.

To reach Křivoklát by car, continue along highway No. 116 to Beroun, then head west for 12 miles along minor roads. By train, you must continue to Beroun and then change for Rakovnik.

Mock medieval
The heavy hand of the architect Josef Mocker (1835–1899) fell on many of the great buildings of Bohemia; not just Karlštejn and, to a lesser extent, Křivoklát, but also Franz Ferdinand's Konopiště, the cathedral at Kutná Hora and many of the ancient buildings of Prague.

Karlštejn Castle in its sublime setting above the Berounka valley

▶▶ Hrad Karlštejn (Karlštejn Castle)   212B2

Karlštejn's towers and battlements crown a rocky summit rising above the glorious woodland of the Berounka valley, giving it the most romantic silhouette of all the castles of Bohemia. It was begun in 1348 by Emperor Charles IV, not as a conventional castle, but as a repository for the crown jewels of the head of the Holy Roman Empire and for the holy relics collected by this most pious of rulers. In the following century it was besieged by the Hussites but, put off by the long climb up from the valley bottom, they went away again.

The castle was partly rebuilt in Renaissance times, but then fell into decay. In the late-19th century, overconscientious restorers refashioned it according to a purist conception of what it should have been like in the Middle Ages, since when it has become so popular a place of modern pilgrimage that its heart, the emperor's Kaple svatého Kříže (Chapel of the Holy Rood) has had to be closed to visitors.

All visits to Karlštejn start far below on the banks of the Berounka. The steep ascent (about 1.25 miles in length) takes you past the souvenir shops of the village and is made on foot, though carriage rides are available. The final approach is made from the rear of the castle, through gateways leading into the outer ward, where you can book the compulsory guided tour in the language of your choice. While waiting, most visitors descend to the gardens around the well tower and admire the stunning views over the surrounding wooded hills.

Eventually, you will be led through the gatehouse of the inner ward into the Imperial Palace. Much restored, and long since deprived of its original furnishings, it now has displays which go some way towards explaining the life led here by the emperor and his court. Beneath the deep coffered ceiling of the Audience Hall, Charles would sit with his back to the light to receive his subjects.

Just up the slope is the second of the castle's principal buildings, the Mary Tower, containing the Chapel of the Virgin. Here an annual Mass is still said on November 29, the date of Charles IV's death. A total of 338 angels grace the painted ceiling, while faded murals show Charles receiving the holy relics which were removed to Vienna long ago.

A narrow passageway, covered in sgraffito decoration, leads to the tiny St. Catherine's Chapel. Here, shut in among the walls of gilded plaster studded with semiprecious stones—including agate, amethyst, and jasper—the emperor would spend whole days in meditation, sometimes in pious preparation for the ascent to the "Great Tower," the holy bunker housing the castle's sacred core, the Chapel of the Holy Rood.

In this chapel, below the gilded vaults lit by 1,400 candles, Charles would pray while enveloped in the mystical atmosphere emanating from the holy relics; as he did so he was watched over by the 100-plus portraits of saints painted by Master Theodorik, set into walls encrusted with no fewer than 2,200 semi-precious stones. Alas, such has been the cumulative effects of tourists' visits and their inclination to finger and even remove objects, that the tower is now closed and may never be opened to the general public again.

►► Zámek Křivoklát (Křivoklát Castle) 212A2

More remote than Karlštejn, and less affected by the restorer's zeal, Křivoklát stands among the deep forests further up the Berounka, a more authentic evocation of medieval Bohemia altogether. Its origins go back to the 11th century; in Charles IV's time it was a royal hunting lodge. Dominated by the tall white cylinder of a tower at its eastern end, at its core is the Royal Palace with its splendidly vaulted Gothic chapel.

In the depths of the castle are the prison and torture chamber, while above them are the Knights' Hall and the King's Hall; the latter has more fine vaulting, graffiti left by 14th-century children and a capital carved to show the demise of Wenceslas' IV's wife, who died as a result of a dog-bite.

In the woods opposite stands a Neo-Gothic monument to the castle's last private owners, the Fürstenbergs, who ceded their possessions to the Czechoslovak State in 1929.

"Hikking" (sic) in the karst
Not a description of the effects of too much Pilsener, but one Prague tour operator's invitation to come rambling in the Český kras (Bohemian Karst), the limestone plateau into which the Berounka has cut its winding course. Because of its splendid forests, not to mention the abundance of plants rare elsewhere and the wealth of limestone features, such as caves and fossils, this is a landscape enjoying special protection. High above the gorge upstream from Srbsko is the ancient hillfort of Tětín, the place where Princess Ludmila was murdered in AD 921.

227

Inside St. Catherine's Chapel, Karlštejn Castle

EXCURSIONS

Drive Plzeň (Pilsen)

Plzeň, famous for its beer, is the busy regional capital of western Bohemia, an industrial city which has nevertheless kept many traces of its long history. The city lies 58 miles southwest of Prague and is reached by car via the D5 expressway and highway No. 5. Express trains run to Plzeň from Prague's Hlavní nádraží (Main Station).

Pils from Plzeň
In the 1840s, several citizens got together to found the Burghers' Brewery (*Bürgerbräu* in German, *Měšťanský pivovar* in Czech). Using prime-quality hops from Žatec and water from the wonderful local springs, they created a pale and delicious bottom-fermented beer, the prototype of all lagers. "Pilsener" soon established an international reputation and many imitation beers were made; to protect the authentic product, the German word *Urquell* (meaning "original source"; *Prazdroj* in Czech) was added to the label.

► **Plzeň (Pilsen)**   *212A2*

Plzeň's main square, the náměstí Republiky (Republic Square) is the biggest in Bohemia and its generous proportions proclaim Plzeň's longstanding importance. The city was founded at the end of the 13th century as a planned settlement, commanding the great trade route linking Prague with the imperial cities of Nuremberg and Regensburg, a strategic advantage it continues to enjoy. The square takes up two blocks of the medieval surveyor's checkerboard plan which still determines the layout of the old city center today, though the walls have long since given way to gardens and roadways.

A feature of the square is the free-standing **Chrám svatého Bartoloměje (Church of St. Bartholomew)** whose steeple, at 310 ft., is the tallest in the land. The church was begun in the early 14th century and given a splendid star vault in the 15th century; its greatest treasure is a Gothic *Madonna and Child*. Lining the square is a medley of other buildings of various dates and degrees of importance, of which the most prominent is the triple-gabled Renaissance Stará radnice (Old City Hall), thoroughly rusticated and sgraffitoed.

The streets running off the square were "modernized" in the late-19th and early 20th centuries, but there are some

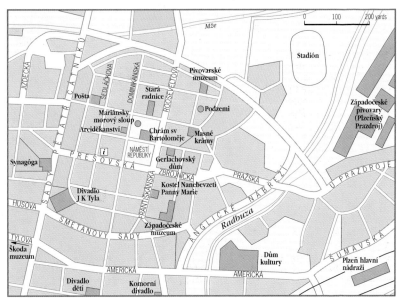

Plzeň's famous brewery, quenching thirsts worldwide

Škoda's Škodas
In the late-19th century, Emil Škoda turned the Plzeň engineering works into the power-house of Austria-Hungary; the great enterprise turned out machine-tools, locomotives, and the armaments that sustained the Habsburgs during World War I and the Nazis in 1939–1945. The Škoda works started manufacturing cars in 1906, a few years after Emil Škoda's death in 1900. The cars which bear his name are now made at Mladá Boleslav, to the northeast of Prague. A pre-war byword for sturdiness, Škodas have since become the butt of many an unkind joke based on their supposed unreliability. Needless to say, such humor forms no part of Plzeň's Škoda museum, which in any case is devoted more to general engineering than to the cars.

fascinating survivors, such as the Gothic house at No. 288 Dominikánská street and the fine Baroque mansion at No. 251 Sedláčkova street. The city's late-19th century civic pride was expressed in pompous public edifices, such as the Divadlo J. K. Tyla (Tyl Theater) and the Západočeské muzeum (the West Bohemian Museum), both located among the parks and gardens which replaced the old walls and moats; the art gallery attached to the museum is a good place to get acquainted with the great variety of work produced by Czech artists of the 19th and 20th centuries.

Brewing Of course, the real reason for visiting Plzeň is to sample its excellent beer in the place where it is made. The main brewery is to the east of the center. The way there takes you past the medieval Masné krámy (Butchers' Stalls) and the 16th-century water tower, part of the old fortifications. Just to the north is the medieval malthouse containing the **Pivovarské muzeum (Brewing Museum)** with its array of beer memorabilia. Beyond the Radbuza river, the **Západočeské pivovary (West Bohemian Brewery)** announces itself—as well it might—with a triumphal arch. The guided tour takes in a tasting as well as a look at some of the 4.5 miles of cellars carved out of the underlying sandstone.

Anatomy of a Škoda

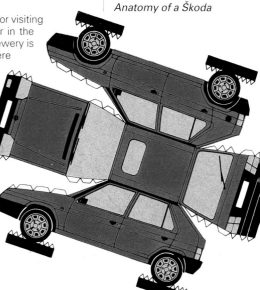

EXCURSIONS

Drive Příbram, Orlík, Zvíkov and Tábor

This round trip of 133 miles takes in the sights that lie to the south of Prague. Příbram is reached after 32 miles along highway No. 4.

Continue along the same highway, then turn right onto highway No. 19 to reach Orlík. Minor roads to the south take you to highway No. 121 where you turn left for Zvíkov. Finally, continue along highway No. 121, then on to highway No. 19, for Tábor. Return to Prague along the same route.

Cupola, court-yard, and statues at Svatá Hora's central complex

► ► **Příbram** 212B2

Highway No. 4 running southwest from the capital is an expressway, one of the first of its kind to be built in Czechoslovakia, supposedly to speed top Party people from their offices in the capital to their exclusive country-side recreation center. The highway gives out near Příbram, an old place with a long history of silver mining and, more recently, of uranium extraction. The rather undistinguished town spreads out around the foot of one of the Czech Republic's most popular places of pilgrimage.

Holy mountain The historic hilltop of Svatá Hora (Holy Mountain) is reached from the town by a covered stairway of 365 steps or, less arduously, from the nearby parking lot. The hilltop is crowned by the domes and cupolas of the Baroque buildings the Jesuits erected in the mid-17th century around the shrine where

230

miraculous cures had been worked for hundreds of years. Even by the standards of these masters of religious spectacle the effect is more than usually theatrical. Many of the greatest artists of the time were employed to create a sense of drama and occasion, the massive cost being covered by the donations of the faithful who flocked here from all over Bohemia and beyond.

Today, pilgrims still gather on the esplanade where they are dominated by the long eastern façade of the complex, with its drum-like corner towers. The entry to the shrine is up some steps and through the elaborate gateway. Inside is an arcaded courtyard with richly stuccoed vaults opening onto a number of chapels whose decoration is equally opulent.

The core of the complex, however, is the central basilica, raised on a plinth whose balustrade seems alive with statuary; three open chapels face east, while inside is the sanctuary itself, its stunning silver altar built around an ancient and time-blackened statuette of the Madonna and Child.

Ancient oak
The approach to Svatá Hora is marked by a venerable oak, preserved since the 19th century as an ancient monument. Oak woods once cloaked much of Bohemia, and the oak (*dub* in Czech) is a much-loved tree, just as Alexander Dubček (= little oak) was a much-loved leader.

231

Orlík Castle on its crag above the Vltava, as depicted in 1815

►► Orlík   212B1

South of Prague the Vltava has been dammed at a number of points, turning the once wild river into a series of placid lakes, ideal water playgrounds for weekenders in their thousands. One effect of taming the river has been to transform the surroundings of Hrad Orlík (Orlik Castle), a medieval fortress converted into a prestigious residence by its Schwarzenberg owners in the 19th century. Old prints in the lavishly furnished interior of the castle show it glowering down from its crag on to raftsmen ferrying timber down from the Bohemian forest on the river far below; nowadays the Vltava, its level raised by 180 ft., laps at the building's foundations.

Orlík is a romantic spot nevertheless, the promontory on which it stands approached through attractive parklands laid out at the same time as the castle was given its pseudo-medieval towers and battlements. Inside are several reminders of the role played by successive Schwarzenbergs in Central European history, including one of Adolf of Schwarzenberg, who incorporated a raven pecking out the eye of a Turk into the family coat of arms after a successful campaign against the Sultan's armies in 1599.

The coat of arms of Orlík

The easily defended approach to Zvíkov Castle

►► Zvíkov   *212B1*

Unlike sprucely restored Orlík, the royal castle of Zvíkov has had the benefit of centuries of neglect; as a consequence it retains an authentically medieval appearance and atmosphere. Like Orlík, it bestrides a rocky spur above the Vltava, at a point where the river is joined by its tributary, the Otava, and here too the rise in water level has deprived the spectacular site of some of its drama. But deep forest stretches away in all directions, and the 10-minute walk along the dusty track atop the peninsula promotes a pleasurable sense of anticipation which is amply rewarded.

Beyond the stone bridge and red-roofed Písek Gate rises the castle's dominant feature, the tall 13th-century Hláska Tower with its conical cap. The inner castle or royal palace has contrasting exterior masonry—bold embossed stonework, as well as smooth stucco and sgraffito. Inside is an irregularly shaped courtyard with two tiers of arcades, giving access to splendid interiors, such as the so-called Wedding Hall, named after the wall paintings of the celebrations accompanying a wedding feast. The chapel, too, has boldly painted walls as well as a splendid late-Gothic carved altarpiece.

►► Tábor   *212C1*

The fortified hilltop town of Tábor was established by Hussite militants as their "holy city" and named after the biblical mountain of Christ's Transfiguration. Thousands of the radical followers of martyred Jan Hus flocked here following the defenestration of Catholics from the windows of Prague's New Town Hall in 1420 (see page 33). The chaotic layout of the town, a labyrinth seemingly

Looking to Tábor
One of the best views of Tábor in its setting is from the suburb of Klokoty just to the west. Here is one of the more exotic sights of Bohemia, a little pilgrimage church of 1730 with a joyous array of copper-green onion domes around its cloister.

Industrial monument
Tábor was in the forefront of engineeering as well as of religion. The town is the terminus of Austria-Hungary's first electric railroad line, completed in 1903 to link the town to the charming little spa and ceramics center of Bechyně, 17 miles away. The line follows the ups and downs of the main road much of the way, then crosses a ravine into Bechyně over a high bridge made of reinforced concrete, one of the first of its kind in Central Europe.

designed to confuse attackers, may be the result of permanent dwellings being built on the very same plots where these first Táborites had pitched their tents.

Secure in their new stronghold, the Hussites felt free to practice their revolutionary religious and social doctrines. All creeds, save straight Catholicism, were tolerated, though eventually the excesses of the Adamites (whose enemies accused them of copulating at random during Mass) had to be put down. Tábor stayed a contrary kind of place throughout its history; even today, it has the lowest proportion of Catholics in the country.

Not a street in Tábor runs straight, but Pražská ulice, with some good sgraffitoed and fancy gabled houses, leads from the newer part of town to its heart, the slightly sloping Žižkovo náměstí (Žižka Square). As well as the Roland Fountain, there is a statue of Jan Žižka, the formidable one-eyed warrior who led the Hussite armies to many a triumph over numerically superior forces.

The north side of the square is dominated by the 235-ft.-high tower of the Děkanský kostel (Deanery Church), whose chancel is covered by one of the intricate diamond vaults characteristic of this part of Bohemia.

Below the surface of the square stretches a labyrinth of tunnels rivaling the street pattern above in complexity and extent. Underground Tábor can be entered from the Stará radnice (Old Town Hall), the picturesque three-gabled building on the west side of the square. Inside, the town museum tells you all you are ever likely to want to know about the Hussites and their doings hereabouts. There is a splendid vaulted Council Chamber of 1515, with a coat of arms incorporating statuettes of both Hus and of one-eyed Žižka.

Old One-eye
Jan Žižka (c1376–1424), a country squire from Trocnov in southern Bohemia, ignored the early loss of an eye in battle to become the fiercest and most successful of the Hussite commanders. In particular, he was the scourge of Emperor Sigismund, defeating the imperial forces many times over, notably on the hilltop overlooking Prague which now carries his name. Incredibly, the loss of his remaining eye in 1421 did not dampen his enthusiasm for a fight, and he continued to harass his enemies, overcoming them on several more occasions before succumbing to a more insidious foe, the plague, while on his way to face the emperor yet again.

233

The indefatigable Jan Žižka astride his charger in Tábor's Old Town Hall

■ The Czech countryside is liberally scattered with castles and country houses. There are the rugged fortresses of the Middle Ages, the lavish palaces of Baroque times and the romantic reconstructions of the 19th century, as well as more modest manor houses of every period. Some are immaculately maintained, others are in a sad state of neglect, reflecting the ups and downs of 20th-century history in Central Europe....■

Top: detail of the wrought-iron gates guarding the Šternbergs' 17th-century Trója Château

234

Right: Count Silva-Taroucčå planted some rare and exotic trees at his neo-Renaissance country residence of Průhonice, 6 miles southeast of Prague

Schwarzenbergs then
The Schwarzenbergs were among those minor German aristocrats whom the Habsburgs invited to replace the native Czech aristocracy after the Battle of the White Mountain. As generals (one of them defeated Napoleon at Leipzig) and as high officials of state (one was Franz Josef's prime minister) they served their masters well. Known as the "Kings of the Bohemian Forest," they acquired estates extending over an area the size of a small state, including 22 castles and countless farms, quarries, breweries, and factories. The Schwarzenbergs came to grief when the Nazis annexed Bohemia-Moravia; refusing the offer of Third Reich citizenship, they lost their estates and one of their number was imprisoned in Buchenwald.

The Czech Lands remained a preserve of aristocracy longer than was the case in most other parts of Europe. After the Battle of the White Mountain (see page 34), the native Protestant nobilty was forced to flee, to be replaced by Roman Catholics loyal to the Habsburgs. This new aristocracy was drawn from all over Europe, but mainly from the German-speaking countries. Its culture was Germanic, though by the late-18th century a distinctive Bohemian patriotism had arisen, focused on the rural residence on the one hand and the Prague palace on the other. Some great families, such as the Lobkovic clan, had a whole group of châteaux as well as several places in town. A Viennese *pied-à-terre* might come in useful, too, though most of these great Bohemians felt more at home in Prague.

In the 19th century, the power and wealth of this class increased; some became industrial entrepreneurs or extended their land-holdings at the expense of smaller proprietors and peasants, many of whom were forced to emigrate to America. Bitterly resented because of this and because of their identification with the hated Habsburgs, the Bohemian nobility found themselves in a distinctly unfriendly environment when the new country of Czechoslovakia was founded in 1918. Land reform took away much of their wealth, and the new social order spurned them in their traditional role as diplomats or other high servants of the state.

Disgruntled, these families turned in on themselves, managing what was left of their great estates, some toying with the new nationalism of the Third Reich just

across the border. Those who had identified themselves with Nazism prudently fled before the arrival of the Red Army, but Allied victory in World War II spelled the end for all of them; further expropriations took place immediately after the Liberation, and even those, like the Schwarzenbergs, who had hung on to the bitter end were forced out by the Communist takeover in 1948.

Communism and after The aristocratic estates were doled out among land-hungry farmers, but they were only allowed to enjoy their new property for a few years before being forced to join collectives. The great houses and castles presented more of a problem to the new rulers. Most of those described in this guide became museums, sometimes still furnished with objects left behind by their former owners. The majority were put to some new use, sometimes appropriate—such as the Writers' Union vacation home installed in a château outside Příbram – and sometimes incongruous, perhaps serving as an ordinary farmstead or even a barn.

Since 1989, a reversal of fortune has begun to take place; lordly residences are being returned to their original owners, or their heirs, though only if they were expropriated after 1948. Some descendants have taken one look at a crumbling palace and returned to their comfortable apartments in a big city elsewhere; others, including the Schwarzenbergs, Bohemian patriots still, are taking their restored inheritance back again.

Schwarzenbergs now
The current head of the Schwarzenberg clan is Karl Johannes Nepomuk Joseph Norbert Friedrich Antonius Wratislaw Menas, 12th Prince Schwarzenberg. "Kari" was born in 1937 in Orlík Castle, which was returned to his family in 1992, 44 years after its confiscation by the Communist regime. In his years of exile, Karl von Schwarzenberg kept his Czechoslovak nationality and, apart from managing the family's Austrian estates, he devoted himself tirelessly to the cause of human rights, becoming president of the Helsinki Committee in 1985. Since returning home, Václav Havel has made him head of the Czech Republic's Presidential Chancellery.

235

Mělník Castle passed into Lobkovic hands in the 18th century

Accommodation

Even before 1989, the provision of accommodation in Prague failed lamentably to meet the needs of the relatively small number of international visitors. Foreigners tended to be directed to one of the small number of expensive luxury hotels, while the few middle-of-the-range establishments catered for locals and fraternal delegations from other socialist countries. Private lodgings were virtually nonexistent. The post-1989 flood of tourists created a crisis, where failure to book a room well in advance could leave the unprepared at the mercy of railroad station scalpers offering an expensive sofa-bed in a dive at the outermost end of a suburban tram-line.

The years since have seen a frenzied effort to remedy the situation. Previously nationalized hotels have been sold or returned to their former owners. New hotels have been built and others are planned. Others are being restored or virtually rebuilt. Private pensiones, a previously almost unknown concept, have appeared. The number of rooms available in private homes has multiplied many times over, and accommodation agencies have also proliferated.

There is still a disproportionate number of bed-spaces at the two extremes of the spectrum, in luxury hotels at the one end, and in private houses and apartments at the other, although the proportion of rooms in moderately priced establishments has steadily grown. At the same time the number of visitors to the city has stabilized or even subsided; now that the allure of previously forbidden fruit has worn off, Prague seems likely to take its place among "normal" vacation destinations in Europe, so visitors will find it increasingly easy to find the kind of lodgings that suit them best.

Alternatives to hotels As well as the more conventional types of accommodation, there are a number of "botels" anchored along the Vltava, an interesting alternative for those with sea-legs, but perhaps not quite as romantic as they might sound. In addition, a ring of campsites surrounds the city, with facilities of varying sophistication, and in very much the same sort of location are a number of motels. Student dormitories provide basic shelter outside term-time.

Doorman standing guard over the Diplomat, one of the city's more prestigious hotels

Booking Although provision is improving, the further in advance you are able to make your plans and reservations, the more options you are likely to have when choosing where to stay.

Hotel ratings Prague hotels were traditionally rated Deluxe, A*, B*, B, or C. This system is in the process of being replaced by a star rating (from five-star luxury to one-star modest) but such is the post-Communist suspicion of government regulation that this new categorization is unlikely to be supervised effectively. The hope is that the free market will eventually sort things out; in the mean time, do not be too surprised if there is the occasional disparity between the price of a room and its quality rating.

Costs Prague is not a cheap place to stay. Luxury hotels charge as much, if not more, as their counterparts in any other Western capital. Establishments in the middle range may be more reasonable, and private rooms are generally excellent value. Rates may be lower out of season, and it is always worth while asking individual hotels if any discounts are available. Breakfast is not necessarily included in the price of the room, though you may be given vouchers which can be traded in the hotel restaurant for a basic, or more substantial, breakfast.

Rent rises II
Many Prague apartments are being returned to their pre-Communist owners. In the past, controls kept rents low, leaving little for spending on what is now a 40-year backlog of maintenance problems. Due to this situation, somewhat rougher methods are being used to persuade tenants to leave, thus making way for new, unprotected occupants, preferably high-paying foreigners.

237

A dual charging system operates in many hotels, depending on whether you are a local or a foreigner. Few Czechs are able to afford the full international price for a hotel room; they will normally pay only a fraction of the rate quoted. This is not a scam, but a logical response to the economic situation, which would otherwise strangle Czech citizens' ability to move around the country.

Another option is to stay in a floating botel—this is the Admiral, moored on the Vltava off Smíchov quayside

Location Where your accommodation is can make or break your stay. It is wonderful to walk out of your hotel and begin your stroll along the Royal Way straight away. On the other hand, Prague is a noisy and polluted city, and a central location could mean breathing in more atmospheric impurities than you might like, or being woken up by trams and garbagemen as the rush hour gets under way shortly after 5 a.m. The air-conditioning and double-paned windows of luxury hotels can be very welcome in such situations. If you are staying outside the central area, proximity to one of the stations on the clean, fast, and reliable metro system can be a great boon.

The hotel listings on pages 276–278 are categorized according to area. There are relatively few places to stay in highly desirable Hradčany, Malá Strana or Staré Město (the Old Town), but there is a much wider choice in Nové

The choices of where to stay in Prague range from modern suburban high-rises such as the Forum...

Město (the New Town). The suburbs obviously cover a very wide range, from the leafy surroundings of the royal hunting park near Bílá Hora (the White Mountain) to inner suburban Vinohrady and Žižkov, parts of which are within walking distance of the historic center. You might consider staying outside the city boundaries altogether if you have a car or can find somewhere near a railroad station. The wooded valley of the Berounka river (where Karlštejn Castle is located) is much in favor among Praguers with weekend homes, and has hotels, pensiones, and private rooms; it also has an excellent electric rail connection which takes you, in a matter of minutes, to Prague's Smíchovské nádraží (Smíchov Station), with its rapid metro link to the city center.

239

...to city center convenience in an old-style hotel such as the Paříž

Accommodation agencies Accommodation in private rooms or hostels is offered by the numerous agencies that you will find crammed into odd corners of Prague's main railroad station, or even operating from portacabins on some of the main road approaches to the city. Even so, the range of accommodation on offer is likely to be limited. An attempt is being made by the official city information service—Prague Information Service (PIS)—to offer a more comprehensive service, including hotel rooms. Agencies are listed below:

● **PIS (Pražská informační služba)**, Na Příkopě 20, Praha 1, Nové Město (tel: 54 44 44).
● **PIS**, Staroměstské náměstí 22, Praha 1 (tel: 2421 2844/5).
● **AVE**, Hlavní nádraží (Main Station), Wilsonova 8, Praha 1 (tel: 2422 3226); one of the larger of the private agencies, specializing in youth accommodation.
● **Prague Bed & Breakfast Association**, Kroftova 3, Praha 5 (formerly R Luxemburgové) (tel: 54 93 44); another fair-sized agency.
● **Czechbook Agency**, 52 St John's Park, Blackheath, London SE3 7JP (tel: 0181 853 1168); useful for UK visitors.

Food and drink

One of the world's heartiest cuisines, Czech cooking is designed to fortify body and soul for hard work and cold winters. Figure-conscious folk and vegetarians will have their work cut out for them: meat and dumplings dominate menus and where often the only vegetables on the menu are pickles, potatoes, and sauerkraut.

Communism tried to keep its subjects happy by loading the supermarket shelves with basic necessities rather than by promoting healthy and varied eating. One of the regime's success stories was ensuring that an abundant supply of crudely butchered pork reached the nation's kitchens; even today, projected rises in the price of pig-meat provoke crisis headlines in the newspapers.

While people ate abundantly, if not particularly well, at home, the restaurant scene was generally uninspiring. Apart from a few places patronized mainly by foreigners, restaurants served a limited range of dishes cooked according to the instructions in a standard manual, involving an absurdly precise calculation and pricing of quantities of ingredients. Even today, you may find yourself served up with 135g of meat costed to the nearest heller.

Since 1989 Prague has seen an explosion of eating places riding on the back of the tourist boom, many of which offer good value, though some fail to meet their pretensions. Many foreign cuisines are now represented, but traditional Czech food should not be disregarded, particularly now that greater care is being taken with the choice of ingredients and their preparation. The restaurant scene is a fluid one, with a constant stream of openings and closings—check that your choice for the evening still exists!

One meal a day
Czechs sometimes claim to keep down the calories by eating only once a day. The trouble with this theory is that the meal starts with breakfast and does not end until after suppertime!

Service with a smile at U pavouka wine-restaurant, on Celetná in Staré Město

Breakfast (*snídané*) Luxury hotels serve their international guests with the usual buffet of cereals, cold meats, cheeses, and excellent local pastries. Typically Czech, in spite of its name, is *hemendeks* (ham and eggs), a delicious fried dish based on Prague's famous ham, served with a pickle sliced into a fan shape to cut through the grease. The first—but by no means the last—of the sausages of the day will be encountered at this time, usually a Frankfurter-like *párky* or one of the more robustly flavored specimens, packed with plenty of fat and sprinkled generously with paprika.

Coffee (*káva*) is often of the Turkish type, excellent as long as you don't try to swallow the thick layer of dregs lurking at the bottom of the cup. Tea (*čaj*) is invariably made with teabags, which seem to have almost no perceptible effect on the tepid water they are supposed to infuse. Whatever the result, tea is probably better drunk without further dilution with milk (*mléko*).

The *knedlík*
"I cannot remember a meal without some sort of dumplings in a Czech home," wrote the Czech-American author and gourmet, Joseph Wechsburg. Every good housewife has her own recipe for this staple element of Bohemian cuisine, which may involve bread, flour, potatoes or semolina, yeast, and an infinite variety of fillings and garnishes—notably *povidla*, a densely textured plum jam.

241

Mid-morning Snacks There is little chance of falling victim to hunger once you are out on the street. Kiosks stand ready to serve further helpings of sausage (plus an obligatory dollop of mild mustard) and other snacks, such as potato pancake (*bramborák*). A delicatessen (*lahůdky*) will provide healthier alternatives in the shape of open sandwiches or rolls made up of slivers of Prague ham, slices of hard-boiled egg, cod's roe, and mayonnaise.

Beer drinkers are often well into their stride by this time, drinking from bottles or from no-nonsense half-liter mugs in the many smoke-filled bars (*pivnice*). Soft drinks are available, of course, some ostensibly fruit-based, while colas continue their triumphant progress here as elsewhere. "Juice" is almost invariably disappointing if you are expecting something vaguely sugar-free and undiluted. A much better bet is mineral water (*minerálka*) from one of the many spas around the country. Don't allow yourself to be fooled into buying bland soda (tap water with bubbles) which somehow seems to have become fashionable.

Café-style society in Old Town Square is strictly for tourists

FOOD AND DRINK

Lunch (*Oběd*) For many Czechs this will be the main meal of the day, consisting of soup, a main course, and perhaps a dessert (the evening meal is a less important affair of cold-cuts or cheese). Soup (*polévka*) comes in great variety and is often very good indeed, usually better value than the appetizers brought around before the meal in the more pretentious restaurants and which often turn out to be surprisingly expensive.

The main course will invariably consist of meat with those dumplings that constitute a national passion among Czechs, but which leave most foreigners completely unmoved. Somehow the gravy (tasty though it may be) is never quite abundant enough to relieve the blandness of the dumpling, particularly if it is not fresh from the oven (as may well be the case in a restaurant). Homemade dumplings are by far the best.

The most popular meat is pork (*vepř*), followed by veal (*telecí maso*) and beef (*hovězí maso*). Chicken (*kuře*) is common, duck (*kachna*) less so, while goose (*hus*) is a real treat. Only minimal vitamins and roughage are supplied by the accompanying salad, which is likely to consist of sliced cucumber and cabbage swimming in sweetened water.

Dessert is most likely to be a crêpe (*palačinka*) awash in chocolate, cream and jam. Fresh fruit is best sought in a market, and cheese plays a far less important role than in some other cuisines.

Afternoon snacks A rest from sightseeing can be enjoyed in the café (*kavárna*) or patisserie (*cukrárna*). Czech patisseurs rival the Viennese in baking cakes of tempting and illusory lightness.

Dinner (*večeře*) It is best to reserve your place in the restaurant (*restaurace*) or wine-cellar (*vinárna*) of your choice well in advance, especially at the height of the season. There are now enough interesting restaurants in Prague to keep visiting gourmets busy for the length of their stay. The evening is perhaps the time to sample some of the less routine specialties of the country. Fish, this far inland, is not common, but trout (*pstruh*) and carp (*kapr*) are netted in their thousands from the vast ponds in the south of the country. Carp is traditionally eaten on Christmas Eve, but visitors may indulge at any time. Beware the bones!

In this country of green-clad huntsmen, game is excellent; hare (*zajíc*), pheasant (*bažant*), partridge (*koroptev*) and venison (*zvěřina*) are all likely to be encountered, best of all in one of the specialist game restaurants.

The *vinarna* (wine bar) is likely to frown on a request for beer; instead, order one of the excellent wines from

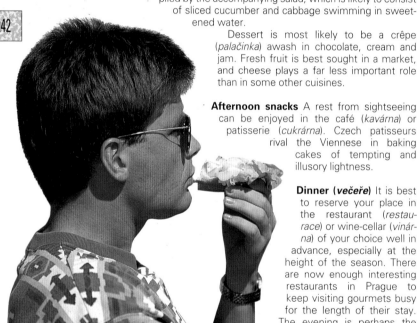

Delicious open sandwiches are a Czech specialty

southern Moravia or from the small vineyard around Mělník, just down the Vltava from Prague. Imported wines are likely to be expensive, as are foreign digestifs or aperitifs. Try the native alcoholic beverages, such as Carlsbad Becherovka (flavored with herbs according to a long-secret recipe) or Moravian *slivovice*, the plum brandy reputed to cure all ills—from the common cold to a hangover!

Old Town style—the interior of U pavouka (At the Sign of the Spider) restaurant

243

Prices The cost of a meal can vary from the full international rates charged by swanky restaurants to the few crowns for the pork and dumplings served up with the beer in a *pivnice* (pub). Watch out for cover charges, note whether tax is included in the basic prices or is charged as an extra, and do look over your check: Prague waiters are still living down a time-hallowed tendency to overcharge.

Pane vrchní!
Under Communism, the prime function of restaurants seemed to be to provide employment and status for staff rather than to give satisfaction to the diners. Traces of the haughtiness this engendered still persist, and you may need to make your needs known firmly and clearly. Paying the check usually involves the senior member of staff, the one with the wallet. Summon him with a robust *pane vrchní!* (*Herr Ober!* in German). Tips are at your discretion: it is normal to round up to the nearest whole number rather than to give a standard 10 or 15 percent.

Shopping

In his first New Year address to the nation, President Havel denounced the Communists' command economy for "producing goods which are of no interest to anyone, while we are lacking the things we need." Communism's failure to keep up with the seductive consumerism of the West was undoubtedly one of the main reasons for its demise. After the Velvet Revolution it sometimes seemed that the country's entire population had deserted in order to go shopping in Germany or Austria, whose sleepy border towns quickly transformed themselves into glittering showcases for the much-desired consumer goodies so long denied the Czechs.

Several years on from 1989, it has become possible to buy almost anything in Prague, though the city is far from a "shoppers' paradise;" international goods are available...at international prices. For the visitor, the main interest may lie in the everyday items whose price tags reflect the low level of local salaries, or in the specialized products (glass, porcelain, marionettes) for which the country has always been famous. The compact nature of central Prague, and the pedestrianization of many streets, make shopping a more pleasant experience here than in other cities. Designer-label goods offered on the street (and sometimes in stores) should be treated with suspicion as they are most unlikely to be authentic.

Stores Privatization of shops has gone ahead rapidly, and innumerable new outlets have opened. The old nationalized shops—with their less-than-inspired fascias proclaiming *Maso* (Meat), *Knihy* (Books) or *Potraviny* (Foods)—are now disappearing, along with their dull displays of pickle jars or canned fish. Praguers tend to do their shopping on a daily basis, rather than stocking up for weeks in advance, and there are virtually no large supermarkets as in the West. Many stores insist that you wait until a shopping basket is available before entering, more as a measure of crowd control than anything else. You

Souvenirs of the Russian retreat

may find it necessary to order what you want at one counter and pay at another before claiming your purchase, a potentially lengthy procedure.

Arts and crafts The classic present to bring back from Prague is Bohemian glass and crystal in both traditional and modern patterns. Try one of the following:
● **Bohemia Glass,** Na Můstku 2 (near Můstek metro).
● **Dana,** Národní 43.
● **Moser,** Na Příkopě 12.
● **Salon Philadelphia,** Vodičková 30.
● **Glass Gallery Böhm,** Anglická 1, Praha 2; glass as an art form.

A traditional favorite is blue-and-white onion-pattern porcelain from Dubi. Porcelain from Carlsbad is popular too, and is available from:
● **Karlovarský porcelán,** Pařížská 2.

Blood-red Bohemian garnets have long been famous, while the northern town of Jablonec maintains its reputation for costume jewelry. Try **Bijoux de Bohème,** Michalská 11.

The various branches of **DÍLO** (for example, at Národní třída 37, Malé náměstí 12 and Uhelný trh 11) have a wide selection of Czech (and, for the time being at least, Slovak) arts and crafts.

Toys and dolls A visit to a marionette performance may well persuade you of the desirablity of taking home an angel, devil, or some other nicely carved reproduction of the traditional wooden figures of the Czech marionette theater. You will find them on sale from street vendors or from **Obchod s loutkami,** Ncrudova 47.

A wide range of sensible and imaginative wooden toys can be obtained from **Dřevěné hračky,** Karlova 26.

Charming metal models of old-time trains in the large O-gauge are made by **ETS** Na Bělidle 34 (Malá Strana).

Puppets on sale in Old Town Square— excellent mementoes of a trip to the National Marionette Theater

Puppet population
A bewildering variety of puppets and marionettes clamor for your attention in stalls and stores. Most are characters from the fairy-tales which are such a feature of Czech literature: the Highwayman, the Devil, the Witch, the Watersprite...

Books abound for browsers; this stall is in Dejvice

Books and antiques Czechs are great readers and, until recently, books were extremely cheap, including many published in a range of foreign languages. A restricted range of new titles meant that secondhand bookstores were thronged by hopeful buyers. Most antiquarian bookshops have a selection of illustrated and foreign books. Begin your browsing at:

● **Melantrich**, Na Příkopě 3–5; new books.
● **Antikvariát, U Karlova mostu** Karlova 2; old books.
● **Antikvariát**, Galerie Můstek, 28 října 13 (basement); old books, maps, and prints.

English readers are well catered for by two American establishments:

● **The Globe Bookstore and Coffeehouse**, Janovského 14, near Strossmayerovo náměstí, Holešovice; incorporates an American-style café.
● **The International Bookstore**, Pařížská 25.

Antique shops (*starožitnosti*) have proliferated, but there isn't much gold to be found among the dross in most of them. Check whether an export license is required for items you may want to take out of the country with you.

● **Athena**, U Starého hřbitova 4.
● **Antiqua**, Panská 1.
● **Čapek**, Dlouhá 32.
● **Hodinářství**, Mikulandská 10; old clocks and watches.

Maps and prints
Philosopher Comenius and draftsman Hollar pioneered the making of accurate maps and topographical views in the 17th century. You are unlikely to find originals of their work, but many Prague *antikvariáts* (antiquarian booksellers) have a good stock of old maps and prints at reasonable prices.

Records First-rate and competitively priced LPs, cassettes and CDs are available of all the classical Czech "greats," such as Mozart, Weber, Wagner, Smetana, and Dvořák, as well as of folk music and the ubiquitous *dechovka* (brass-band polkas, waltzes, and marches). You can also sample the distinctive local pop music played by groups such as Laura a její tygři (Laura and her Tigers), Support Lesbiens (*sic*), and Žlutý pes (Yellow Dog), while

the Original Prague Syncopated Orchestra reproduces the sound of the 1920s with uncanny authenticity. Try:
● **Popron**, Jungmannova 30.
● **Goltz-Kinský Palace**, Staroměstské náměstí 12.

Markets, food and department stores For cheap souvenirs, try the following:
● **Bílá labut** (White Swan), Na Poříčí 23; the most traditional of the city's department stores and the one where you are most likely to find cheap, though not particularly stylish, household goods and other items produced for the domestic market.
● **K-Mart**, Národní 2; the heroically named former "May" department store is now American-run.
● **Kotva**, náměstí Republiky 8; large and modern.
● **Krone,** Václavské náměstí 21; German-run.
  The market in **Havelská** is good for fresh fruit and vegetables.
  For a change from the standard offerings of the Potraviny, try:
● **Country Life**, Melantrichova 15; health foods and café.
● **Fruits de France**, Jindřišská 9; not just fruits, but food imports of all kinds.
● **SYP**, Senova 2232, Prague 4 (Chodov metro station); Western-European-style supermarket.

Bohemian glassware maintains its long-standing reputation for quality

247

Nightlife and culture

A stroll along the Royal Way between Staré Město (Old Town) and the castle will be sufficient to convince any visitors that they have arrived in a culturally vibrant city, eager to display its talents. As well as sword-swallowers, fire-eaters and the vendors of knick-knacks, an array of other performers line the streets and squares; jazz artists, solo singers, classical instrumentalists, folk groups, mime artists. Posters, placards, and press listings confirm this first impression, and few visitors will find difficulty filling their engagement diary, whatever their tastes and however extended their stay.

Music The city makes the most of its musical heritage, with frequent performances of the Czech classics and of the music of its favorite adopted son, Mozart. The performance settings often enhance the experience enormously; they range from the magnificent 19th-century interiors of the Národní divadlo (National Theater) or the more intimate ambience of the Bertrámka (the Mozart Museum) and the Vila Amerika (the Dvořák Museum) to the twilight magic of the gardens of the Valdštejnský palác (Wallenstein Palace). No visitor will want to miss a performance of a Mozart opera in the gloriously refurbished 18th-century Stavovské divadlo (Estates Theater), while palaces and churches create an equally inspirational setting for chamber or religious music. Tickets are on sale at various agencies but may be cheaper if bought at the door:

● **Národní divadlo** (National Theater), Národní třída 2 (tel: 2491 3437); opera, concerts, and plays from the classical repertoire.
● **Státní Opera Praha** (State Opera), Wilsonova 4 (tel: 2422 7696); opera and ballet.
● **Stavovské divadlo** (Estates Theater), Ovocný trh 6 (tel: 2421 5001; the theater where *Don Giovanni* had its première has the ideal ambience for performances of all Mozart operas.

Musical spring
Music pervades Prague at all seasons of the year, but the high point is reached in the Prague Spring, the annual music festival held in May and early June when the city is at its freshest and most glamorous. The proceedings traditionally open at the Obecní dům (Municipal House) with a rousing rendering of Smetana's *Má Vlast* (*My Country*).

248

A sold-out concert fills Smetana Hall in the Obecní dům

- **Rudolfínum**, Alsovo nábřeží 12 (tel: 2489 3352); orchestral and chamber concerts in the Dvořák Hall and the Little Hall. Home of the Czech Philharmonic Orchestra.
- **Bertrámka** (Mozart Museum), Mozartova 169 (tel: 54 38 93); frequent early-evening chamber concerts (not just Mozart) at the Smíchov home of Mozart's Prague friends, the Dušeks.
- **Vila Amerika** (Dvořák Museum), Ke Karlovu 20 (tel: 29 82 14); evening evocations of the life and works of the master.

Among the palaces with regular concerts are:

- **Nostický palác** (Nostic Palace), Maltézké náměstí (tel: 53 60 62).
- **Dům U kamenného zvonu** (the House at the Stone Bell), Staroměstské náměstí 13 (tel: 232 7677).
- **Lobkovický palác** (Lobkovic Palace), in the castle' Jirska 3 (tel: 53706).
- **Trojský zámek** (Trója Château), Trója (tel: 84 07 61).

There are also regular concerts in the Mirror Hall of the Clementinum, Valdštejnské náměstí, and Wednesday evening summer concerts in the gardens of the Valdštejnský palác (Wallenstein Palace), náměstí Primatora dr V Vacka.

The following churches have regular concerts:

- **Chrám svatého Mikuláše** (St. Nicholas' Church), Malostranské náměstí.
- **Basilika svatého Jiří** (St. George's Basilica), in the castle.
- **Kostel svatého Františka** (St. Francis' Church), Křížovnické náměstí.
- **Basilika svatého Jakuba** (St. James's Church), Malá Štupartská.
- **Loretánská kaple** (Lorreto Shrine), Loretánské náměstí.

Jazz Readers of Josef Škvorecký's novels and short stories (such as *The Bass Saxophone*) will be aware of the hold jazz has on many of his fellow-countrymen, in spite of—or perhaps because of—Communist disapproval. If the same applies to you, and the street offerings are not sufficient for your appetite, head for the following venues:

- **Reduta** Národní třída 20 (tel: 2491 2246). Performances by professional and amateur groups from 9 p.m. daily except Sundays.
- **AGhaRTA Jazz Centrum** Krakovská 5 (tel: 2421 2914). Jazz café and shop plus music from 8 p.m. every evening.
- **Viola** Národní 7 (tel: 235 8779). Literary wine-bar with Saturday-night jazz.

> **Strictly ballroom**
> As well as being fervent followers of the fast-changing pop scene, many young Czechs are schooled in the disciplines of traditional ballroom dancing, the climax of their school careers being the graduation ball. There has also been a revival of the excellent Czech bands of the 1930s and 1940s, an era that was anathema to the Communists.

249

Sax and strings at the Viola jazz club

Pop music Rock 'n' roll received the presidential seal of approval when Václav Havel invited Mick Jagger to Hradčany and proposed that the late and much-lamented Frank Zappa should serve as his roving cultural attaché. John Lennon's image stares out from its Wall in Malá Strana (see page 114), gazed at by reverent pilgrims gathered on the sidewalk, while today's Czech rock, from a background of dissidence represented by the likes of the Plastic People of the Universe (see pages 21 and 129), attempts to create its own traditions. The following venues seem well established, but the pop scene is a shifting one; consult the *Prague Post* or *Prognosis* for up-to-date information:

● **Bunkr**, Lodecká 2, near náměstí Republiky (tel: 2481 0661); the archetypal post-1989 club, always lively and very crowded. True to its name, it really used to be a bunker! Good music from 9 p.m. nightly.

● **Lávka** Novotného lávka 1 (tel: 2421 4797); fascinating riverside location by Karlův most (Charles Bridge). Music starts daily at 9 p.m.

250

Dramatic lighting effects at the Laterna Magika, which puts on music and mime concerts, as well as showing plays and movies

Nightclubs
These still abound around Václavské náměstí (Wenceslas Square), and the more prestigious hotels run their own. Floorshows can be enjoyed at a number of establishments, including:
Alhambra Václavské náměstí 5 (tel: 22 04 67).
Lucerna Štepánská 61 (tel: 235 0909).
Variete Praga U Novaků, Vodičkova 30 (tel: 50861).

Friedrich Dürrenmatt

MINOTAURUS

LATERNA MAGIKA

● **Malostranská beseda**, Malostranské náměstí 21 (tel: 53 90 24); ska (white reggae), folk, reggae, and blues, as well as rock.
● **Radost FX**, Bělehradská 120 (tel: 25 12 10); favored by both locals and tourists. Music nightly from 9 p.m.
● **Rock Café**, Národní třída 20 (tel: 2491 4414); daytime café, night-time disco and live music.

Dechovky Prague's favorite brass bands (see page 128) blare out their waltzes, polkas, and marches every Saturday afternoon in the Národní dům Vinohrady (Vinohrady National House), Náměstí Míru 9 (metro line A to Náměstí Míru station).

Theater Even if you only understand English, you can get some drama into your stay by attending one of the foreign-language performances on offer, or by enjoying the highly accomplished techniques of the Prague marionette tradition and the famous Laterna Magika. The **Rokoko Theater** (Václavské náměstí 38, tel: 2421 7113) puts on English plays, while a look at the posters on any central street will put you in touch with one effort or another to recycle the life and times of Franz Kafka. Alternatively, you can check out the English-language magazines (see panel) for dramatic offerings (perhaps even a performance of President Václav Havel's plays).

Where and when
The weekly English-language newspapers *Prague Post* and *Prognosis* both give comprehensive coverage to all the events and attractions likely to be of interest to non-Czech speakers. In addition, there is a monthly publication in English, *Cultural Events*, a summary of the fully comprehensive *Přehled Kulturních Pořadů v Praze*. Perusal of this latter publication with your dictionary or with the help of a Czech friend will reveal the incredible range of entertainments on offer in the city.

251

The magical synthesis of film, music, theater and mime of the **Laterna Magika** can be experienced at its new home in the extension to the National Theater, the Nová scéna, Národní třída 2 (tel: 2491 4129), while the not-dissimilar **Black Light Theater** can be seen in the Divadlo Za bránou II, Národní 40 (tel: 2423 0421).

Prague puppetry can be enjoyed at any number of locations. The following are the best:
● **Národní divadlo marionet** (National Marionette Theater, a venerable institution also known as the Říše loutek—the Realm of Puppets), Žatecká 1 (tel: 232 3429); also at Celetná 13. Features puppet adaptations of operas.
● **Muzeum české hudby** (Museum of Czech Music), Novotného lávka (tel: 2422 9075); similar operatic offerings to the above, cabaret style.
● **Divadlo Spejbla a Hurvínka**, Římska 45 (tel: 25 16 66); features the antics of the city's famous comic duo, Špejbl and Hurvínek.
● **Česky soubor písní a tanců** (The Czech Folklore Ensemble), Divadlo na Klarově, nábřeží E Beneše 3 (tel: 2451 1077). Performances most evenings.
● **Letní scéna AUS Praha**, Pohořelec 25 (tel: 2451 1027); shows based on Moravian and Slovak folklore.

Welcome to our wonderful world! Entrance to the Říše loutek (the Realm of Puppets)

Prague for children

Dining out
For incorrigible junior consumers, familiar food can be enjoyed at the steadily increasing number of McDonald's outlets opening up in the city, while some may find the youthful ambience of the American Hospitality Center, at Melantrichova 8 (tel: 2422 9961) reassuring.

Gadgets with youth appeal at the National Technical Museum

Many children will enjoy the tourist trail along the Royal Way from Staré Město (the Old Town) to the castle with its throngs of people and performers of all kinds. A protracted tour of the castle can easily become tedious for the young, but entertaining moments are provided by the Changing of the Guard (daily at noon), especially on Sunday morning when the ceremony is fleshed out by a military band and by buglers bugling from on high. There are also military band concerts on Saturday mornings. Most children will enjoy the fairytale cottages of Zlatá ulička (Golden Lane) to the north of the castle (see page 91). The castle, of course, has plenty of towers to explore, and there are several others (such as Charles Bridge—page 103; Powder Tower—page 145; Old Town Hall Tower—page 150; Cathedral Tower—page 63), all of which can be fun to climb as long as energy lasts.

Childrens' exploration of the city can be varied by taking different kinds of transportation. The horse-drawn carriages leaving from Staroméstské náměstí (Old Town Square) are a good bet, as is the "train" that takes its pas-

sengers from here up to the castle. There are rowboats to be rented from Slovanský ostrov (Slavonic Island), while steamers ply from the quay beside Palackého most (Palacký Bridge), going upstream (towards the Vltava dams) and downstream (to Trója Château—see page 200—to the zoo and beyond). Check on the length of the trip before committing the family to what could turn out to be a long day on board.

Tram rides will be unfamiliar to many children, and there is a useful old-timer which runs a circular route beginning and ending at the Výstaviště (Exhibition Grounds—see page 202). Here there is a whole array of attractions, including an amusement park, playgrounds, fountains, the amazing painted panorama of the Battle of Lipany, and even visiting circuses.

Adjoining the Exhibition Grounds is Stromovka park with its lake, where ducks can be fed in summer and ice skating enjoyed in winter. The hockey rink in the Exhibition Grounds themselves is open for public skating at times when it is not in use for tournaments. There are a number of swimming pools in Prague, but for a day out rather than just a quick dip it might be a good idea to head for one of the artificial lakes on the edge of the city. These include the Džbán Dam, in the attractive Šárka valley, and the Hostivař Dam Oaze in the suburb of Hostivař, where you can take part in boating, windsurfing, and many other activities.

253

An excursion to Petřín (see page 81) will also help keep children busy. The easiest way up to these western heights is by the *lanovka* (funicular railroad), with its dramatically unfolding views over the city. Once at the top, there is the miniature Eiffel Tower (the Rozhlédna) to climb, the Bludiště (Hall of Mirrors) to explore and the Hvězdárna (Planetarium) to marvel at.

The whirring and clicking puppets that form a procession around the Astronomical Clock at the Old Town Hall (see page 149) will reduce the most fidgety child to temporary awe. Puppets and marionettes are on display at many stalls, while the puppet theater is sure to be a hit (especially when the antics of Špejbl and Hurvínek are involved—see page 251).

Prague's popular zoo can be found in the suburb of Holešovice

Older and technically-minded children will find plenty to interest them in the cars, locomotives, aircraft and the hands-on exhibits of the National Technical Museum (see page 195). Others will be fascinated by the uniforms and hardware of the two military museums (pre-World War II in the Schwarzenberg Palace in Hradčany—see page 57, and more recent conflicts at the foot of Žižkov hill—see page 211).

Further away from Prague, romantic castles, such as Karlštejn (see page 226) and Konopiště (see page 220) might cast their spell on the more imaginative, especially in the case of Karlštejn if you take the horse-drawn carriage up the long hill to the castle gates.

Prague on a budget

Though Czechs may not agree, living costs in Prague remain low and it may take a few years yet before they catch up fully with the rest of Europe. For the time being this makes the city a relatively inexpensive place to take a vacation.

Haggles and hassles
Store prices are generally not negotiable, but most stallholders will not be averse to some friendly bargaining. When in a restaurant, always verify your check, and in a bar compare the price you are charged with that on the tariff list displayed.

Somewhere to sleep The fly in the ointment is accommodation. This is likely to be your main expense, as prices here are close to, or even greater than, those in other countries. Mainstream hotels can easily absorb a disproportionate amount of your budget, and the number of moderately priced establishments is still limited. The best solution is to take advantage of the burgeoning numbers of private rooms, checking first that there are good public transportation links to the center. The young have the further alternative of hostels and dormitories (see pages 236–239 and pages 276–278).

Getting around Exhausting yourself by excessive walking and then taking a taxi home can make a big dent in your finances. Make yourself familiar with the public transportation network as a whole (not just the metro) and plan your movements accordingly. The system is reliable and still extremely good value (though locals will disagree, especially after one of the fairly regular price hikes). Single tickets are cheap, but buy a day- (or several-day) ticket if you are going to make lots of journeys. Avoid tour-operators' excursions to out-of-town destinations, such as Karlštejn Castle, and take the train or normal bus instead at a fraction of the cost.

254

Souvenirs such as these local-made shirts are excellent value

Dining out Food and drink will cost you as much as anywhere else if you insist on patronizing

places along the tourist trail and spending your evenings in the ($$$) restaurants recommended in this guide (see pages 278–281). Stick to the ($) establishments, and enjoy your evenings in the local bar whose beer will be as good as that served up in the fancy hotel at several times the price. Buy delicious open sandwiches from the delicatessen rather than from kiosks, and make up picnics with ingredients bought from supermarkets. Get bottled beer, mineral water or canned fruit juices from the same source in preference to buying cola from street vendors.

Where am I? The city plan (often available free of charge) will help

Nightlife Entertainments designed for foreign visitors (plays and opera in languages other than Czech) don't come particularly cheap, though many performances are well worth the money. You may find that your ticket for an ordinary concert will cost more than the one sold to a local. This is not a deception, but a rational response to the fact that Czechs are not as wealthy as most visitors.

Make the most of the amazing array of free entertainment on offer from the street performers thronging the tourist trail between Staroměstské náměstí (Old Town Square) and the castle. The jazz, chamber music or solo performances of these entertainers are often as good as those provided in a concert hall or club (not that clubs, discothèques and the like are expensive by international standards). The bands serenading the elderly clientele at the open-air dance floor in the Výstaviště (Exhibition Grounds) play for free (once you've paid the entrance fee); another spot to enjoy rousing music is at the Saturday morning military-band concerts in the castle gardens.

Museums The entry fee to museums and galleries is likely to be a fraction of that charged in your home country, though here again a dual-pricing system, favoring Czech citizens, may be in operation. If your command of the language is near perfect, you might get in at the local rate, but keep in mind that most institutions of this kind need all the financial support they can get.

Youth movement
Hitchhiking is widely practiced in the Czech Republic, and you may be tempted to join other hopefuls at the entrance to the highway. However, the less adventurous alternative, the long-distance bus, is still amazingly cheap, and will also get you reliably to your destination.

Shopping Excellent souvenirs are on sale on street stalls and specialist shops. Cheaper alternatives can be found in department stores, record shops, and bookstores (see pages 244–247).

Practicalities

Unlike many capital cities, Prague is comfortably sized and easy to grasp as a whole. A walk along the Royal Way from Staré Město (the Old Town) to the castle, with plenty of pauses along the route and a climb to one of the many panoramic viewpoints, will introduce you to many of the city's charms. Prague thus makes a wonderful weekend destination; the visual impact and liveliness of the city is such that even 48 hours spent here is enough to make visitors feel they have more than scratched the surface. On the other hand, to enjoy all the attractions listed in this book would take a good month of your time, without undertaking any excursions. A possible compromise, if you want to spend a summer holiday of three weeks or so, would be to spend at least part of the time in the more relaxed surroundings of Prague's countryside; bearing in mind the small size of the Czech Republic it is also very easy to tour some of the outstanding provincial towns and landscapes (covered in Fodor's *The Czech Republic and Slovakia*).

The immaculate Malá Strana metro station

Transportation The historic four towns of Prague are best explored on foot, with some help from the comprehensive public transportation system. In spite of the city's relative compactness, to attempt to do everything on foot can leave you exhausted, particularly in view of some of the hills to be overcome. The metro is very useful, the trams perhaps even more so, and it is well worth taking a little trouble to master the route map. Walking downhill is always easier than climbing up, and excursions which start at the castle, or further up the hill at Strahov, can make life a lot easier.

TRAVEL FACTS

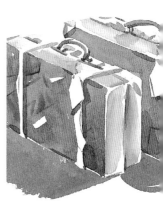

Getting there

By air Prague is served by its venerable Ruzyně airport, located about 10 miles west of the city center. A major expansion program is planned, the present facilities (car-rental and bureaux de change) being adequate rather than lavish. Between them, the national airline, ČSA, and numerous foreign companies operate services to most major European cities as well as to the U.S. and Canada, and the number of destinations served is increasing. In addition there are internal flights to Brno, Ostrava, and Karlovy Vary. The cheapest way to get from the airport to the city center is to take the service bus to Dejvická metro station and travel onwards by the clean and efficient subway. There is also an airport shuttle bus service and a taxi stand.

By train Prague can be reached from all the neighboring countries by express train, and there is also a link to Paris, and to Ostend in Belgium. Most trains terminate at Prague's main station (Praha Hlavní nádraží), though Berlin and Dresden expresses operate from the modern Praha Holešovice station in the northern suburbs. This is easily reached by metro. Smíchov station, in the southern suburbs, is also served by international trains to western Germany, and it may shorten your journey to get off here and continue by metro to your final destination.

By bus Express bus services link Prague with a number of European cities, including London. Fares and journey times (24 hours from London) compare favorably with trains, but there are no sleeper cars or couchettes! Prague's principal long-distance bus station is Autobusové nádraží Florenc (linked to the metro). For details of the London service call:
● Kingscourt Express (Prague tel: 6121 1668; London 0181 769 9229), or
● Adco Travel (Prague tel: 6631 0061; London 0171 372 0323).

An international express leaves Prague's Main Station, Praha Hlavní nádraží

Bringing a bike will give you much more freedom once you arrive

By boat As well as carrying local pleasure boats, the Vltava sees an occasional steamer which has come up the Elbe from far-off Hamburg via Dresden and the spectacular scenery of the river's gorges in both Germany and Bohemia. For travelers from Britain this gives the intriguing possibility of sailing from Harwich into the heart of Central Europe (changing craft at Hamburg). Details from:
● **Weisse Flotte**, Otto Wagner Strasse 6, Dresden, Germany.

By car Good main roads link Prague to all frontier crossings, though as yet there is no direct connection with the expressway network of adjoining countries. Some recently reopened minor border crossings may only be usable by locals or by pedestrians and cyclists. Those driving over from Britain should consider the overnight Harwich–Hamburg ferry service as a relaxing alternative to the shorter Channel crossing; from Hamburg to Prague is a day's drive. The Harwich–Hamburg service is operated by Scandinavian Seaways:
● **Scandinavian Seaways**, Scandinavia House, Parkeston Quay, Harwich, Essex CO12 4QG (tel: 01255 241234).

Customs regulations
The duty-free allowance is up to 250 cigarettes (or the tobacco equivalent) plus 2 liters of wine and 1 liter of alcohol. Expensive gifts may attract duty fees. You can export items paid for with hard currency, but officially there are strict limits on the duty-free export of goods purchased with Czech crowns. Enforcement seems lax, but it is a good idea to check the latest situation and keep receipts for all the goods you buy. It is forbidden to take antiques out of the country without proof of payment and a certificate from a museum or national gallery giving permission.

Insurance
Most visitors are entitled to free emergency medical treatment (medicines are extra, but are not expensive). Even so, medical insurance still makes sense if you would like to be able to return home without fuss in the event of an emergency.

Visas
Visitors from the U.S. and most European and Commonwealth countries do not need visas.

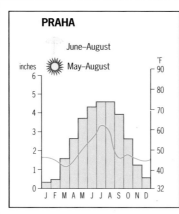

PRAHA

June–August

inches ☀ May–August °F

Weather and when to go

With its glittering array of attractions, Prague is an all-year destination, an ideal city for a winter break just as much as for a summer vacation. The city is probably not at its best during the height of summer, when the temperatures can be very high, the rainfall at its most abundant and the humidity oppressive.

April can still be surprisingly wintry, but in May there is usually plenty of sunshine; this is the month when the fruit trees on Petřín hill are gloriously covered in blooms and the music of the Prague Spring Festival fills all the available concert halls.

September is still sunny, but from mid-October onwards the weather tends to deteriorate; air pollution is at its worst in winter, when temperature changes can trap coal smoke and exhaust emissions for days, if not weeks, on end.

National holidays
- January 1 New Year's Day
- Easter Monday (variable)
- May 1 Labor Day
- May 8 Liberation from German occupation
- July 5 Saints Cyril and Methodius' Day
- July 6 Anniversary of the death of Jan Hus
- October 28 Independence Day
- December 24 Christmas Eve
- December 25 Christmas Day
- December 26 St. Stephen's Day

Time
The Czech Republic observes Central European Time, one hour ahead of GMT and seven hours ahead of U.S. Eastern Standard Time. Clocks go forward an hour between March and late September.

Money matters
The unit of currency is the Czech crown (Kč = Koruna česká). This is divided into a hundred hellers, annoying little coins which you will amass in your change at the supermarket and elsewhere. The full range of coins includes 10, 20, and 50 hellers, 1, 2, 5, 10, 20, and 50 crowns, while bills come in denominations of 20, 50, 100, 200, 500, and 1,000 and 5,000 crowns.

The 200-crown bill features the 17th-century Czech philosopher Comenius

Foreign money is best changed at a bank, though Směnárna (bureaux de change) abound; their rates and commission charges should be compared before making a transaction. Those at border crossings mostly charge a reasonable commission. The crown is not yet a convertible currency (though this may change). If you wish to change crowns back into a foreign currency, make sure you keep the receipts from your original transactions. When Czechs and Slovaks first went their separate ways, existing Czechoslovak bills were overstamped with a Czech or Slovak emblem; these are no longer valid,

There is no shortage of bureaux de change in the city, but banks may offer a better rate

having been replaced by the new currency. The Slovak crown is now a distinct currency from the Czech crown.

Although the once-thriving black market in foreign currency scarcely exists nowadays, you should resist the temptation if accosted by anyone offering to change your pennies for crowns—you may well be ripped off.

Credit cards are in increasing use, particularly in the kind of places likely to be frequented by tourists.

Car rental

Hertz and Europcar have offices in the city center and at Ruzyně airport. There are many other operators (who may be cheaper, with local Škodas available as well as international models); try one of the following:

● **Avanticar**, Evropská 178 (tel: 316 5204).
● **A K MÜ**, Dačická 178 (tel: 786 9318).
● **Dancar**, Bělohorská 186 (tel: 35 74 74).
● **Esocar**, Husitská 58 (tel: 691 2244).

Driving

No special documents are required for drivers bringing their own vehicles into the Czech Republic, though officially the registration should be available for inspection. Green Card insurance cover is recommended.

Prague is a far-from-ideal city for a car, with a labyrinth of one-way streets, an acute shortage of parking spaces, and zealous police eager to pounce on traffic offenders. That said, a car gives you flexibility in visiting suburban locations and for making excursions beyond the city limits. Czechs drive on the right, and road signs are the familiar international ones. Seatbelts must be worn, and children under 12 must not sit in the front seat. Driving after consuming any amount of alcohol is forbidden. Serious accidents must be reported to the police. Vehicles must show an international identity plate and carry a first-aid kit, a warning triangle, and replacement bulbs.

Driving in Prague can be hazardous, and any serious accidents should be reported to the police

Speed limits are low compared with some neighboring countries (60km in town, 90km outside, 110km on highways); speed traps and on-the-spot fines are common. At tram stops motor vehicles must stop and yield to passengers boarding or leaving the tram. Gas stations are not as numerous as in the rest of Europe, and lead-free gas (identified by its German name *bleifrei*, or as "Natural") is not available at all of them.

If you insist on bringing a car into the city center, avoid the risk of being towed away or clamped by using a designated parking lot or garage (for example, at the main station or the Kotva department store on náměstí Republiky). In case of a breakdown, contact any of the following 24-hour repair services:

● **ADOS** (tel: 6731 0713).
● **Automotoklub** (tel: 123).
● **Pragis Assistance** (tel: 75 81 15).
● **Travel Agency Autoturist** (tel: 154).
● **ÚAMK** (tel: 123/0123/154).

Most international makes of car can be serviced in Prague, though parts may take a long time to order from abroad.

Public transportation

One of the positive legacies of Communism is Prague's comprehensive and integrated public transportation system, centered around the metro, trams, and buses (plus the Petřín hill funicular). Carrying up to 2½ million passengers a day, the system gives reliable access to virtually any destination within the city, though it may take a while, and is likely to be unpleasantly overcrowded during rush hour. There is a scanty night service too. Tickets, which are valid on any part of the system, must be bought in advance from news kiosks, tobacconists, metro stations or at hotel reception desks; validate them by putting them in the clipping machine as you enter a station or board a vehicle. Tickets are cheap—even more so if you buy a tourist pass, valid for one to five days.

For public transportation information, tel: 29 46 82.

Traffic conditions are far from ideal, so stick to public transportation

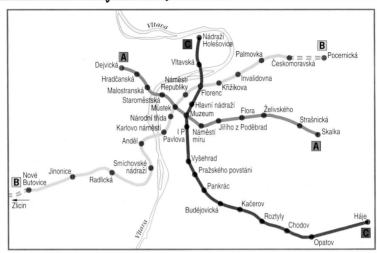

Metro, tram, and bus Swift, clean, and safe, the metro consists of a network of three lines (A, B, and C) with widely-distanced stations. It was designed to be used in conjunction with trams and buses, and it is worth studying the city map to identify the connections most useful to you. A favorite for tourists is Malostranská metro station, with an adjacent stop for Tram 22 up to Hradčany or Strahov monastery (Hradčany metro is quite a walk from the castle).

Trams fill most of the gaps left by the metro, while buses mostly link suburban metro stations to the far-flung housing developments.

Taxis The poor reputation of Prague's taxi drivers may be tough on that majority of cabbies who are honest, but it is not undeserved. The official charge per kilometer is quite modest, but as a visitor you are likely to be charged several times this rate. Even if the meter is working, it will probably be illegally switched to the night tariff. Journeys which should cost a handful of crowns can end up costing hundreds. If you have to use a taxi, check the likely fare beforehand and refuse to be overcharged. Requesting a receipt is a useful tactic. If you're a resident of one of the more expensive hotels, you will be able to use their own taxi service, whose rates, though high, are at least predictable.

Prague's metro

The up-side in all this is the sheer number of taxis (ranging from battered Škodas to plush Mercedes); you should have no difficulty in finding one, whether at a stand or in the street.

Central Taxi Control (tel: 2491 1559/1538/1225) is the control center for all taxi drivers who are members of the Taxi Guild.

Public transportation stops show their location and routes served

Around-the-clock services are provided by:
- **AAA Radiotaxi** (tel: 3399 or 312 2112).
- **City Taxi Radiodispatch** (tel: 20 20 51).
- **DMV Taxi** (tel: 692 0214 or 43 49 18).
- **Microlux Taxi** (tel: 35 03 20, 35 48 19 or 35 61 47).
- **Profitaxi** (tel: 692 1332).

Student and youth travel

Young people should find Prague a cheap city. Travel within the Czech Republic is inexpensive, too, which may make you think twice about whether you really need to purchase an Inter-Rail Pass if you are spending most of your time within the Republic. All aspects of youth travel, including accommodation in student hostels, are dealt with by the **CKM** agency, at Žitná 12 (tel: 29 99 49). An International Student Identity Card is useful for getting reduced-rate entry to galleries and museums. Young visitors tend to visit, for company and news, the American Hospitality Center at Melantrichova 8 (tel: 2422 9961).

Prague has a huge number of taxis in all shapes and sizes

Media
Newspapers The English-language weekly *Prague Post* and the bi-weekly *Prognosis* both contain a wealth of events, travel tips, and so on.

TV and radio Of the four local TV stations, the commercial Premiera station broadcasts some American news programs. The more expensive hotels invariably have satellite television.

Post offices
Prague's main post office is at Jindřišská 14 (tel: 2422 8588) and offers 24-hour mail, telegram, fax, telephone, and poste restante services. For the latter, address correspondence to: Post Restante,

A wide range of publications, both local and international, is on sale

Jindřišská 14, 110 00 PRAHA 1. Present your passport when collecting mail. Postage stamps can be obtained at kiosks and hotel reception desks as well as at post offices.

Telephone and fax
The inefficiency of the Czech telephone service is legendary, but improvements are under way (which means all Prague telephone numbers are being changed—check before calling). Hotel rates are up to four times the cost of a call made from a public phone. These are of two types; the older, orange model is inferior to the newer, gray version,

Prague mail/boxes are bright orange in color

which takes a greater range of coins making (expensive) international calls at least theoretically possible. Card phones are on the increase, or you can go to a post office and book a call. Give the clerk the full number you want and wait until your name is announced. Pay on completion of the call. There are no off-peak rates. International dialling codes: Australia 0061, Ireland 00353, New Zealand 0064, U.K. 0044, U.S. and Canada 001. Faxes can be sent and received (at 232 0878) at the main post office, Jindřišská 14.

Language guide

Generally regarded as "difficult," Czech is closely related to Russian and Polish, and anyone with a knowledge of these tongues should have no great problems getting by. Written Czech looks intimidating, and it even has its own unique sound—ř as in Dvořák. As in any country, it is worth mastering a few basics, so that street signs at least become comprehensible. Czech is pronounced as it is written. The stress is always on the first syllable.

Vowels

a	as in mammoth
á	as in father
é	as in air
ě	as in yes
i,y	as in city
í, ý	as in meet
o	as in top
ó	as in more
u	as in book
ú	as in boom

Consonants

c	as in its
č	as in china
ch	as in lock
j	as in yes
ň	as in onion
r	a 'rolled' r
ř	a combination of r and z (as in Dvořák)
š	as in shine
z	as in zero
ž	as in pleasure

Basic words and phrases

yes	ano
no	ne
please	prosím
thank you	děkuji
do you speak English?	mluvíte anglicky?
I don't understand	nerozumím
I don't speak Czech	nemluvím česky
hello	ahoj
good morning	dobrý den
good evening	dobrý večer
good night	dobrou noc
goodbye	na shledanou
sorry	promiňte
where?	kde?
how much?	kolik?
when?	když?
what?	co?

Numbers

1	jeden/jedna/jedno
2	dva/dvě
3	tři
4	čtyři
5	pět
6	šest
7	sedm
8	osm
9	devět
10	deset

City police on patrol—in a Škoda of course!

Crime and police

Before the Velvet Revolution, many seemingly innocent activities (like speaking your mind) were regarded as a crime, and the enforcement of the law by a grim, khaki-uniformed police force was rigorous, to say the least. One interpretation of the democracy that succeeded Communism is that anything goes; crime has certainly increased by leaps and bounds, and is one of the favorite topics of conversation among locals, who will do their best to frighten you about the perils that await you on the city streets. Even so, you need not be unduly worried. What has happened could be seen as another aspect of a move towards normality, and the likelihood of your becoming a victim of crime is still much less than in most other western cities.

Nevertheless, you should take all the usual precautions. Theft of, and from, cars is particularly common. Don't leave any valuables in a vehicle, and park it, if possible, in a super-vised parking lot. Pickpockets operate routinely along the tourist trail, particularly in Václavské náměstí (Wenceslas Square) and on Karlův most (Charles Bridge). Remember that you are an object of envy to many locals, whose legitimately earned salaries are likely to be a tenth of yours; cameras and camcorders may represent many months' wages to most people and could prove an irresistible temptation.

The police, once forbiddingly known as the VB ("Public Security") have now reverted to the more innocuous name of *policie*. They are supplemented by an increasing number of black-clad municipal police, known as "black sheriffs," and by an army of swaggering security men whose behavior often leaves a lot to be desired.

The police emergency telephone number is 158.

Embassies
● **Canada**, Mickiewiczova 6 (tel: 2431 1108; fax: 2431 0294).
● **United Kingdom**, Thunovská 14 (tel: 2451 0439 and 2451 0443); this embassy handles matters for Irish, Australian and New Zealand citizens.
● **U.S.**, Tržiště 15 (tel: 2451 0847 or 2451 1001).

Emergency telephone numbers
● **Ambulance** 155.
● **Doctor** (*lékař*) 158.
● **Police** (*policie*) 158.
● **Fire department** 150.

Lost property
The lost property office is at Karolíny Světlé 5, tel: 2422 6133.

Health
Emergency medical treatment is generally free for foreign visitors, but medical insurance is still advisable to cover all the incidental costs of a disrupted vacation. If you need regular medication it is best to bring your own supplies. Two institutions are used to dealing with sick visitors from abroad:

● **Diplomatic Health Center**, Na Homolce 724, Roentgenova ulice, Prague 5 (tel: 5292 2146; for emergencies, tel: 5292 2191). Na Homolce is located in Motol, in the western suburbs, reached by bus 167 from Anděl metro station. It used to be the exclusive preserve of high-ranking Party members. Since 1990 its multilingual staff have provided in-patient and out-patient care for foreigners. Bring your passport. Dental treatment is also available.
● **Fakultní poliklinika**, Karlovo náměstí 32, Nové Město (tel: 2496 1111); less well-appointed facilities than at Na Homolce.

There are 24-hour pharmacists all over Prague. Two examples in the city center are at Na Příkopě 7 (tel: 2421 0229) and at Ječná 1 (tel: 29 29 40); for others check the *Yellow Pages*.

Air pollution is so bad in Prague that anyone with respiratory problems should think twice before making an extended stay here, particularly in the winter.

Old-fashioned pharmacy

Camping

Camping is possible on the outskirts of Prague at a number of sites, among them:
● **Caravan-Camp**, Plzeňská (tel: 52 47 14); conveniently located on the main road in from the west.
● **Kotva Bráník**, U ledáren 55 (tel: 46 17 12 or 46 13 97); by the Vltava to the south of the city, with better-than-average facilities and chalets to rent.

Visitors with disabilities

Under the old regime, people with disabilities were encouraged to stay at home and keep quiet. The issue of access is now a live one, but the habit has a long way to go before it catches up even with the minimal level of provision that exists in other European cities. Standards range from excellent in the more modern and expensive hotels to nonexistent in many other places.

Opening times

Banks Relatively liberal opening hours are kept by:
● **Komerčni banka**, Na Příkopě 28 (8 a.m.–6 p.m. Monday to Friday).
● **Česká spořitelna**, Václavské náměstí 42 (8 a.m.–6 p.m. Monday to Friday, 9 a.m.–1 p.m. Saturday).
● **Živnostenská banka**, Na Příkopě 20 (8 a.m.–5 p.m. Monday to Friday and 9 a.m.–1 p.m. Saturday).

Food stores These may open as early as 6 a.m., closing between 6 and 7 p.m. on wekdays, and at noon on Saturdays. A few also open on Sunday.

Other shops From 8 or 9 a.m. to 6 or 7 p.m. during weekdays, and from 9 a.m. to 2 p.m. on Saturdays. Department stores may stay open until 4 p.m. on Saturdays and there may be late-night shopping on Thursdays. More and more private shops are opening on Sundays, especially in areas frequented by tourists. The habit of closing for days on end for *inventura* (stock-taking) or for "technical reasons" will diminish as private ownership takes hold.

Galleries, museums, and historic buildings From 9 or 10 a.m. to 5 p.m. (or sometimes 6 p.m.) from Tuesday to Sunday. Monday is the universal day off except for the Národní muzeum (National Museum), which closes its doors on Tuesday instead.

Stores no longer close at will

The National Museum is open on Mondays, unlike other museums

Places of worship
Anglican
St. Clement's Church (svatého Klimenta), Klimentská (in the north-ern part of Nové Město); Sunday service in English at 9:30 a.m.

Baptist
International Baptist Church Vinohradská 68 (tel: 311 7974); Sunday service in English at 11 a.m.

Roman Catholic
St. Joseph's Church (svatého Josefa), Josefská 4, Malá Strana; Sunday service in English at 10:30 a.m.

Tipping
Despite occasional poor service, it is expected that you will tip 10 percent in a restaurant and when paying a taxi driver. Small tips are also given to tour guides and hotel porters.

Toilets
Most metro stations have a toilet (*muži/páni* = men, *ženy/dámy* = women), but other public toilets are few and far between, so it is a good idea to plan your daily needs around the facilities in your hotel and in cafés and restaurants. The toilet is often guarded by an attendant whose livelihood depends on the tip you give her.

Photography
In contrast to the situation of only a few years ago, when only rather dubious brands of East German film were available, photographic supplies of all kinds are now widely on sale and outlets compete in providing express processing services.

Electricity
220 volts, 50 cycles AC. Standard continental European two-prong plugs are in general use, so any appli-ance fitted with a three-prong plug will need an adaptor (though shavers are usually compatible).

Etiquette
Like other Central Europeans, Czechs are fond of titles, such as Doctor and Professor, and these will be used in introductions and corres-pondence. Introductions tend to be formal, with each person announcing his or her own name and shaking hands. Dress has become steadily less formal in recent years, and neat casual wear is acceptable in almost any situation.

The sharing of tables is customary in ordinary restaurants. Wish your neighbors *dobrou chut!* (have a good meal!), *na zdraví!* (cheers!) and *na shledanou!* (goodbye!) at the appro-priate moments.

If you are invited to someone's home, take flowers or a small gift.

The evolution of social attitudes was frozen under Communism and political correctness has as yet to make inroads. Expect antediluvian

West window of St. Vitus' cathedral

Informal clothing is acceptable everywhere

CONVERSION CHARTS

FROM	TO	MULTIPLY BY
Inches	Centimeters	2.54
Centimeters	Inches	0.3937
Feet	Meters	0.3048
Meters	Feet	3.2810
Yards	Meters	0.9144
Meters	Yards	1.0940
Miles	Kilometers	1.6090
Kilometers	Miles	0.6214
Acres	Hectares	0.4047
Hectares	Acres	2.4710
Gallons	Liters	4.5460
Liters	Gallons	0.2200
Ounces	Grams	28.35
Grams	Ounces	0.0353
Pounds	Grams	453.6
Grams	Pounds	0.0022
Pounds	Kilograms	0.4536
Kilograms	Pounds	2.205
Tons	Tonnes	1.0160
Tonnes	Tons	0.9842

MEN'S SUITS

U.K.	36	38	40	42	44	46	48
Rest of Europe	46	48	50	52	54	56	58
U.S.	36	38	40	42	44	46	48

DRESS SIZES

U.K.	8	10	12	14	16	18
France	36	38	40	42	44	46
Italy	38	40	42	44	46	48
Rest of Europe	34	36	38	40	42	44
U.S.	6	8	10	12	14	16

MEN'S SHIRTS

U.K.	14	14.5	15	15.5	16	16.5	17
Rest of Europe	36	37	38	39/40	41	42	43
U.S.	14	14.5	15	15.5	16	16.5	17

MEN'S SHOES

U.K.	7	7.5	8.5	9.5	10.5	11
Rest of Europe	41	42	43	44	45	46
U.S.	8	8.5	9.5	10.5	11.5	12

WOMEN'S SHOES

U.K.	4.5	5	5.5	6	6.5	7
Rest of Europe	38	38	39	39	40	41
U.S.	6	6.5	7	7.5	8	8.5

views to be freely expressed on subjects such as race and sex. Anything that smacks of restriction has been rejected, so you will see plenty of freely displayed pornography, uncontrolled advertising (and smoking!) of cigarettes, and numerous billboards disfiguring the highways.

Women travelers

Women visitors face no special problems in Prague. The public behavior of Czech men is no better or worse than that of their counterparts in any other Western city, although attitudes to women remain largely unenlightened.

Tourist information

The formerly monolithic state travel agency, Čedok, has not only been privatized, it has also been split into separate Czech and Slovak sections. It still offers the most comprehensive tourism service for the country as a whole, with numerous offices both in the Czech Republic and abroad.

● **Čedok in Prague**, Na Příkopě 18, 111 35 Praha 1 (tel: 2419 7111).
● **Čedok in the U.K.**, 49 Southwark Street, London SE1 1RU (tel: 0171 378 6009).
● **Čedok in the U.S.**, 10 East 40th Street, New York, NY 10016 (tel: 212 689 9720).

With 800 staff commanding a range of languages, the **Prague Information Service** (**PIS**) provides comprehensive information about the city, makes reservations of all kinds, runs tours, and operates a number of attractions itself, including the Powder Tower and Charles Bridge towers (one of which may soon house the Museum of Musical Instruments, displaced from its original home). **PIS** aims to supplant the numerous private accommodation agencies, most of which offer only a limited range of accommodation. The organization has several offices, at:

● Staroměstské náměstí 22 (tel: 2421 2844/45).
● Panská 4 (tel: 2421 2757).
Other helpful agencies are:
● **CKM**, Žitná 12 (tel: 29 99 49); the specialist agency for youth travel in the republic.
● **Balnea**, Pařižská 11 (tel: 2481 2657/1927); arranges accommodation and treatment in the country's spa towns, such as Carlsbad and Marienbad.

No visitor to Prague need go short of information

HOTELS AND RESTAURANTS

HOTELS AND RESTAURANTS

ACCOMMODATION

The following hotels have been divided into three price categories:

- budget ($)
- moderate ($$)
- expensive ($$$)

HRADČANY

Diplomat ($$–$$$) Evropská 15 (tel: 2439 4111). Strictly speaking, this glittering modern establishment on the road in from the airport is in the middle-class suburb of Dejvice. However, its location, within a 10-minute walk of the castle, merits its inclusion here. A further plus is its proximity to Dejvice metro station, bringing the city center within equally convenient reach. This is the ideal place to stay in its price range.

Pyramida ($$) Belohorská 24 (tel: 311 3075). This vast glass palace lies just up the street from the Strahov monastery end of the Hradčany quarter.

Savoy ($$$) Keplerová 6 (tel: 53 74 59). This Art Nouveau structure has been completely rebuilt to luxurious specifications.

U Raka Pension ($$) Černínská 10 (tel: 35 14 53). An exclusive pensione in a timber chalet sitting strangely among the stuccoed houses in the charming quarter of Nový Svět.

MALÁ STRANA

Hoffmeister ($$$) Pod bruskou 9 (tel: 2451 0381). In a historic building subjected to total modernization, this highly recommended hotel enjoys a romantic (but somewhat noisy) location just below the eastern end of the castle.

Kampa ($) Všehrdova 16 (tel: 2451 0409). In a delightful corner of Malá Strana, this conversion of an old building is popular with tour groups.

U pava ($$$) U lužického semináře 32 (tel: 53 22 51 or 2451 0922). The well-appointed "Peacock" has a

perfect location at the foot of the castle.

U tří pštrosů ($$$) Dražického náměstí 12 (tel: 2451 0779). The ancient gabled building known as the "Three Ostriches" (look for the coat of arms of the original owner—a supplier of ostrich feathers) has an unbeatable location overlooking the Karlův most (Charles Bridge) with all its 24-hour activity. Otherwise only average facilities and service are on offer.

NOVÉ MĚSTO

Adria ($$$) Václavské náměstí 26 (tel: 2421 9274). Completely refurbished old hotel right in the center of things on Wenceslas Square.

Albatros ($$) Nábřeží L Svobody (tel: 2481 0547). One of the city's so-called "botels," floating hotels that are less romantic than they sound.

Ambassador Zlatá Husa ($$$) Václavské náměstí 5–7 (tel: 2419 3111). The Ambassador is two hotels in one, once the haunt of the rich and privileged, lately somewhat gone to seed, although this is a situation the new owners intend to remedy. It is always thronging with the life that spills in from Wenceslas Square, and is home to the Alhambra nightclub.

Atlantik ($$) Na Poříčí 9 (tel: 2481 1084). This pleasant hotel with attentive staff is situated on a busy shopping street.

Atrium ($$$) Pobřeží 3 (tel: 2484 1111). Built, as its name implies, around a splendid atrium, this huge modern hotel (nearly 800 rooms) had just enough space for President Clinton's staff on the occasion of his 1994 visit. Just beyond the Magistral expressway at the northern end of Nové Město.

Axa ($) Na Poříčí 40 (tel: 2481 2580). Much patronized by the young.

City Hotel Moran ($$$) Na Morani 15 (tel: 2491 5208). Austrian comfort provided in a historic building close to

Karlovo náměstí (Charles Square).

City Pensión ($) Belgická 10 (tel: 691 1334). Pleasant pensione close to Náměstí míru metro station.

CKM Junior Hotel Žitná 12 (tel: 2491 5767). This is a well-run youth hostel, and as a result is often booked up long in advance.

Esplanade ($$$) Washingtonova 19 (tel: 2421 1715). Extreme luxury close to the city's main railroad station.

Evropa ($$) Václavské náměstí 25 (tel: 2422 8118/9). The temptation to take a room at one of the most succulent of Prague's Art Nouveau buildings should be resisted until you have actually inspected the room itself, whose décor is unlikely to match that of the hotel's exterior or its wonderful café.

Harmony ($$) Na Poříčí 31 (tel: 232 0016 or 232 0720). A stylish and welcoming building dating from the 1930s that has been thoroughly freshened up.

Hybernia ($) Hybernská 24 (tel: 2421 0439). Prices may rise once this rather grim establishment has undergone renovation.

Jalta ($$$) Václavské náměstí 45 (tel: 2422 9133). Not surprisingly, in view of its name and general ambience, this was a favorite with fraternal delegations from other Communist countries. Not a lot has changed since.

Julius ($$) Václavské náměstí 22 (tel: 2421 7092/6). This restored hotel has a very convenient central location.

Juventus ($) Blanická 10 (tel: 25 51 51/2). Former youth hostel undergoing gradual refurbishment, the Juventus is located one metro stop (Náměstí míru) from the Národní muzeum (National Museum).

Meteor-Plaza ($$$) Hybernská 6 (tel: 2422 0664). Emperor Franz Josef once stayed in this venerable hotel with its Baroque entrance hall and medieval wine cellar.

Opera ($) Těšnov 13 (231 5735). Double-paned windows keep out some of the din from the adjacent Magistral expressway overpass.

Palace ($$$) Panská 12 (tel: 2409 3111). Art Nouveau outside, ultra-modern inside, the Palace is proud to be Prague's most expensive hotel.

Páv ($$) Kremencová 13 (tel: 2491 2893). This tiny pensione is ideal for those who would like to be close to Prague's most popular beer hall and garden (U Fleků).

Penta ($$$) V Celnici (tel: 2481 0396). This newly opened link in the Penta chain offers many facilities, and is located close to Masaryk station. It also offers reduced rates on weekends.

STARÉ MĚSTO

Bohemia ($–$$) Kralodvorská 4 (tel: 232 3417). The Bohemian provides clean and comfortable accommodation close to the Obecní dům (Municipal House).

Centrál ($) Rybná 8 (tel: 2481 2041). Rundown and potentially noisy, but true to its name.

InterContinental ($$$) náměstí Curieovych 5 (tel: 2488 1111). In an enviable location where Pařížská avenue meets the Vltava, this was the city's pride when built in the 1970s and it strives to maintain high standards. Works of art and fine antiques adorn its public spaces.

Pařiž ($$$) U Obecního domu (tel: 2422 2151). The luxurious Paris hotel occupies a historic building just behind the Art Nouveau Obecní dům (Municipal House).

President ($$–$$$) náměstí Curieových 100 (tel: 231 4812). The InterContinental's neighbor is slightly less stylish and correspondingly less expensive.

Ungelt ($$$) Stupartská 1 (tel: 2481 1330). Attractive apartments in a Gothic building on one of the narrow streets leading into Staroměstské náměstí (Old Town Square).

Unitas Pension ($) Bartolomějská 9 (tel: 232 7700/09). This former convent was confiscated by the Czechoslovak State Security system, and the nuns' cells were used for the interrogation and detention of political prisoners—including President Václav Havel, whose cell is marked by a plaque. The convent has since been returned to the nuns, who now offer secure and affordable (but strictly no alcohol) accommodation in the very heart of the city, with thick walls that help to shut out the noise. This is a favorite with young tour groups.

SUBURBS

Admiral ($$) Hořejší nabřeží (tel: 2451 1697). Large floating botel anchored off a Smíchov quayside.

Ariston ($) Seifertova 65 (tel: 627 8840). Rock-bottom prices for rock-bottom accommodation in inner suburban Žižkov.

Balkan ($) Svornosti 28 (tel: 54 01 96). Basic accommodation in the suburb of Smíchov.

Belvedere ($$) Milady Horákové 19 (tel: 37 47 41/9). This new and somewhat characterless building is located near Letná plain, just about within walking distance from Staré Město (the Old Town).

Bílý lev ($) Cimburkova 20 (tel: 27 11 26). Reliable, simple and value-for-money accommodation is offered at the "White Lion" in Žižkov.

Coubertin ($$) Atletická 4 (tel: 35 40 69 or 35 28 51). This small, modern establishment is favored by sportspeople, not least because it is located in the middle of the Strahov stadium complex.

Florenc ($– $$) Křižková 11 (tel: 2422 3260). Basic lodgings located amid the main roads and railroad tracks surrounding the Florenc long-distance bus station.

Forum ($$$) Kongresova 1 (tel: 6119 1111; reservations in U.K. tel: 0171 741 9000). Vast luxury hotel complex adjoining the Nusle expressway bridge, with magnificent views back towards the city center. The hotel lies five minutes from the city center by metro.

Golf ($$) Plzeňská 215 (tel: 52 10 98). This big motel is conveniently sited on the main route into the city from the west.

International ($$) Koulová15 (tel: 331 9111). Take a time-trip back to the heyday of the Soviet Empire in this Socialist-Realist skyscraper in Dejvice.

Kafka ($) Cimburkova 24 (tel: 236 8192). An alternative to the Bílý lev (see above).

Lauda ($) Kubišova 10 (tel: 6641 1491). A pleasant suburban pensione located on the hills above the north bank of the Vltava, convenient for the expressway to northern Bohemia and Dresden.

Lunik ($) Londýnska 50 (tel: 25 27 01). This reliable small hotel lies just outside Nové Město (the New Town).

Obora ($$) Libocká 271/1 (tel: 36 77 79). A small, well-appointed establishment in the attractive surroundings of the royal hunting park on the western outskirts close to the airport.

Ostaš ($) Orebitská 8 (tel: 627 9418). Almost in the shadow of the statue of Jan Žižka high up on Žižkov hill, this inner suburban hotel offers simple rooms at prices that may rise once the current renovations are complete.

Panorama ($$–$$$) Milevská 7 (tel: 6116 1111). Faceless high-rise with good facilities, close to Pankrac metro station and thus within minutes of the city center.

Parkhotel ($$$) Veletržní 20 (tel: 3807 1111). A 1960s slab in Holešovice, on the north bank of the Vltava, but reliable.

HOTELS AND RESTAURANTS

Praha ($$$) Sušická 20 (tel: 2434 1111). A hill-top location in the affluent western suburbs of the city makes this former Party-members-only hotel a privilege to stay in.

Racek ($$) Dvořecká louka (tel: 6121 4383). This floating botel is located in the southern suburb of Podolí, close to the city's favorite swimming-pool complex.

Splendid ($–$$) Ovenecká 33 (tel: 37 33 51/9). This small family-run hotel is located in a turn-of-the-century street close to Letná plain.

Vaníček ($$–$$$) Na Hřebenkách 60 (tel: 35 28 90). A ziggurat of a hotel climbing up the steep slopes above the smoke and fumes of industrial Smíchov. The establishment is both comfortable and welcoming.

Vila Voyta ($$$) K Novému dvoru 124/54 (tel: 472 5511). A small villa hotel with luxury facilities. It is buried in the southern suburbs, but lies close to the southern traffic circle.

EXCURSIONS
Černošice
Pension Horka ($) Pod Horkou 203, Černošice (tel: 643 4056). You will find a friendly welcome in this family villa overlooking Černošice in the picturesque Berounka valley. On the down side, it is only accessible via an interminable flight of stairs from the road.

Slánka ($) Černošice (tel: 643 4326). This modernized station hotel is an ideal spot for railroad buffs, who will appreciate the frequently passing trains on the main line to the west.

Karlštejn
Mlýn ($) Karlštejn (tel: 0311 942 08 if calling in Karlštejn, or contact Prima Hotels, Na Výtoni 10, Praha, tel: 29 29 96 in Prague). The "Mill," as the name translates, is in a tranquil location on the far side of the river from Karlštejn castle.

Průhonice
Club Hotel Průhonice ($$$) Průhonice (tel: 643 6501). Průhonice, with its vast and tree-rich park, is where the real countryside begins just southeast of Prague, and only minutes from town via the Brno expressway. This 1960s establishment boasts a wide range of sports facilities.

Parkhotel Průhonice ($–$$) Uhříněvská 12, Průhonice (tel: 643 6090 or 643 6094). Pleasant, newly built small hotel in the village center of Průhonice, just off the Brno expressway.

Štiřín
Zámek Štiřín ($$) Štiřín (tel: 99 20 33 or 99 21 60). This splendid country château and its park have been impeccably restored to make a quiet retreat some 15 miles southeast of Prague just off highway No. 603 towards Benešov. Golf course.

RESTAURANTS

In addition to the establishments listed below, nearly all the major hotels have their own restaurants; some of them—including the InterContinental's top-floor Zlatá Praha, or the Club at the Palace—have a very fine reputation indeed.

The following restaurants have been divided into three price categories:

- budget ($)
- moderate ($$)
- expensive ($$$)

HRADČANY
Peklo ($$) Strahovské nádvoří (tel: 2451 0032). "Hell" is situated in the nether regions of Strahov monastery and serves excellent Italian, as well as Czech, dishes.

Stará radnice ($$) Loretánská 1 (tel: 53 27 32). At the top of the winding steps known as Radnické schody (Council House Steps) stands the Old Council House itself, a hostelry since the 15th century. Here you are served unpretentious Czech food at prices which are reasonable considering the restaurant's location along the main tourist trail.

U Zlaté hrušky ($$$) Nový svět 3 (tel: 53 11 33 or 53 51 80). The "Golden Pear" once had one of the city's most enviable reputations for fine food, though it may now be relying too much on past achievements. That said, it still enjoys the exquisite setting of a Rococo house in romantic Nový svět.

MALÁ STRANA
David ($$–$$$) Tržiště 21; also accessible from Nerudova 13 (tel: 53 93 25). Faultless food is offered in a gracious and intimate setting. Lamb is a house specialty.

Floriánův dvůr ($$$) Újezd 16 (tel: 53 05 02). Erratic excellence with some fine fish specialties.

Lobkovická vinárna ($$) Vlašská 17 (tel: 53 01 85). Imaginative international cooking in the wine restaurant run by the Lobkovic family and featuring the wines from their estate at Mělník.

Nebozízek ($$) Petřínské sady 411 (tel: 53 79 05). There is fine food here, but the view is the thing from this elegant establishment, half-way up the funicular on Petřín hill.

U Malířů ($$$) Maltézské náměstí 11 (tel: 2451 0269). Vies for the title of the city's most expensive restaurant, with French food to match expectations.

U Maltézkých rytířů ($$) Prokopská 10 (tel: 53 63 57). Gourmet cuisine at more than usually affordable prices in the heart of Malá Strana.

U Mecenáše ($$$) Malostranské náměstí 10 (tel: 53 38 81). Ancient and atmospheric establishment on Malá Strana Square, frequented by Mydlář the Executioner in his time, and by distinguished foreign guests in ours.

U Modré kachničky ($$–$$$) Nebovidská 6 (tel: 20 38 22).

An intimate and welcoming restaurant, full of antiques, the "Blue Duckling" offers first-rate game dishes at reasonable prices. One of the best new restaurants in Prague.

NOVÉ MĚSTO
Country Life ($) Jungmannova 1 and Melantrichova 15. Two city-center branches for that rare commodity in the Czech Republic: vegetarian sandwiches.
Fakhreldine ($$–$$$) Klimentská 48 (tel: 232 7970). Lebanese food served in sumptuous style.
Fregata ($$) Ladová 3 (tel: 29 31 21). The "Frigate" specializes in fish dishes.
Indicky Snack Bar Mayur ($) Štěpánská 61 (tel: 2422 6737). Dishes up Indian specialties, which are also available in the more stylish (and more expensive) adjoining restaurant.
Klašterní vinárna ($$) Národní třída 8 (tel: 29 05 96). The "Monastery" wine-restaurant specializes in good-value steaks.
Na Rybárně ($$) Gorazdova 17 (tel: 29 97 95). Excellent-value fish dishes are served here, one block away from the Vltava near Karlův most (Charles Bridge). The restaurant was once frequented by President Havel and his international acquaintances (look for the signatures of Paul Simon and Mick Jagger).
Pezinok ($–$$) Purkyňova 4 (tel: 29 19 96). No need for an excursion to Slovakia—everything has been done in the Cultural Center of what used to be the eastern part of Czechoslovakia to create a cheerful Slovak ambience and cuisine.
Pizzeria Kmotra ($) V jircháfích 12 (tel: 20 35 64). Excellent pizzeria with a reputation that makes reservations advisable.
Premiéra ($$$) V Jircháfích 6 (tel: 29 91 62). Unbeatable range of fish dishes prepared and served with aplomb two blocks away from the Národní divadlo (National Theater).

Principe ($$) Anglická 23 (tel: 25 96 14). Italian professionalism not far from the Národní muzeum (National Museum).
Rotisserie ($$–$$$) Mikulandská 6 (tel: 2491 2334). Formerly one of the few oases in a culinary desert, the Rotisserie now has plenty of competition in the city.
U Čížků ($) Karlovo náměstí 34 (tel: 29 88 91). Charming Czech atmosphere and authentic Bohemian food in Charles Square. Popular with tour groups.
Vltava ($$) Rašínovo nábřeží (tel: 29 49 64). The riverside is an eminently suitable location for this restaurant offering fish specialties and a lot else besides.

STARÉ MĚSTO
Brasserie Mozart ($$–$$$) Náměstí Republiky 5 (tel: 2481 1057). Closed for restoration until 1997, but when it opens expect international-standard cuisine to match the stunning décor of the Art Nouveau Obecní dům (Municipal House) in which it is located.
Canadian Lobster ($$$) Husova 15 (tel: 2421 3530). Impeccable international food prepared from imported ingredients. The prices are international, too—though the *prix fixe* menu may help you economize.
Fotbal ($) Kozí 7 (tel: 231 2394). Value-for-money fast-food two blocks away from Staroměstské náměstí (Old Town Square).
Kosher Restaurant Shalom ($–$$) Maislova 18 (tel: 2481 0929). Kosher food (some of it brought in from Vienna) served up in the former meeting room of the ghetto's town hall.
Mucha ($$) Melantrichova 5 (tel: 26 35 86). Good Czech food in a narrow street just off Starméstské náměstí (Old Town Square).
Opera Grill ($$$) Karolíny Světlé 35 (tel: 26 55 08). Expensive elegance close to the Národní divadlo (National Theater).

Parnas ($$$) Smetanovo nábřeží (tel: 2422 7614). Sophisticated international cuisine to be savored together with the unbeatable view across the Vltava to the castle. Reserve a window table.
Pod křídlem ($$) Corner of Národní třída and Voršilská (tel: 2491 2377). Traditional Czech food is dished up here in untraditional surroundings. Vegetarian Czech dishes are also available.
Reykjavik ($$) Karlova 20 (tel: 2422 9251). This fish restaurant is strategically located on the tourist trail through Staré Město (the Old Town).
U červeného kola ($$–$$$) Anežská 9 (tel: 231 8941). Tasty steaks can be washed down with good Moravian wine.
U Golema ($$) Maiselova 8 (tel: 232 8165). A convenient stop while sightseeing in the ghetto, the Golem serves specialties with predictable titles such as "Wrath of the Golem" and "Elixir of Life soup."
U Modré růže ($$) Rytířská 16 (tel: 26 38 86). Deep in a Staré Město (Old Town) vault, a refined restaurant offering excellent game and fish.
U Pavouka ($$–$$$) Celetná 2 (tel: 2481 1436). The "Spider" is a wine-restaurant conveniently placed on one of the main thoroughfares in Staré Město (the Old Town).
U Sixtů ($$$) Celetná 2 (tel: 2422 5724). This vaulted medieval wine cellar lies deep below the Staré Město (Old Town). The prestigious establishment is run by an award-winning chef, but it may be resting on its laurels.
U Supa ($$) Celetná 22 (tel: 2421 2004). Substantial food is offered at "The Vulture," also a beer hall.
U Velryby ($$) Jilská 24 (tel: 26 69 33). Stylish and healthy food is available in "The Whale," on the corner of Karlova in the heart of Staré Město (the Old Town). The service tends to be unhurried.

HOTELS AND RESTAURANTS

U Zlatého hada ($$) Karlova 18 (tel: 2422 0843). The "Golden Snake" used to be one of the oldest and best-known cafés in town, but it is now better noted for its American-style steaks and hamburgers.

U Zlatého jelena ($$$) Celetná 11 (tel: 2423 0244). As you might expect, the cellars of the "Golden Stag" offer venison as their specialty.

V zátiší ($$–$$$) Náprstkova 11 (tel: 2422 8977). Czech and international dishes are available in this restaurant, located in the square dominated by the chapel in which Jan Hus once preached.

Zlatá ulička ($$) Masná 9 (tel: 232 0884). This re-creation of the castle's Golden Lane is not in Hradčany but in "Meat Street," close to the butchers' church of St. James. The restaurant's meat dishes, especially veal, are appropriately appetizing.

SUBURBS

Ali Baba ($–$$) Vodičkova 5 (tel: 2491 2084). Arabian delights are dished up here in the eastern, but decidedly unexotic, surroundings of suburban Žižkov.

Austria ($) Štefánikova 25 (tel: 54 98 79). Excellent Czech food is served at this restaurant, located a block away from Andel metro station in Smíchov.

Crazy Daisy ($$) Vinohradská 142 (tel: 6731 0378). American atmosphere close to Flora metro station.

Dlouhá zed ($$) Marie Pujmanové 10 (tel: 692 2374). At one time it claimed to be the city's only authentic Chinese restaurant, but today the "Great Wall" is not always able to maintain its authenticity in the face of unreliable supplies of the right ingredients.

Elite ($) Korunní 1 (tel: 25 71 50). A good range of pasta is offered here at appetizing prices. The Elite is located on the main road running east from Náměstí míru metro station.

Emir Hoffman ($$) Mahlerovy sady 1 (tel: 27 63 07). This restaurant is located in the TV tower, hence the unrivaled views over the city. It also has a snack bar.

Fenix ($$) Vinohradská 88 (tel: 25 03 64). Chinese food in great variety served up by Chinese cooks.

Harlekýn ($) Jugoslávských partyzánů 6 (tel: 311 0713). Good Czech food served in a friendly setting in Dejvice.

Impera ($) Vinohradská 44 (tel: 25 15 03). Serves up unpretentious but reliable Czech food.

Myslivna ($$) Jagellonská 21 (tel: 627 0209). The "Hunters' Lodge" is the best of the city's game restaurants, despite its unlikely location in a suburban residential street in Vinohrady. Excellent value.

Na Ořechovce ($$) Východní 7 (tel: 312 4872). Deep in Dejvice (and probably best reached by taxi), this bar/restaurant provides superlative traditional Czech food and has the bonus of a beer garden.

Nürnberger Stub'n ($$) Vinohradská 10 (tel: 2421 8032). Just up Vinohradská from the Národní muzeum (National Museum), a reminder of the difference between Czech and German cooking.

U Cedrů ($) Na Hutích 13 (tel: 312 2974). Delicious and inexpensive Lebanese cuisine makes a change from dumplings. The U Cedrů is located in Dejvice, with an entrance on Národní obrany.

U Govindy ($) Na Hrázi 5. This Hare Krishna establishment close to Palmovka metro station, in the eastern suburbs, will help vegetarians in their sometimes difficult quest. Open weekdays noon–6 p.m. Donations welcome.

U Kláštera ($) Bělohorská 169 (tel: 35 48 60). Pleasant restaurant and bar conveniently situated opposite the Břevnov monastery on one of the main roads into the city from the west.

U Mikuláše Dačického ($) Viktora Huga 2 (tel: 54 93 12). Situated two blocks north of Andel metro station in Smíchov, this welcoming family-owned wine bar/restaurant dishes out generous portions of hearty food.

U Sloupu ($$) Lucemburská 11 (tel: 27 14 57). Above-average Czech cuisine is served at this restaurant near the foot of the TV tower in Žižkov.

U Vojáčků ($–$$) Vodní 11 (tel: 53 56 68). Unpretentious but recommended fish restaurant in Smíchov.

U Zlatého rožne ($$) Československé armády 22 (tel: 2431 1161). Under the same ownership as the U Sixtů wine cellar (see Staré Město above), this Dejvice restaurant is not in quite the same category, but it serves excellent steaks and interesting fish dishes.

Victoria Saloon ($) Seifertova 44 (tel: 27 05 81). Frogs legs, shark and T-bone steaks in the atmosphere of the Old West, re-created in the improbable surroundings of suburban Žižkov.

EXCURSIONS

Stará myslivna ($) Konopiště. Another "Hunters' Lodge," this time in the wooded grounds of Konopiště castle, serving tasty and value-for-money main courses and excellent desserts.

Terasy Barrandov ($–$$) Barando vská 1 (tel: 54 54 09). This stylish and recently renovated out-of-town leisure complex was *the* place to head for in the 1930s.

Zámecký penzión ($–$$) Zbraslav, Ke krnovu 630 (tel: 59 15 07). You may not want to stay overnight in Zbraslav, but this immaculate establishment is an excellent place to lunch after visiting the National Gallery's modern sculpture collection just opposite.

CAFÉS AND BARS
Hradčany

U Černého vola Loretánske

náměstí 1. With its beer from the Velké Popovice brewery, this is a place for serious drinkers.

Malá Strana
Café Savoy Vitězná 1. Highly recommended café at the Malá Strana end of the Most legií (Legionaries' Bridge).
U Čerta Nerudova 4. The "Devil" is well placed to pull in thirsty tourists schlepping up picturesque Nerudova street on their way to the castle.
U Kocoura Nerudova 2. The famous old "Tom Cat" caters to its resilient locals as well as to visitors taking a break from the long climb up to the castle.
U Svatého Tomáše Letenská 12. Originally a monastic brewery, St. Thomas's and its beer garden make the most of their historic associations and are very popular with tour groups. Folk music performances.
U Zeleného čaje Nerudova 19. The "Green Tea" provides just this useful kind of refreshment on the long haul up to the castle, but you may have to wait to get in.

Nové Město
Ambassador Denní bar Václavské náměstí 5. The Ambassador Hotel's "day bar" is one of the most central and luxurious cafés in which to sit and plan your day.
Bránická formanka Vodičkova 26. The Braník brewery's outlet in the city center.
Café Monica Charvátova 11. Good coffee and desserts are served in the elegant ambience of this café.
Černý pivovar Karlovo náměstí 15. Serves snacks, Czech restaurant food, and dark beer as a bonus.
Česká hospoda v Krakovské Krakovská 20. This comfortable pub proffers beer from the Braník brewery, and is located just a step away from the top end of Václavské náměstí (Wenceslas Square).

Evropa Václavské náměstí 29. The archetypal turn-of-the-century café, bearing up despite its extreme popularity (note that there is an entrance fee).
H&S Café Slovanský ostrov (Slavonic Island). Rent your rowboat from what is possibly the city's most attractive open-air café.
U Fleků Křemencova 11. After 200 years, Flek's beer garden is still serving its unique black beer (brewed on the premises) to the thousands who visit daily.
U Jelínků Charvatova 1. A favorite with city-center employees when work becomes too boring.
U Kalicha Na Bojisti 12–14. Thanks to the Good Soldier Švejk, this is the city's best-known pub/restaurant, a hit with tour groups.
Velryba Opatovická 24. In spite of its name ("The Whale"), this is not a fish restaurant but a popular café serving a mixture of Czech, pasta, and vegetarian dishes.

Staré Město
Café Nouveau Obecní dům. Art Nouveau elegance in the turn-of-the-century Municipal House (currently under restoration—reopening in 1997).
James Joyce Liliová 10. In the almost unlikely event that you get tired of drinking Czech beer, there is a trio of Irish beers on tap here.
Lávka Novotného lávka 1. Disco, restaurant, garden bar, and a waterside café with arguably the best view in Prague.
Slavia Narodní třída 1. Together with the Evropa, this used to be the classic Prague café. It is hoped that its new owners (who closed the café down in 1993) will wake up to this fact and reopen it.
U Medvídků Na Perštýně 7. Budvar, from Budejovice, is on tap here, and a big beer garden is open in the summertime.
U svatého Anny denní bar Na Zábradlí. Close to the famous Divadlo Na Zábradlí

(Theater on the Balustrade), this bar serves good, cheap eats and some of the best coffee in town. The restaurant is more expensive.
U Zlatého tygra Husová 17. The "Golden Tiger" has long been a haunt of the literary and intellectual set who, in a conspiracy with the waiters, insist on arcane rules of conduct which you may find difficult to fathom. You will also have to wait a long time for a table. The place was so popular—even before the U.S. president's visit—that some of its original luminaries, such as the writer Bohumil Hrabal, deserted it. The Pilsener, drawn from the pub's 13th-century cellars, tastes particularly good.

Suburbs
FX Radost Café Bělehradská 120. Trendy vegetarian café, open all night.
Globe Bookstore and Coffee House Janovského 14. Embedded in the inner suburban streets of Holešovice, on the north bank of the Vltava, is this (excellent) piece of England serving teas and other British staples.
Hanavský pavilón Letenské sady (Letna Gardens). There is a wonderful view of the Vltava and its bridges from this exuberant little pavilion, first built for the 1891 Expo.
Na Zvonařce Šafaříkova 1. Solid "bar snacks" (soups, chicken liver) and good beer in the lively setting of "The Bell," located in Vinohrady.
U Berana Jana Masaryka 45. Family pub in the inner suburbs not too far from Náměstí míru metro station.
U Bohouše Polská 34. While some central pubs have been overwhelmed by a wave of foreign patrons, Prague life goes on unabated in this Vinohrady establishment.
U Hronků Nad hradním vodojemem 11. Freshly restored family pub in the middle-class suburb of Střešovice.

Index

INDEX

INDEX

INDEX

PICTURE CREDITS AND CONTRIBUTORS

Picture credits

The Automobile Association would like to thank the following photographers, libraries and associations for their assistance in the preparation of this book:

MARY EVANS PICTURE LIBRARY 22–23 Kepler and Emperor Rudolf II; 22b Rudolf II; 22c Kepler; 31b Wenzel; 32c Charles IV; 34b Defenestration of Prague; 35b Albrecht von Wallenstein; 36c Joseph II; 38–39a Independence celebration; 39b Edward Beneš; 40b Sudetenland invaded by Germans; 70–71 Prague 1648; 86–87a President Masaryk enters Prague; 136b Franz Werfel; 137b Rainer Maria Rilke. REX FEATURES LTD 12b Václav Havel; 47b Václav Havel; 87b President Havel. ROBERT HARDING PICTURE LIBRARY 197 pink tank. THE HULTON DEUTSCH COLLECTION 40–41a Liberation of Prague; 41b Liberation of Prague 1945; 44–45a Soviet troops in Prague 1968; 44b Alexander Dubček; 45b Soviet invasion Prague 1948; 46c Jan Palach. M. IVORY two jazz men in Old Town square; 26c 1920s tour bus; 49 South Gardens; 75b Communist sign; 80 Nový Svět; 158 figure; 216 Veltrusy; 230 Příbram; 232 Zvíkov; 251 Marionette theater. LATERNA MAGIKA 20b Laterna Magika. THE MANSELL COLLECTION LTD 32–33 Jan Hus; 33c Jan Hus; 38–39d President Masaryk in carriage; 86b President Masaryk. NATIONAL GALLERY IN PRAGUE 71 Jakub Schikaneder, *Winter Evening in the City*; 77 Lucas Cranach the Elder *Adam and Eve*; 78 Albrecht Dürer, *Feast of the Rosary*; 79 Oskar Kokoschka, Charles Bridge, and Hradčany; 225 Zbraslav Castle. PICTURES COLOUR LIBRARY Cover, The Old Town. POPPERFOTO 42–43a Congress of Czech. youth union; 42b Göttwald; 43b Jan Masary;, 43c Czech. president accepts the oath. ROYAL GEOGRAPHICAL SOCIETY 34–35 map of Prague 1574. J. VOTRUBA, FUN EXPLOSIVE, PRAGUE 50 This is Prague; 103 The Charles Bridge; 136 Kafka & Svějk; 197 No More Tanks in Prague. JUSTIN WILLIAMS, THE PRAGUE POST 8 Alan Levy.

The remaining photographs are held in the Automobile Association's own photo library (AA PHOTO LIBRARY) and were taken by Clive Sawyer, with the exception of the spine and the following pages: 7, 10b, 12–13, 23b, 35c, 37b, 50, 54, 55a, 57, 61b, 84–85, 95, 100, 136–137a, 138, 141, 144, 145, 147, 179b, 183, 191 and 238, which were taken by Antony Souter; and the back flap and pages 6, 10c, 17b, 20–21, 21b, 21c, 24b, 29a, 31a, 36–37, 45c, 60, 62, 63b, 64b, 66b, 68, 75c, 81, 88, 93, 94, 97b, 104–105, 104b, 105b, 105c, 106, 111, 112, 114, 117, 120, 121, 126, 127, 128–129a, 132, 152, 153b, 154, 157, 158–159, 159, 160, 161b, 164, 165c, 167, 168–169, 169, 174, 177, 180, 184–185, 184, 185, 190, 192, 193, 198, 199, 208, 212, 215b, 218, 219, 220, 221, 222–223, 222, 229, 232–233, 234–235, 234, 235, 236, 240, 243, 244, 246, 248, 249, 250, 252, 254, 256, 257, 260, 265, 267, 270, 271, 273 and 275, which were taken by Jon Wyand.

Acknowledgments

The author would like to thank the following for their help in the production of this book: Alexandra Bolla, J Crickettová of Atelier Jé-Cé, Ljuba Horáková of the Presidential Chancellery, Alan Levy of the *Prague Post*, Václav Novotný of the Prague Information Service, Ivan Plicka of the City Architects' Department, Aram Simonian of Mladá Fronta Dnes, George and Kathy Šmíd, and Wolfgang Teufel.

Contributors

Series advisor: Christopher Catling   **Designer**: Kingfisher Design
Joint series editor: Susi Bailey   **Indexer**: Marie Lorimer
Copy editor: Christopher Catling   **Verifiers**: Philip O'Neil, Iba and Hanka Blasko